Research in Informatics

Volume 5

Computer Analysis of Images and Patterns

Computer Analysis of Images and Patterns

Proceedings of the
IVth International Conference CAIP '91,
Dresden, September 17–19, 1991

edited by

Reinhard Klette

Akademie Verlag

Herausgeber:

Prof. Dr. rer. nat. Reinhard Klette
Technische Universität Berlin
Fachbereich 20 (Informatik)
Computer Vision — FR 3-11
Franklinstraße 28—29
W-1000 Berlin 10

Die Titel dieser Schriftenreihe werden vom Originalmanuskript der Autoren reproduziert.

Lektorat: Dipl.-Math. Gesine Reiher
Herstellerische Betreuung: Christian P. Biastoch

Die Deutsche Bibliothek - CIP-Einheitsaufnahme

Computer analysis of images and patterns : proceedings of the IVth International Conference CAIP '91, Dresden, September 17 - 19, 1991 / ed. by Reinhard Klette. - Vom Orig.-Ms. reproduziert. - Berlin : Akad.-Verl., 1991
   (Research in informatics ; Vol. 5)
   ISBN 3-05-501299-2
NE: Klette, Reinhard [Hrsg.]; CAIP <04, 1991, Dresden>; GT

ISBN 3-05-501299-2
ISSN 0863-4300

© Akademie Verlag GmbH, Berlin 1991
Erschienen in der
Akademie Verlag GmbH, O-1086 Berlin (Federal Republic of Germany), Leipziger Str. 3—4

Gedruckt auf säurefreiem Papier.

Druck und Bindung: Druckhaus „Thomas Müntzer" GmbH, O-5820 Bad Langensalza
Umschlaggestaltung: Verlag
Bestellnummer: 2192/5
Printed in the Federal Republic of Germany

IVth International Conference CAIP´91
Computer Analysis of Images and Patterns
Dresden, September 17-19, 1991
sponsored by the IAPR

Conference chairman:

Gerald Sommer, Jena

Organizing committee:

Klaus-Dieter Müller

Elvira Bahn

(WGMA - Wissenschaftlich-Technische Gesellschaft für Meß- und Automatisierungstechnik, Berlin)

Chairman of the program committee:

Reinhard Klette, Berlin

Program committee:

D. Chetverikov, Budapest

W. Coy, Bremen

M.J.B. Duff, London

B. Gudmundsson, Linköping

S. Fuchs, Dresden

C.-E. Liedtke, Hannover

N. Petkov, Sofia

J. Pitas, Thessaloniki

A. Rosenfeld, College Park

F. Sloboda, Bratislava

J. Sklansky, Irvine

K. Voss, Jena

L.P. Yaroslavsky, Moscow

Y.I. Zhuravlev, Moscow

Sponsors:

The conference CAIP´91 is sponsored by the *IAPR* (International Association for Pattern Recognition), *KONTRON Bildanalyse GmbH*, the periodical *BILD UND TON*, and *Jenoptik Carl Zeiss Jena GmbH*.

Preface I

CAIP '91 is the fourth of a biennial conference on computer analysis of images and patterns. Do we need such a conference in addition to the broad spectrum of established international conferences on pattern recognition, image processing, and related fields? Remembering the initial intention to establish this conference series, the answer ist - Yes, we need it more than ever.

CAIP was floated in 1985 to promote personal contacts of scientists who are working in this very dynamic developing discipline in different political systems. GDR was a good place to realize this because of its central location in Europe. Apart from this, there was a soft currency in GDR, and there were good conditions for western colleagues to get a permit for Berlin, Wismar or Leipzig.

CAIP '89 took place in Leipzig on the eve of great political changes in Germany and Eastern Europe. As a pleasing result frontiers are more penetrable, but unfortunately currency boundaries are still existing. We hope that CAIP will survive. To reach this we need to achieve three goals: new models for realization, financial support by political organizations as for example, the European Commission and the German goverment, and goodwill of all the friends of CAIP's basic idea.

CAIP was created by the Image Processing Group in the Scientific-Technological Society for Measurement and Automated Control (WGMA). In this year, we can celebrate the 10th anniversiary of this group. The unification of Germany brought consequencies also in the necessity to define new working fields for this Image Processing Group.

CAIP will remain an important activity. Perhaps in future its profile should accentuate more than in the past applicative aspects, because meanwhile automatic and computer supported interpretation of sensoric data has established in various application fields.

CAIP '91 owes its existence in the present instable economic situation in some European areas, the unbroken interest of speakers and participants and the idealism of some individuals. Our thanks is due to the members of the Program Committee of CAIP '91 especially to Prof. R. Klette, to E. Bahn and K.-D. Müller from WGMA, and to the staff of Akademie Verlag. All of them spared no efforts to ensure that this conference will be successful.

Jena, June 1991

Gerald Sommer
Conference Chairman

Preface II

Computer Vision deals with the manipulation and interpretation of pictorial information by computers. Pictures result in many application areas in science, engineering, industry, office automation etc. According to the desired interpretation of the visible structures, pictorial information may be subdivided into the class of patterns in the case of a two-dimensional interpretation, or into the class of images if the picture is considered to be a scene projection visualizing three-dimensional objects or structures.

The conference series "CAIP - Computer Analysis of Images and Patterns" was started in 1985 to be a meeting place for specialists working in a certain discipline of Computer Vision, without limiting the different disciplines which may be represented at the conference. Looking back to the conferences at Berlin (1985), Wismar (1987) and Leipzig (1989), this conference strategy was of importance especially because of the location of the conference sites at the East-West border, to avoid additional restrictions. But, as at the conferences before the submitted papers to CAIP '91 did not cover all the essential disciplines of Computer Vision - they were mainly related to the fields of picture processing and pattern analysis, and in just a few cases to aspects of image understanding.

According to the judgement of the members of the program committee, 48 papers were selected for conference presentation out of 82 submitted papers. This evelution procedure was based on extended abstracts, which was difficult to realize in some cases because of the restricted information. These proceedings contain 37 papers, which were sent to us in time until June 1991.

I like to thank all the authors and members of the program committee for their efforts to ensure an interesting and good quality program at CAIP '91. Also I like to thank Elvira Bahn for her assistence in program preparation, Gesine Reiher for cooperation in editing this volume, and Sabine Mertke for help in preparing this volume.

I hope you will enjoy your stay at CAIP '91 and at the city of Dresden, the historic capital of Saxonia.

Berlin, June 1991

Reinhard Klette
Chairman of the program committee

List of authors

Contents

Image reconstruction and 3D vision

Picture grammars and picture models

Color picture processing

Picture transforms

* accepted conference papers not arriving in time for inclusion into the proceedings

Filtering

Segmentation

Picture   topology

Classification   and   pattern   analysis

Matching

Applications

Systems

FAST GENERATION OF VOLUME PROJECTION SEQUENCES

Björn Gudmundsson[1], Michael Randén[1]

Abstract

The large datasets constituting 3D–volumes inflict high costs in terms of storage space and computation time. Visualization of 3D–volumes by means of ray–casting is a very time–consuming operation, especially if a sequence of projections for animation purposes is to be generated. In this paper we present an algorithm that computes projections for rotation sequences **incrementally**. A projection in the sequence is computed from a 2D–transformation of the previous one plus a few new samples from the volume. Experiments indicate that speed–up factors in the range 10–15 are achievable for small angle increments.

1. Introduction

Visualization of 3D–volumes has attracted considerable interest in the last few years. Although special purpose display devices for true 3D display have begun to emerge, a conventional 2D display device is still the only available option in most cases. Thus, the basic problem to be solved is how to make projections from 3D to 2D in such a way that the 3D–structures in the volume are faithfully revealed to the viewer. A number of methods have been proposed [5], [7], [8], [1], [6], [9]. Most of them are based on ray–casting, i.e. imaginary rays emanating from grid–points in the projection plane pierce the volume and generate sample points in the projection plane. The viewers perception of the third dimension can be enhanced by means of object surface shading, stereo–viewing and animation. The most prevalent form of animation technique in cases where the object in the volume can be segmented from the background, is rotation of the object around some axis.

The illusion of a rotating volume is achieved by computing a sequence of projections from different angles and then displaying the sequence, possibly under interactive control. Smooth rotation requires a sequence where two successive projections are only a few degrees apart, and thus a large number of projections is needed. For volumes of reasonable resolution the task of generating such sequences tends to become computationally expensive, unless special–purpose hardware is used. However, the fact that the projections are only a few degrees apart means that there is a high degree of coherence between successive projections in the sense that if an object surface point is visible in one projection, then it is highly probable that it will also be visible in the next. This observation is the basis for an algorithm that computes successive projections in the sequence **incrementally**, thereby avoiding a costly full–fledged ray–casting operation for each projection.

In this paper we will present the incremental algorithm. An earlier version of the algorithm confined to depth–shaded projections was presented in [3]. We will first describe

1. Linköping University, Department of Electrical Engineering, S-581 83 LINKÖPING, Sweden

12

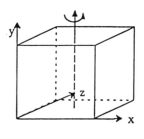

Figure 1

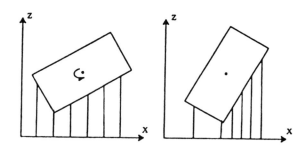

Figure 2

generation of depth–shaded projections and then consider the modifications required for surface–shaded projections.

2.   Incremental generation of sequences

We assume orthogonal parallel projection and a geometry as shown in Figure 1.

The xy–plane is the image plane (projection plane) and the rotation axis is parallel to the y–axis. The 2–dimensional slices, obtained for example from a CT–scanner, are stacked in the y–direction to form a volume. Parallel projection means that we transform in x and z only and thus we can limit our discussion to a plane of constant y, i.e. a slice. Also, we assume that the volume contains opaque objects whose surfaces we will render.

When the volume is rotated a certain angle some points on the surface will become visible while others will become hidden. The incremental algorithm applies a two–dimensional geometric transformation (rotation in x and z) to the currently visible surface points, then it removes those that have become hidden and finally casts a few new rays to detect points that have gone out of hiding, i.e. have become visible. When the rotation angle is small, the vast majority of surface points will remain visible from one projection to the next. More specifically, the algorithm proceeds in the steps shown on page 3.

Steps 2)–5) are integrated so that they are all executed in essentially one left–to–right scan of the current list. Note that there is one coordinate list per plane of constant y (slice). In the lists, coordinates are maintained with high precision (in our experiments we have used 32–bit floating point numbers).

In step 1) the volume is uniformly sampled, but the transformation in the next step results in a non–uniform distribution of the samples along the x–axis. See Figure 2.

In some regions the distance between successive samples increases while in others it decreases. Thus, in step 4) new rays are cast not only to detect surface points that were previously hidden but also to fill in the gaps between samples that are sliding apart.

1) Detect the visible surface points by means of full ray–casting (one ray per image plane pixel). Save the coordinates of the surface points in a list. This is an initialization step that yields the first projection in the sequence.

2) Transform the points in the list by a 2D rotation matrix.

3) Remove from the list points that have become hidden.

4) Cast new rays to detect points that have become visible and insert them in the list.

5) Interpolate in the list to create an image for display.

6) Go to 2).

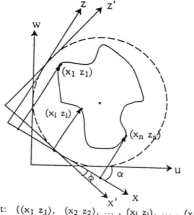

Figure 3

List: $((x_1\ z_1),\ (x_2\ z_2),\ \dots,\ (x_i\ z_i),\ \dots,\ (x_n\ z_n))$

The volume is accessed in (u, w)–space (object–space). See Figure 3. A counterclockwise rotation of totally α degrees corresponds to a rotation of the object coordinate system into a system (x, z) (current image space). To obtain the next projection in the sequence, the points in the current list are rotated an angle increment ϕ into a new current image space (x', z').

3. Visibility of surface points

Step 3) in the algorithm requires that we have a method to detect which surface points have become hidden after the transformation. The way the algorithm works guarantees that the current list of points, i.e. the currently visible points, is always sorted in x.

A visible point $(x_i\ z_i)$ is transformed into $(x_i'\ z_i')$. Since the list is sorted in x we know that

$$x_i > x_{i-1}$$

14

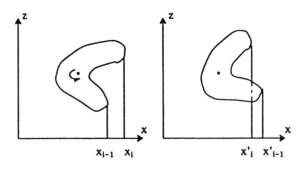

Figure 4

If $(x_i'\ z_i')$ is hidden, the following must hold:

$$x_i' < x_{i-1}' \tag{1}$$

This is illustrated in Figure 4.

Thus the points in the list are transformed from left to right (assuming counterclockwise rotation) and those transformed points for which (1) holds are simply thrown away. However, relation (1) is a necessary but not sufficient condition for $(x_i'\ z_i')$ to become hidden as illustrated in Figure 5 where the slice contains disjoint objects.

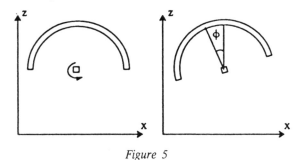

Figure 5

The surface points in the marked sector in Figure 5 will be deemed invisible by the algorithm. However, this creates a "gap" between neighboring samples that will be filled in with samples from new rays, which are fired in step 4) of the algorithm according to rules that will be described in the next section.

4.   Interpolation and new rays

A depth–shaded image for display is created via interpolation in the lists of surface points (one list per slice). In the experiments that we have done so far, nearest neighbor interpolation has been used, i.e. the x–values in the list have been rounded to yield positions on the integer grid of the display.

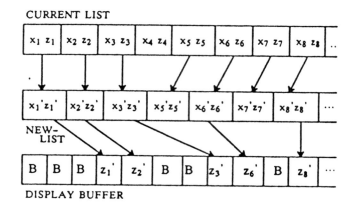

Figure 6

As was mentioned earlier, steps 2)-5) in the algorithm are executed in essentially one left-to-right scan of the list. We will now give an informal description of the total process.

It takes as input the current list of surface points and it produces a new list and a depth-shaded image for display. Let us for a moment ignore that new rays are cast to supplement the new list and the display buffer. See Figure 6.

For each projection in the sequence:

Initialize the display buffer with background intensity (B, maximum depth). Start scanning the current list left-to-right.

For each point in the list:

Transform the point.

If the point becomes hidden (relation (1)), then ignore it, otherwise append it to the new list.

Round the x-value of the transformed point of the nearest integer. Use this value as an index in the display buffer and store the z-value in this buffer (in fact, what is stored is not the z-value but rather a decreasing function of z to achieve the depth-shading effect). If more than one point rounds to the same index, then the nearest one is selected.

In the example in Figure 6, $(x_4\ z_4)$ becomes hidden. Also, x_5', x_6' and x_7' round to the same integer but x_6' is nearest and is thus selected. Note that $(x_5'\ z_5')$ and $(x_7'\ z_7')$ are appended to the new list.

In step 4) of the algorithm selective ray-casting is used to detect surface points that have become visible. Assuming counter-clockwise rotation, it is easy to show that a point that goes out of hiding will appear to the left of a visible point. Thus, when a value has been stored in the display buffer the following is done:

16

1. Check the position to the left of the current position in the display buffer.

2. If this position does NOT contain B then STOP.

3. Cast a ray from this position.

4. If the ray hits the background then STOP.

5. A new point has been obtained. It is inserted in the new list and the display buffer.

6. Check one position further left in the display buffer.

7. Go to 2.

This procedure detects new visible points and also takes care of the problem indicated in Figure 5. It does not, however, solve all problems. If a slice contains disjoint object parts between which the background is visible, then artefacts can appear in certain projections. Consider the situation depicted in Figure 7.

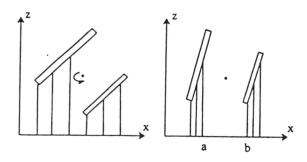

Figure 7

A new ray will be cast to the left of b but this ray will hit the background and the left-scan will stop. Thus, on the display we will see background between a and b. The way to remedy this problem is to make a slight change in the procedure so that the left-scan is not stopped the first time a ray hits the background. Rather, a parameter n > 1 determines the maximum number of background hits before the left-scan is stopped. In the experiments reported in this paper parameter n had value 1. Artefacts were observed in some projections when the angle increment was large (8 degrees) [3].

5. Surface-shaded projections

Surface-shading models show how light from light-sources is reflected from surfaces. We have used the well-known Phong shading model [2]. The intensity I of a surface point is a function of the surface normal, the direction to the light-source and the direction to the viewer.

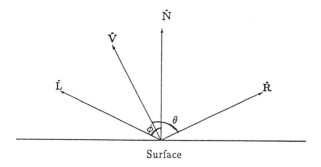

Surface

Phongs shading formula computes the intensity in the following way:

$$I = k_A + k_D(\overline{N} \cdot \overline{L}) + k_S(\overline{R} \cdot \overline{V})^n$$

or the equivalent

$$I = k_A + k_D \cos \phi + k_S \cos^n \theta$$

where

I	intensity assigned to the pixel
k_A	fraction of ambient reflection (from background light)
k_D	fraction of diffuse reflection (from light source)
k_S	fraction of specular reflection (from light source)
$\overline{N}$	normal vector for surface
$\overline{V}$	viewing vector (direction to observer)
$\overline{L}$	light vector (direction to incident light)
$\overline{R}$	reflected light vector
n	exponent for modeling highlights
ϕ	angle between $\overline{L}$ and $\overline{N}$
θ	angle between $\overline{R}$ and $\overline{V}$

Calculating the reflection vector $\overline{R}$ requires mirroring $\overline{L}$ about $\overline{N}$ and some simple geometry yields

$$\overline{R} = 2(\overline{N} \cdot \overline{L})\, \overline{N} - \overline{L}$$

The shading equation can be rewritten as

$$I = k_A + k_D(\overline{N} \cdot \overline{V}) + k_S(2(\overline{N} \cdot \overline{L})(\overline{N} \cdot \overline{V}) - (\overline{L} \cdot \overline{V}))^n$$

We have made two simplifications: the viewer and the lightsource are assumed to be at infinite distance (parallel rays) and $\overline{L}$ and $\overline{V}$ coincide.

With $\overline{L}$ and $\overline{V}$ coinciding we get

$$\cos \theta = \cos 2\phi = 2 \cos^2 \phi - 1$$

18

and

$$I = k_A + k_D(\overline{N} \cdot \overline{V}) + k_S\left[2(\overline{N} \cdot \overline{V})^2 - 1\right]^n$$

When a ray hits a surface point, the unit normal is estimated from the 3D–gradient of the volume data. The gradient was computed by means of filter kernels of size 3 x 3 x 3 [8].

The list of coordinates of visible surface points (Figure 3) is supplemented with the normals:

$$[(x_1, y_1), \overline{N}_1], [(x_2, y_2), \overline{N}_2], \ldots , [(x_n, y_n), \overline{N}_n]$$

Whereas the surface points are stored in current image space coordinates (Figure 3), the normals are stored in object space coordinates. The reason for this is that the normals are computed in object space and there is no need to transform them until they are actually needed.

Evaluation of the shading equation requires that we compute $\overline{N} \cdot \overline{V}$. We have

$$\overline{V}_{obj} = [0, 0, 1] \cdot R_a$$

$$\overline{V}_{im} = [0, 0, 1]$$

$$\overline{N}_{obj} = [n_u, n_v, n_w]$$

$$\overline{N}_{im} = \overline{N}_{obj} \cdot R_{-a} = [n_x, n_y, n_z]$$

where R_α is the rotation matrix. Whether we compute $\overline{N} \cdot \overline{V}$ in image– or object–space we end up with

$$\overline{N} \cdot \overline{V} = n_u \cdot \sin a + n_w \cdot \cos a = n_z$$

Thus we need to store only two components of the normal: n_u and n_w. The shading equation becomes

$$I = k_A + k_D \cdot n_z + k_S(2n_z^2 - 1)^n$$

6.   Implementation and results

In our experiments we have used a volume obtained from Computer Tomography (CT). The volume contains a human skull from a cadaver and it is embedded in a plastic material that has been moulded into the shape of a human head. The volume consists of 99 slices, each with a resolution of 256 x 256 pixels. In computing the projections generated by the incremental method (INC) that are shown in this paper, new rays were cast according to the procedure described in Section 4. The horizontal artifacts are caused by damaged slices. They rays were generated by a DDA–algorithm. Figure 8 shows surface–shaded projections generated by INC. The corresponding projections generated by full ray–casting (FR), i.e. the conventional method, are identical for all practical purposes.

Figure 8

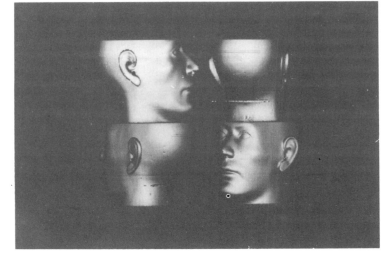

Figure 9 shows depth–shaded projections where the threshold was set higher than in Figure 8. The surface points that were hit by new rays in the process of computing the projection from the previous one in the sequence are marked with white pixels. We use the following notation:

α: accumulated rotation angle (see Figure 3)

φ: angle increment ($\alpha = m \cdot \phi$, m = 1, 2, 3 ...)

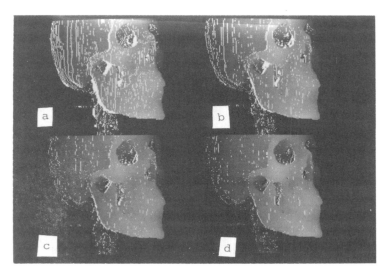

Figure 9 INC, α = 48°

a) φ = 8°   *b)* φ = 4°   *c)* φ = 2°   *d)* φ = 1°

The idea behind INC is that speed can be gained if costly ray–casting operations are as far as possible replaced by 2D geometric transformations of the currently visible surface points. INC significantly reduces the number of ray-casting operations needed. Increasing the angle increment (ϕ) diminishes the coherence between successive projections and thus more rays are required. As ϕ is further increased, INC gradually degenerates into FR.

The table below shows a comparison between INC and FR in terms of computational speed. Four sequences of the skull covering 0–360 degrees with angle increments 1, 2, 4 and 8 degrees were generated by INC and FR on a SUN4/280 computer. The source code was written in C. The times are given in seconds.

	ϕ	P	T_{FR}	T_{INC}	T_{FR}/T_{INC}
Depth–shading	1°	360	3455	226	15.3
	2°	180	1728	128	13.5
	4°	90	864	77	11.2
	8°	45	432	49	8.8
Surface shading	1°	360	3804	315	12.1
	2°	180	1902	172	11.1
	4°	90	950	101	9.4
	8°	45	475	63	7.5

P: number of projections in the sequence
T_{FR}:   total time to generate the sequence by means of FR
T_{INC} total time to generate the sequence by means of INC

As could be expected, the gain in computational speed decreases as the angle increment increases, i.e. as the number of rays per projection increases. Still, the gain is significant even for the relatively large increment of 8 degrees. The difference in speed–up between depth–shading and surface–shading is due to the fact that in the former case the speed is mainly determined by the number of ray–casting operations, while in surface–shading it is mainly determined by the number of 3D–gradient calculations. The ratio between the number of rays for FR and INC is larger than the ratio between the number of gradient calculations since only about half of the rays in FR actually hit the object.

7.   Concluding remarks

We have described an algorithm for fast generation of sequences of depth–shaded and surface–shaded projections of 3D–volumes. As a byproduct, the algorithm generates a compressed representation of the projection sequence. By saving only the new surface points detected when going from one projection to the next, a data compression factor of 32 was achieved for depth–shading and a 1 degree angle increment [4].

8. References

[1] Farell, Zapulla: *Three-Dimensional Data Visualization and Biomedical Applications*. CRC Critical Reviews in Biomedical Engineering, 16 (1989), 323–363.

[2] Foley, van Dam, Feiner, Hughes: *Computer Graphics: Principles and Practice*. Addison–Wesley, 1990.

[3] Gudmundsson, Randén: *Incremental Generation of Projections of CT–Volumes*. Proc. First Conference on Visualization in Biomedical Computing, Atlanta, Georgia, USA (1990).

[4] Gudmundsson, Randén: *Compression of Sequences of 3D–Volume Surface Projections*. Proc. XIIth International Conference on Information Processing in Medical Imaging, Wye, England (1991).

[5] Herman, Lui: *Three-Dimensional Display of Human Organs from Computed Tomograms*. Computer Graphics and Image Processing, 9 (1979), 1–21.

[6] Levoy: *Efficient Ray Tracing of Volume Data*. ACM Transactions on Graphics, 9 (1990), 245–261.

[7] Lenz, Gudmundsson, Lindskog, Danielsson: *Display of Density Volumes*. IEEE Computer Graphics and Applications, 6 (1986), 7, 20–29.

[8] Magnusson, Lenz, Danielsson: *Evaluation of Methods for Shaded Surface Displaly of CT–Volumes*. Proc. Ninth International Conference on Pattern Recognition, Rome, Italy, (1988).

[9] Tiede, Hoehne, Bomans, Pommert, Riemer, Wiebecke: *Investigation of Medical 3D–Rendering Algorithms*. IEEE Computer Graphics and Applications, 10 (1990), 2, 41–55.

COMPRESSION AND PARALLEL CALCULATION OF THE PROJECTION MATRIX IN IMAGE RECONSTRUCTION

Wieslaw Lucjan NOWINSKI

Institute of Computer Science, Polish Academy of Sciences
P.O. Box 22, PKiN, 00-901 Warsaw, Poland

ABSTRACT

The paper is concerned with the compression and parallel calculation of the projection matrix being used in series expansion methods of image reconstruction. Several factors allowing to compress the projection matrix have been analysed and attainable rates of compression evaluated. Three ways of parallelization of an algorithm for calculation of the projection matrix [5] have been proposed and adequate procedures expressed in *occam* presented. Finally, the parallel implementation of the algorithm on the processor farm has been discussed.

1. Introduction

Image reconstruction, allowing to visualize the internal structure of an object from its projections, is exploited in many fields. To reconstruct images, two groups of methods are being used: *transform methods* and *series expansion methods* [2,4]. In general, series expansion methods require more computations than transform methods. On the other hand, however, series expansion methods have many advantages, like a wider range of applicability, geometrical versatility, and ease of dealing with incomplete projection data.

In series expansion methods the reconstruction problem is stated in a discrete form. It consists in estimating the image vector $\vec{x} = [x_0, x_1, \ldots, x_{J-1}]^T$, J – the number of pixels (or voxels in a 3-D case), from the system of equations

$$\vec{y} = R\vec{x} + \vec{e}, \tag{1}$$

provided that the measurement vector $\vec{y} = [y_0, y_1, \ldots, y_{I-1}]^T$, I – the number of rays, and the projection matrix $R = [r_{i,j}]_{I \times J}$ are given. Alternatively, the system (1) with the unknown error vector $\vec{e}$ can be replaced by the system of inequalities.

In general, the projection matrix R contains the information about the measurement geometry and the basis pictures [4]. In the herein paper we will consider the most common case, i.e., measurements are taken along straight lines (like in computerized tomography) and the j-th basis picture equals 1 inside the j-th pixel (voxel) and 0 outside it. Then, the components of the projection matrix have a simple geometrical interpretation. Namely, $r_{i,j}$ is the length of intersection of the i-th ray with the j-th pixel (voxel).

The number of components of the projection matrix is big. For example, the matrix has over 10^9 components for a 256×256 image reconstructed form 250 projections each containing 250 rays. Moreover, the amount of data is much higher in a 3-D case. Therefore, one of main problems in implementing series expansion methods is in an efficient calculation and storage of components of the projection matrix.

In general, there are two approaches in implementing series expansion methods. First, the projection matrix is precalculated and stored before a reconstruction process starts.

Second, the necessary components of the projection matrix are calculated during a reconstruction process without storing them.

The first approach demands much more memory but results in faster reconstruction. Therefore, it can be useful, especially, in real-time applications. Moreover, it is efficient to use this approach in iterative methods in order not to calculate the projection matrix many times. For example, in iterated discrete backprojection (one of the most popular simultaneous methods) the projection matrix is needed two times in every iteration, since

$$\vec{x}^{(k+1)} = \vec{x}^{(k)} + \lambda^{(k)} R^T(\vec{y} - R\vec{x}^{(k)}), \quad k = 1, 2, \ldots, \tag{2}$$

where k is the iteration index, λ is the relaxation parameter, and T denotes transposition. The second approach does not require the memory to be big enough to hold the projection matrix; on the other hand, however, it is much slower. This approach can be used in situations when the size of available memory is restricted (especially when big values of I and J are required, like in high accuracy reconstruction).

The aim of the paper is to discuss some ways of reducing the disadvantages of both approaches. Namely, in the first approach the amount of required memory has been decreased by compressing the projection matrix. In the second approach the calculation of the projection matrix has been accelerated exploiting parallelism.

2. Compression of the projection matrix

The number of components of the projection matrix is big even for medium numbers of rays and pixels. On the other hand, however, it is not efficient to store all the $I \times J$ components of the projection matrix, as most of them equals zero. Note that a ray intersects at most $2L - 1$ pixels of all the $J = L \times L$ pixels, so the number of the non-zero components is less than $2/L$. For example, if $J = 256 \times 256$ pixels, the number of the non-zero components is less than 1 per cent. Therefore, the projection matrix can be stored without distortion in a compressed form. To store only the non-zero components of the projection matrix, we introduce two 1-D arrays: integer `ProjectionMatrixIndices[]` to hold the indices of the non-zero components and real `ProjectionMatrixValues[]` to keep the values of these components.

In addition, there is no need to store components of the projection matrix for pixels lying outside the reconstruction region. This results in the rate of compression equal $4/\pi$ (i.e., the square to circle ratio).

Let us evaluate the rate of compression of the projection matrix C_R taking into account both mentioned factors. Since a ray intersects less than $2L$ pixels, we get

$$C_R > \frac{4}{\pi} \frac{L^2 I}{2LI} = \frac{2}{\pi} L. \tag{3}$$

On the other hand, a ray intersects at least L pixels, so

$$C_R < \frac{4}{\pi} \frac{L^2 I}{LI} = \frac{4}{\pi} L. \tag{4}$$

Hence

$$\frac{2}{\pi} L < C_R < \frac{4}{\pi} L. \tag{5}$$

Consider examples. Suppose P denotes the number of components of the compressed projection matrix. For the constant number of rays and $L \in \{32, 64, 128\}$, the following results have been obtained:

— $P = 9328$ for $I \times J = (10 \times 33)(32 \times 32) = 337920$; then $C_R \approx 36$;
— $P = 19174$ for $I \times J = (10 \times 33)(64 \times 64) = 1351680$; then $C_R \approx 70$;
— $P = 38895$ for $I \times J = (10 \times 33)(128 \times 128) = 5406720$; then $C_R \approx 139$.

For the constant number of pixels and various number of rays, the results obtained are as follows:

— $P = 19174$ for $I \times J = (10 \times 33)(64 \times 64) = 1351680$; then $C_R \approx 70$;
— $P = 37725$ for $I \times J = (20 \times 33)(64 \times 64) = 2703360$; then $C_R \approx 71$;
— $P = 38462$ for $I \times J = (10 \times 65)(64 \times 64) = 2662400$; then $C_R \approx 69$.

Thus, the rate of compression of the projection matrix increases practically linearly with increasing L, and is pretty nearly constant with respect to I.

The rate of compression of the projection matrix can be even higher provided that there exist certain regularities of the measurement geometry. Suppose M denotes the number of projections, each containing N rays. Let us assume that the projections are equally spaced, that the geometry of each projection is the same, and that the number of projections for each quadrant of the reconstruction region is the same, i.e.,

$$M = 4K, \qquad K - \text{an integer.} \tag{6}$$

Consider four pixels, which indices with respect to a ray are the same, intersected by the n-th rays of the m-th, $(m+K)$-th, $(m+2K)$-th, and $(m+3K)$-th projections (Fig. 1).

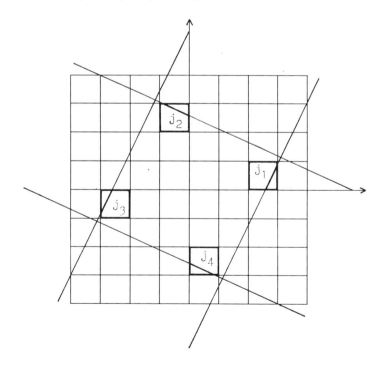

Figure 1. Symmetry of the projection matrix

Then, for those pixels the value of $r_{i,j}$ is the same. Therefore, the rate of compression of the `ProjectionMatrixValues[]` array is four.

To determine the rate of compression of the `ProjectionMatrixIndices[]` array, let us calculate the indices of the pixels j_2, j_3, j_4 provided that the index of the j_1-th pixel is given (Fig. 1). For the j-th pixel the following relationship holds

$$j = lL + k, \qquad l = 0, 1, \dots, L-1, \quad k = 0, 1, \dots, L-1, \tag{7}$$

where l is the horizontal layer index and k is the vertical layer index. Furthermore, the coordinates x, y of the central point of the j-th pixel are the following

$$\begin{cases} x = (k + 0.5)d - \varrho, \\ y = (l + 0.5)d - \varrho, \end{cases} \tag{8}$$

where d denotes the width of a pixel and ϱ is the radius of the reconstruction circle. Since $Ld = 2\varrho$, we get

$$\begin{cases} k = \frac{x}{d} + \frac{L-1}{2}, \\ l = \frac{y}{d} + \frac{L-1}{2}. \end{cases} \tag{9}$$

Denoting by

$$\bar{x} = x/d, \qquad \bar{y} = y/d, \qquad L_0 = (L-1)/2, \tag{10}$$

relationship (9) can be rewritten as

$$\begin{cases} k = \bar{x} + L_0, \\ l = \bar{y} + L_0. \end{cases} \tag{11}$$

Suppose x_1, y_1 are the coordinates of the central point of the j_1-th pixel. Then, the coordinates of the central points of the j_2, j_3, j_4 pixels can be determined due to the symmetry in the following way (Fig. 1)

$$(x_2, y_2) = (-y_1, x_1), \qquad (x_3, y_3) = (-x_1, -y_1), \qquad (x_4, y_4) = (y_1, -x_1). \tag{12}$$

Finally, the indices of the considered pixels are obtained from (7), i.e.,

$$j_2 = l_2 L + k_2, \qquad j_3 = l_3 L + k_3, \qquad j_4 = l_4 L + k_4, \tag{13}$$

where the layer indices $k_q, l_q, q = 2, 3, 4$, are calculated from (11) and (12) as follows

$$\begin{cases} k_2 = -\bar{y}_1 + L_0, \\ l_2 = \bar{x}_1 + L_0, \end{cases} \quad \begin{cases} k_3 = -\bar{x}_1 + L_0, \\ l_3 = -\bar{y}_1 + L_0, \end{cases} \quad \begin{cases} k_4 = \bar{y}_1 + L_0, \\ l_4 = -\bar{x}_1 + L_0. \end{cases} \tag{14}$$

Thus, it is possible to attain the rate of compression of the `ProjectionMatrixIndices[]` array equal four, but it demands some processing.

It should be noted that the equally spaced rays assumption may result for certain projections in an additional symmetry of the projection matrix. Moreover, the above considerations may be generalized provided that the condition (6) is generalized as follows

$$M = 2^{K_1} K_2, \qquad K_1, K_2 - \text{integers}. \tag{15}$$

3. Parallel calculation of the projection matrix

To calculate or approximate the projection matrix, many different approaches have been proposed, e.g., [1,5,8]. Below we will consider parallelization of an algorithm presented in [5]. The algorithm has many advantages, like:

— determination of the exact values of components of the projection matrix;
— efficiency;
— calculation of the projection matrix in the compressed form.

Recall that the considered algorithm contains three loops: projection loop, ray loop, and pixel loop. The quickness of the algorithm consists in an efficient implementation of the innermost loop, i.e., the pixel loop. This is attained by a suitable grouping of rays and dividing them into four groups. Rays are processed in steps, and for a given ray its step is constant. Then, $r_{i,j}$ is equal to the step or can be calculated by dividing the step in an appropriate ratio (without using mathematical functions, like sin(), cos(), sqrt(), which are time-consuming). Therefore, the innermost loop makes use of data which are produced mostly outside it, and processing is concerned mainly with the determination of indices of the non-zero components of the projection matrix. The algorithm expressed in an *occam* type syntax is following

```
PROC CalculateProjectionMatrix (VAL INT J, M, N)
  INT m, n, kmin, kmax, lmin, lmax, p :
  REAL x0, y0 :
  SEQ
    p := 0      -- p - the index of the compressed projection matrix
    SEQ m = 0 FOR M      -- projection loop
      SEQ
        -- calculate the coordinates of the source of emanation
        SEQ n = 0 FOR N      -- ray loop
          SEQ
            -- calculate the angle α of the x axis with a ray
            -- calculate the first and the last layer to be processed
              -- and the coordinate of the starting point, i.e.,
              -- (lmin,lmax,x0) for layers processed vertically, or
              -- (kmin,kmax,y0) for layers processed horizontally
            IF
              (α = π/2) OR (α = 3π/2)                 -- case a)
                ProcessCaseA(lmin,lmax,p,x0)
              (α ∈ [π/4,3π/4]) OR (α ∈ [5π/4,7π/4])   -- case b)
                ProcessCaseB(lmin,lmax,p,x0)
              (α = 0) OR (α = π)                       -- case c)
                ProcessCaseC(kmin,kmax,p,y0)
              (α ∈ (-π/4,π/4)) OR (α ∈ (3π/4,5π/4))   -- case d)
                ProcessCaseD(kmin,kmax,p,y0)
```

In the cases a) and c) the value of $r_{i,j}$ is constant for all pixels lying inside the reconstruction circle along the i-th ray (i.e., from the layer indexed by $lmin$ (or $kmin$) to the layer indexed by $lmax$ (or $kmax$)) and equals the width of a pixel d (Fig. 2a).

Consider the case b). Suppose s, dx denote the steps along a ray and the x axis, respectively (Fig. 2b). The condition $\alpha \in [\pi/4, 3\pi/4]$ OR $\alpha \in [5\pi/4, 7\pi/4]$ assures that passing along a ray from the current to the next horizontal layer, just two cases are possible:

— a ray does not quit the current vertical layer;
— a ray enters the next (or previous) vertical layer (but not farther).

In the first case, the value of $r_{i,j}$ for the pixel lying in the next horizontal layer equals s. In the second case, the values of $r_{i,j}$ for two pixels lying in the next horizontal layer are determined by dividing s in an appropriate ratio. The indices of pixels to be processed are easily determined by means of the lat() function (which divides its argument by d and returns the integer part of the result [5]). The case d) is similar to the case b), however, layers are processed not vertically but horizontally.

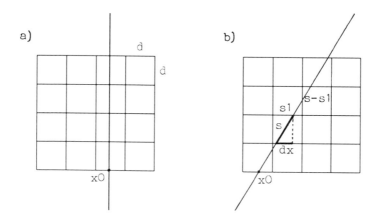

Figure 2. Geometrical interpretation of the cases a) and b)

Let us consider parallelization of the above algorithm. In general, image reconstruction algorithms may be parallelized by exploiting forms of parallelism specific to image reconstruction. These forms have been defined by means of *occam* and presented in [6]. They include:

— *pixel parallelism*, i.e., pixels (or voxels) are processed in parallel;
— *projection parallelism*, i.e., projections are treated concurrently;
— *ray parallelism*, i.e., rays are processed simultaneously;
— *operation parallelism* which refers to all forms of concurrency in operations.

Consider projection parallelism. Let us decompose the projection matrix as follows

$$R^T = \left| \, R^T_{N J_0} \, R^T_{N J_1} \, \cdots \, R^T_{N J_m} \, \cdots \, R^T_{N J_{M-1}} \, \right|, \tag{16}$$

where

$$\cdot \, R_{N J_m} = [r_{i_m, j}]_{N \times J}, \qquad i_m = mN \ldots (m+1)N - 1, \quad j = 0 \ldots J - 1. \tag{17}$$

Then, the considered algorithm can be parallelized in the following way

```
PROC CalculateProjectionMatrix.ProjectionParallelism (VAL INT J, M, N)
  INT m :
  PAR m = 0 FOR M
    CalculateProjectionSegment(m,J,N)
:
```

The CalculateProjectionSegment(m,J,N) procedure calculates $R_{N J_m}$ in the compressed form (i.e., it performs the body of the projection loop).

Let us discuss ray parallelism. Then, the projection matrix is decomposed as

$$R^T = \left| \begin{array}{ccccc} R_{1 J_0}^T & R_{1 J_1}^T & \cdots & R_{1 J_i}^T & \cdots & R_{1 J_{I-1}}^T \end{array} \right|, \tag{18}$$

where

$$R_{1 J_i} = [r_{i,j}]_{1 \times J}, \qquad j = 0 \ldots J - 1. \tag{19}$$

In this case parallelization is following

```
PROC CalculateProjectionMatrix.RayParallelism (VAL INT I, J)
  INT i :
  PAR i = 0 FOR I
    CalculateRaySegment(i,J)
:
```

The CalculateRaySegment(i,J) procedure calculates $R_{1 J_i}$ in the compressed form.

It should be noted that in spite of the similarity in formulation, there exist essential differences between both procedures. First, the degree of parallelism of the latter procedure is N-times higher than that of the former (as $I = MN$). Furthermore, the granularity of component processes of the latter procedure is various, since the number of pixels intersected by a ray is variable. In the former procedure, on the other hand, the granularity of component processes is constant provided that the geometry of each projection is the same. Assuming that a processor runs a single component process, projection parallelism results in a constant while ray parallelism in a variable workload amongst processors.

Theoretically, the projection matrix may also be decomposed as

$$R = \left| \begin{array}{ccccc} R_{I 1_0} & R_{I 1_1} & \cdots & R_{I 1_j} & \cdots & R_{I 1_{J-1}} \end{array} \right|, \tag{20}$$

where

$$R_{I 1_j} = [r_{i,j}]_{I \times 1}, \quad i = 0 \ldots I - 1. \tag{21}$$

This approach is equivalent to the use of pixel parallelism. For this decomposition, however, the algorithm [5] is inadequate, as it processes successive pixels lying along rays.

Projection parallelism parallelizes the projection loop, whereas ray parallelism parallelizes the projection and ray loops. Operation parallelism, on the other hand, is inherent mainly in the pixel loop. Let us consider parallelization of the ProcessCaseA() procedure

```
PROC ProcessCaseA.OperationParallelism (VAL INT lmin, lmax, INT p, REAL x0)
  INT k, l :
  SEQ
    k := lat(x0)
    SEQ l = lmin FOR (lmax - lmin)        -- pixel loop
      SEQ
        PAR
          ProjectionMatrixIndices[p] := (L * l) + k
          ProjectionMatrixValues[p] := d
        p := p + 1
:
```

Parallelization of the case b) may be expressed as follows

```
PROC ProcessCaseB.OperationParallelism (VAL INT lmin, lmax, INT p, REAL x0)
  INT k0, k1, l, Ll :
  REAL dx, x1, s, s1 :
  SEQ
    -- calculate s, dx (see Fig. 2b)
    x1 := x0 + dx
    SEQ l = lmin FOR (lmax - lmin)        -- pixel loop
      SEQ
        PAR
          k0 := lat(x0)
          k1 := lat(x1)
          Ll := L * l
        IF
          k0 = k1        -- the ray does not quit the layer
            SEQ
              PAR
                ProjectionMatrixIndices[p] := Ll + k0
                ProjectionMatrixValues[p] := s
              p := p + 1
          k0 <> k1       -- the ray enters the next vertical layer
            SEQ
              -- calculate s1 (see Fig. 2b)
              PAR
                ProjectionMatrixIndices[p] := Ll + k0
                ProjectionMatrixValues[p] := s1
                ProjectionMatrixIndices[p+1] := Ll + k1
                ProjectionMatrixValues[p+1] := s - s1
              p := p + 2
        x0 := x1
        x1 := x0 + dx
```

Thus, the degree of operation parallelism is low in comparison with the degrees of projection and ray parallelisms.

4. Parallel implementation of the algorithm on the processor farm

The projection matrix may be calculated during reconstruction or, alternatively, its calculation may precede a reconstruction process. Therefore, it seems reasonably to use for the parallel calculation of the projection matrix the same computational model as for parallel series expansion methods.

For parallel series expansion methods, the processor farm computational model has been proposed [7]. Recall that the processor farm introduced in [3] consists of a controller and linear array of worker processors. The controller generates tasks for the workers and collects results produced by them. A worker contains two parts: an application and harness being used for message routing. The processor farm model is especially useful for applications demanding repeated execution of the same code with different data and little or no communication between processors. Thus, the model is particularly well suited to parallel series expansion methods, since component processes of a decomposed reconstruction process form arrays of similar processes having no need to pass information to one another.

Let us discuss the parallel implementation of the considered algorithm on the processor farm. Then, either parallelization by projection parallelism or by ray parallelism may be exploited, as in each case component processes form an array of similar and independent processes.

Consider projection parallelism. Then, the controller transmits to a worker a packet containing the information about the measurement geometry and the projection index, whereas a worker performs the `CalculateProjectionSegment()` procedure. For ray parallelism, the controller sends the information concerning the measurement geometry and the ray index, while a worker runs the `CalculateRaySegment()` process. It should be noted that the processor farm copes easily with the problem of the various granularity of component processes for ray parallelism, as it provides an automatic mechanism for dynamic load balancing.

For both parallelizations, there are two ways of keeping results produced by the workers. First, the calculated segments of the projection matrix are sent to the controller. This results in the extensive communication, as well as demands the controller to compose the compressed projection matrix from its segments. Moreover, during a reconstruction process the segments have to be sent back to the workers what slows down reconstruction. The second way consists in remaining the calculated segments of the projection matrix in local memories of the workers. This solution has many advantages, as it decreases substantially the amount of communication as well as there is no need to compose the projection matrix. In addition, the memory requirements with respect to the controller (or a host computer) are essentially reduced, because the projection matrix is distributed to local memories. On the other hand, however, this way has a vital disadvantage. Namely, the processor farm is not able to provide during reconstruction an automatic mechanism for dynamic load balancing, since a free worker cannot process a packet if an adequate projection matrix segment is not available at the worker. Therefore, work has to be partitioned manually, so as to ensure the even distribution of work amongst workers. Fortunately, it can be done before reconstruction, as a workload depends on the measurement geometry (i.e., it is independent of projection data).

5. Summary

To cope with a big amount of data of the projection matrix, two approaches have been proposed: compression and parallelism.

The basic compression consists in storing only the non-zero components of the projection matrix for pixels lying in the reconstruction region. This results in the rate of compression $C_R \in (2L/\pi, 4L/\pi)$. Moreover, examples show that the rate of compression grows (practically) linearly with the square root of the number of pixels and is independent of the number of rays. It is worth noting that the compressed projection matrix (i.e., kept as the arrays of indices and values) facilitates to formulate image reconstruction algorithms. A higher rate of compression may be achieved assuming certain regularities of the measurement geometry.

The algorithm for calculation of the compressed projection matrix has been parallelized in three ways exploiting projection, ray, or operation parallelisms. Projection and ray parallelizations are especially useful, since they are applicable either to 2-D or to 3-D reconstruction. In addition, both parallelizations are well suited to be implemented on the processor farm.

References

[1] Colsher, J. G.: *Iterative three-dimensional image reconstruction from tomographic projections.* Computer Graphics and Image Processing, **6** (1977) 513–537.

[2] Herman, G. T.: *Image Reconstruction from Projections. Fundamentals of Computerized Tomography.* Academic Press, New York 1980.

[3] May, D.; Shepherd, R.: *Communicating process computers.* Inmos Technical Note 22, Inmos Ltd., Bristol 1987.

[4] Nowinski, W. L.: *Image reconstruction methods and a tool for their investigation.* Journal of New Generation Computer Systems, **1** (1988) 4, 327–352.

[5] Nowinski, W. L.: *Fast calculation of the projection matrix in image reconstruction.* Proceedings of the III. International Conference on Computer Analysis of Images and Patterns – CAIP'89, 8–10 September 1989, Leipzig, 51–53.

[6] Nowinski, W. L.: *Parallel implementation of the convolution method in image reconstruction.* Lecture Notes in Computer Science, **457** (1990) 355–364.

[7] Nowinski, W. L.: *Parallel implementation of series expansion methods of image reconstruction using the processor farm.* Presented at the Transputing'91 World Conference, 22–25 April 1991, Sunnyvale, CA, USA.

[8] Schott, D; Isernhagen, V.: *Zur Bestimmung der Projektionsmatrix bei der Bildrekonstruktion aus Projektionen.* Wiss. Zeitschrift der PH Guestrow, **27** (1989) 2.

A MULTI-VIEW STEREOVISION APPROACH
FOR POLYHEDRON RECONSTRUCTION

Volker Steinhage [‡], Ingo Daniels [‡], Albrecht Schick [‡]

1   Introduction

We present a method to derive a reliable 3D description of polyhedral scenes based on stereovision using multiple camera views. This multi-view stereo technique has been successfully applied to many scenes and has proved more reliable and more accurate than the well known binocular and even trinocular stereo techniques. Our method turns out to be applicable for the fast recognition of objects in robot picking tasks using only two or three views as well as using a greater number of images for complete and accurate measurements of objects. The method has the following attractive features:

- **Flexibility:** Arbitrary positions of an arbitrary amount of different camera views are allowed.
- **Automatic Calibration** of each camera view.
- **Automatic Feature Extraction** of corner points and edge lines from each image.
- **Reliable Stereo Analysis:** The matching of corresponding image features uses the basic paradigm of Hypothesis Prediction and Validation. Each additional camera view increases the reconstruction reliability and accuracy.
- **Knowledge Base:** Fast and reliable object identification will be supported by stored object prototypes.
- **CAD–Interface** for measurement tasks: The 3D description of the reconstructed object can automatically be converted to DXF and is available for the most CAD–systems.
- **Low Costs:** No special and expensive technical equipment like a laser or an UV range finder is necessary.

2   Binocular and Trinocular Stereovision

Stereo analysis has been developed to measure positions and shapes of 3D objects for applications in aerial cartography, automatic surveillance, parts identification in industrial automation, and passive robot navigation. The main problem in stereo analysis is the matching of stereo images to ascertain the corresponding points, the so called *correspondence problem* by [Ullman79].

[‡]   University of Bonn, Department of Computer Science,
D-5300 Bonn 1, Römerstr. 164, F.R.G.

In conventional binocular stereo analysis, various matching techniques have been used to avoid ambiguous matches: relaxation in [Barnard&Thompson80], coarse-to-fine in [Marr82], [Grimson85], and [Posch88], and dynamic programming in [Otha&Kanade85]. Although these schemes are useful as stereo analysis strategies, they cannot avoid ambiguous matches which are attributed to the appearence of scene points with similar features or to local vanishing of true match points caused by occlusions or due to noises in video signals.

In trinocular stereovision a third camera view is added to solve the correspondence problem geometrically. While in binocular stereovision the search for corresponding points is a search along conjugated epipolar lines, in trinocular stereovision the search for corresponding points between two images can be reduced to simple verification at a precise location in the third image. A survey about approaches in trinocular stereovision is given in [Steinhage89].

Figure 1 shows the epipolar geometry for trinocular vision: each camera is modeled by its optical center C_i and its image plane B_i. An image point P_i of the image plane B_i defines together with the optical center C_i and the second optical center C_j the epipolar plane (P_i, C_i, C_j). The intersection of this plane with the image plane B_j yields the epipolar line L_{ji} on which the corresponding image point P_j in the image B_j must lie. To verify the correspondence of the two image points P_i and P_j the corresponding image point P_k in the third image B_k has to lie on the intersection point of both epipolar lines L_{ki} and L_{kj}.

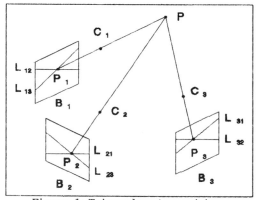

Figure 1: Trinocular stereovision.

While the use of a third view increases the reliability of the correspondence analysis in general, there are still certain cases where correspondence cannot be established. These cases are often not mentioned in other references or occluded by definition like the so called *general position assumption* in [Binford81] and [Marr82]. But our experiences with trinocular vision show that these cases quite often occur and are not negligible because they result in wrong matches. We have examined the following error cases:

(1)   A visible point in two images does not appear in the third image. The third image cannot verify a true correspondence found in the two images.

(2)   Two distinct pairs of corresponding points in two images are both verified by the same point in the third image. This happens whenever one point of the scene is hidden by another similar point in one camera view. The computation of the 3D position will yield a wrong value for the hidden point.

(3)   A false correspondence between two points in two images is verified by a third false correspondence in the third image. This case appears when the lines of sight from the three cameras to three distinct points of the scene intersect at one point. A non-existing scene point will be computed.

3   The Multi-View Algorithm

The three error cases described above indicate that additional information is needed to solve correspondences more reliable. So we propose a multi-view stereovision system POLYOC which derives the correspondences in principle via three images. But the algorithm takes in account a user-defined number of additional images. Each additional camera view provides an additional measurement which increases the reconstruction reliability and accuracy of each 3D point. The three error case can be solved much more reliable. POLYOC includes the following steps:

(1) image processing and feature extraction for each image,
(2) calibration of the camera views,
(3) object reconstruction via multi-view stereovision,
(4) object identification via object prototypes.

3.1   Image Processing and Feature Extraction

The image features used for the multi-view stereo matching and the polyhedron reconstruction are corner points and edge lines. To extract the desired features the following steps are applied:

We use a 5x5 Median operator to reduce the noise signal and the Sobel operator to extract edge points. The edge picture is processed by a thinning algorithm described in [Pavladis82]. To obtain connected edge lines a weighted polarized Hough transform proposed in [Lie/Chen90] is applied. Unlike the standard Hough transform, the weighted polarized Hough transform restricts the transform mapping to within a polarizing zone of the local fitting line, thus eliminating noisy votes on parameter space. The corner points are derived by investigating the intersections of the edge lines. The result of the feature extraction procedures are two lists for each image: one list holds all extracted corner points of the image, while the second list contains all edge lines connecting the corner points of the first list.

3.2   Calibration

Within the robot picking task we choose a cube with known dimensions and known location to be the calibration object and use a simple calibration algorithm described in [ChenEtAl89] to determine the location and orientation of the camera relative to the cube. The algorithm uses the 2D coordinates of the vanishing points obtained from the perspective projection of the cube to express the 3D line equations and the 3D plane equations of the cube. Furthermore the dimensions and the edge perpendicularity property of the cube are used to determine the 3D coordinates of the cube vertices. Due to errors brought by image processing, image quantization and other possible camera distortion, the coordinates of the projected vertices and the vanishing points are usually not very accurate and will be iteratively modified so that the derived 3D corners comply with the given geometric constraints of the cube and the cube image data given by the back projection is also in close agreement with the TV image.

3.3   Multi-View Stereo Analysis

Two CCD-cameras are used within the robot picking task. One camera is fixed on a tripod to get a top view of the whole scene while the second camera is mounted on the robot arm. The top view and views of the robot arm camera made from different positions are matched to derive a 3D description of the scene.

The matching of corresponding image features is driven by corner points and edge lines. The corner points are the image features to match while the edges which connect neighbouring corner points are used as constrains for the matching process. The whole multi-view stereo matching uses the basic paradigm of Hypothesis Prediction and Validation.

3.3.1   Hypotheses Prediction

The hypotheses for corresponding corner points are derived via the epipolar constraint which requires that each pair of corner points along the conjugated epipolar lines between two images has to be confirmed by a corner point lying at the intersection of the pair of conjugated epipolar lines in a preset number of the other images.

3.3.2 Hypotheses Validation

The hypotheses for corresponding corner points are verified via a neighbourhood constraint which requires for each set of three connected corner points in one image that the corresponding three corner points in a preset number of the other images are also connected in the same manner. Furthermore the difference between the 3D positions for a corner computed from each pair of images may not exceed a preset small threshold.

3.4 Knowledge Based Object Identification

To identifiy and locate objects of the scene in a fast and reliable fashion a knowledge base is currently in work to hold 3D descriptions of the scene objects. The object models of the knowledge base are generated via a geometric modeling system which uses a boundary representation. A graphical interface including construction operations like slicing, gluing and set operations allows a clear and comfortable way of defining the object models of the knowledge base. The identification of the scene objects is derived via a matching process of the 3D description of the partial scene reconstruction derived by the multi-view stereo analysis against the 3D object descriptions of the knowledge base.

4 Other Multi-View Approaches

Other multi-view approaches are reported in [Moravec79], [Thorpe&Shafer83], [Tsai83], and from the INRIA group in [Faugeras87], [Ayache&Faugeras87], [Ayache&Lustman87], and [Ayache&Hansen88].

The matching step in the approach of [Thorpe&Shafer83] uses the notion of trihedral vertices based on a Huffmann-Clowes junction dictionary and therefore works only for trihedral objects.

In contrast to [Moravec79] and [Tsai83] we have chosen a feature based matching algorithm to find corresponding cornerpoints instead of area based matching.

Arbitrary camera positions demand the use of such an algorithm because significant changes in camera position result in a totally different illumination of object surfaces making area correlation an unusable approach to the correspondence problem. Regarding computational cost, area correlation is very expensive whereas the implementation of the epipolar constraint for matching cornerpoints only requires the computation of the distance of each point to the current epipolar line. The costs involved with the extraction of features is not as great a disadvantage if one keeps in mind that with area correlation the areas to be matched have to be selected as well, for example by an interest operator as described by Moravec.

With edge line segments and its orientation and length as features the INRIA group uses a feature based stereo matcher. However, for polyhedral objects, corner points are more reliably extracted than edge line segments. Moreover, since the illumination intensity of the scene object seen by cameras located at different locations are different, edge lines can be missing in one image or another.

5   Experimental Results

The multi-view stereovision system POLYOC that we have sketched has been successfully applied to many scenes and has proved reliable and accurate results. Reliability and accuracy increase with each additional camera view. Using four or more images within the multi-view stereo algorithm an accuracy of the reconstructed 3D positions within 1 mm is reachable.

The following figure 2 shows the experimental set-up: One CCD camera is fixed on a tripod to get a top view of the whole scene while the second camera is mounted on the robot arm. In the working space of the robot the cube for camera calibration and a test object are visible.

Figure 3 shows the reconstruction steps for the test object seen in figure 2: (a) an original video image, (b) the edge picture extracted via the Sobel operator, (c) the Hough space of the thinned edge picture, (d) seven peaks found in the Hough space corresponding the seven line equations of the connected edge lines of the Sobel picture, (e) the computed corner points projected in the original video image, and (f) the complete object reconstruction derived from four video images via the multi-view stereo analysis.

Of cause this approach yields a trade-off between reliability and accuracy on the one hand and speed on the other hand. But the user is able to decide whether he wants a quick but not complete object reconstruction like in robot navigation and picking tasks supported by a knowledge base or whether he wants a complete and accurate object reconstruction like in measurement tasks. All the matching algorithms that we use are highly parallel, and this is an obvious way of improving the performance of the system.

38

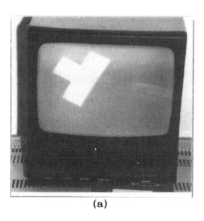

| (a) | (b) |

Figure 3: (a) the original video image of a test object, (b) the edge picture extracted via the Sobel operator.

(c)

(d)

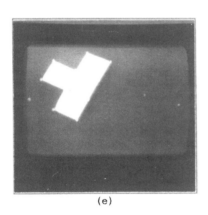

(e)

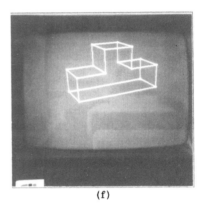

(f)

Figure 3: (c) the Hough space of the thinned edge picture, (d) the peaks found in the Hough space corresponding the line equations of the connected edge lines of the Sobel picture, (e) the computed corner points projected in the original video image, and (f) the complete object reconstruction derived from four video images via the multi-view stereovision algorithm.

6   References

[Ayache&Faugeras87] : N. Ayache, O. D. Faugeras, *Combining a Consistent 3D Representation of a Mobile Robot Environment by Combing Multiple Stereo Vievs*, in Proc. 10th IJCAI, 808–810, 1987.

[Ayache&Lustman87] : N. Ayache, F. Lustman, *Trinocular Stereovision: Recent Results*, in Proc. 10th IJCAI, 826–828, 1987.

[Ayache&Hansen88] : N. Ayache, C. Hansen, *Rectification of Images for Binocular and Trinocular Stereovision*, in IEEE 9th Intern. Conf. on Pattern Recognition, 11–16, 1988.

[Barnard&Thompson80] : S. T. Barnard, W. B. Thompson, *Disparity Analysis of Images*, in IEEE Transact. Pattern Analysis and Machine Intelligence, Vol. PAMI-2, No. 4, 333–340, 1980.

[Binford81] : T. O. Binford, *Inferring Surfaces from Images*, in Artificial Intelligence 17, 205–244, North Holland, Amsterdam, 1981.

[Faugeras87] : O. D. Faugeras: *Artificial 3D Vision*, in Proc. 10th IJCAI, 1169–1171, 1987.

[GerhardEtAl86] : A. Gerhard, H. Platzer, J. Steuer, R. Lenz, *Depth Extraction by Stereo Triples and a Fast Correspondence Estimation Algorithm*, in IEEE 8th Intern. Conf. on Pattern Recognition, 512–515, 1986.

[Grimson85] : W. Grimson, *Computational Experiments with a Feature Based Stereo Algorithm*, in IEEE Trans. Pattern Anal. Machine Intell., Vol. PAMI-7, No. 1, 1985.

[GurewitzEtAl86] : E. Gurewitz, I. Dinstein, B. Sarusi, *More on the Benefit of a Third Eye for Machine Stereo Perception*, in IEEE 8th Intern. Conf. on Pattern Recognition, 966–968, 1986.

[Huffman71] : D. A. Huffman, *Impossible Objects as Nonsense Sentences*, in Machine Intelligence 6, B. Meltzer, D. M. Michie (eds.), 295–323, Edinburgh Univ. Press, Edinburgh, 1971.

[HungEtAl89] : K.-C. Hung et al., *Polyhedron Reconstruction Unsing Three-View Analysis*, in Pattern Recognition, Vol. 22, No. 3, 231–246, 1989.

[Ito&Ishii86] : M. Ito, A. Ishii, *Three-View Stereo Analysis*, in IEEE Trans. Pattern Anal. Machine Intell., Vol. PAMI-8, No. 4, 524–532, 1986.

[Marr82] : D. Marr, *Vision*, Freeman, San Francisco, 1982.

[Moravec79] : H. P. Moravec, *Visual Mapping by a Robot Rover*, in Proc. 6th IJCAI, Vol. 1, 598–600, 1979.

[Posch88] : S. Posch, *Hierarchische linienbasierte Tiefenbestimmung in einem Stereobild*, in Informatik-Fachbericht 181 der 12. GWAI, Springer Verlag, Berlin et al., 275–285, 1989.

[Ohta&Kanade85] : Y. Ohta, T. Kanade, *Stereo by Intra- and Inter-Scanline Search Using Dynamic Programming*, in IEEE Trans. Pattern Anal. Machine Intell., Vol. PAMI-7, No. 2, 1985.

[OthaEtAl86] : Y. Ohta, M. Watanabe, K. Ikeda, *Improving Depth Map by Right-Angled Trinocular Stereo*, in IEEE 8th Intern. Conf. on Pattern Recognition, 519–521, 1986.

[Steinhage89] : V. Steinhage, *Objektrekonstruktion durch trinokulare Stereoanalyse*, KI-Bericht Nr. 12, Universität Bonn, 1989.

[Thorpe&Shafer83] : C. Thorpe, S. Shafer, *Correspondence in Line Drawings of Multiple Views of Objects*, in Proc. 9th IJCAI, 959–965, 1981.

[Tsai83] : R.Y. Tsai, *Multiframe image point matching and 3D surface reconstruction*, in IEEE Trans. Pattern Anal. Machine Intell., Vol. PAMI-5, 159–173, 1983.

[Ullman79] : S. Ullman, *The Interpretation of Visual Motion*, MIT Press, Cambridge, Mass., 1979.

[YachidaEtAl86] : M. Yachida, Y. Kitamura, M. Kimachi, *Trinocular Vision: New Approach for Correspondence Problem*, in IEEE 8th Intern. Conf. on Pattern Recognition, 1041–1044, 1986.

COMPENSATION OF MOTION BLUR IN BINARY IMAGES

B. Michaelis and T. Heimburger[1]

INTRODUCTION

Blurring in an image can arise for a number of reasons including aberration in the image system, lens out of focus, object and/or camera movements or any combination of these.

Today CCD-cameras are used very often for industrial applications [1,2,3,4]. In industrial image processing moving and swinging objects are frequently. This results in a rounding of edges in the received image. In the case of quick motion some pixels in the region of edges are illuminated only in a part of integration time. Shutter cameras can diminish this effect, but the system needs a large light intensity [5,6]. The use of pulsed light sources requires sufficient power, stability and repetition rate. In many cases other methods are desirable.

Assuming nearly binary images (transmitted light, sharp contours) an algorithm for reconstruction of the binary image in the case of motion blur can be derived.

MATHEMATICAL DESCRIPTION OF THE SHAPE OF EDGES

Binary images are important for the estimation of geometrical quantities. The arrangement for linear CCD-image sensors is shown in the left side of Fig. 1. A measured object which is swinging with a high frequency results in the shape of edges in the right side of Fig. 1. In the more general case (including area array imagers too) the motion of an edge parallel to the imager is analysed (see Fig. 2). The edge is assumed perpendicular to the direction of motion.

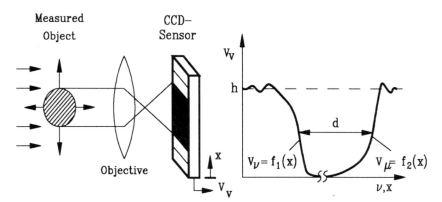

Fig. 1: Estimation of geometrical quantities with CCD-Sensors.

Rounding of edges in the received image by vibration of the measured object.

[1] Technical University "Otto von Guericke" Magdeburg
Institut für Prozeßmeßtechnik und Elektronik
Postfach 4120, O-3010 Magdeburg, Germany

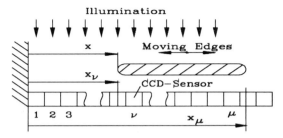

Illumination

x

Moving Edges

x_ν

CCD–Sensor

1 2 3 ν x_μ μ

Fig. 2: Motion of the edge parallel to an imager (simplified without the optical system)

For derivation of the following equations the motion should be in direction of a line of the imager. The numbers ν and μ describe the number of pixel in the line. Small displacements along the optical axis are compensated by a suitable optical system [8]. The motion blur should be the most important quantity.

Assuming an exact integration in the sensor elements the model in Fig. 3 can be used for the derivation of the shape of edges [4]. The edge is moving with x(t), T_i the integration time of the imager and t_k the sampling point.

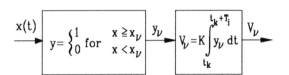

Fig. 3: Model for calculation of voltage in the sensor elements

From

$$x_\nu(t_\nu) = f(t_\nu)$$

follows

$$t_\nu = g(x_\nu) \tag{1}$$

For constant illumination intensity the model in Fig. 3 gives

$$V_{const} = h = K * T_i \tag{2}$$

At the edges the shape depends on the direction of motion. We can derive for motion in the direction of the coordinate x for edges according Fig. 2.

left edge:
$$V_\nu = f_1(x_\nu) = h - K * (g(x_\nu) - t_k) \tag{3}$$

right edge:
$$V_\mu = f_2(x_\mu) = K * (g(x_\mu) - t_k) \tag{4}$$

If motion is against the direction of coordinate x Eq. (3) and Eq. (4) are interchanged.

Assuming some conditions (constant illumination and so on) a simple relation between $f_1(x)$ and $f_2(x)$ can be given. It follows with the denotation in Fig. 1 independent of direction of motion

$$f_1(x_\nu) = h - f_2(x_\mu). \tag{5}$$

The two edges in Fig. 2 have the distance **d** corresponding to the number of pixels n. From this follows

$$x_\mu = x_\nu + d \quad or \quad \mu = \nu + n \tag{6}.$$

If the estimation of the distance **d** occurs by a simple threshold decision the threshold voltage V_s is described by

$$V_S = V_\nu(x_0) = V_\mu(x_0+d) = f_1(x_0) = f_2(x_0+d) \qquad (7)$$

where x_0 and x_0+d are the coordinates of binarisation.

Introducing Eq. (5) in Eq. (7) we get directly

$$V_S = f_1(x_0) = f_2(x_0+d) = 0.5 * h \qquad (8).$$

A threshold voltage $V_S = 0.5 * h$ gives the right result for the distance **d** <u>independent</u> of the time course of motion. Using a starting point the distances in the image can be reconstructed (see Fig. 4).

But Eq. (8) is true only for a constant illumination along the CCD-Sensor. The exact fulfilment of this condition is very difficult in real conditions (e. g. [9]).

Assuming now a constant illumination only in the region of every edge follows more general:

$$V_\nu = f_1(x_\nu) = h_1 - K_1 * (g(x_\nu) - t_k) \qquad (3a)$$
$$V_\mu = f_2(x_\mu) = K_2 * (g(x_\mu) - t_k) \qquad (4a)$$

Introducing Eq. (4a) in Eq. (3a) and defining new constants α and β results in

$$f_1(x) = \alpha + \beta * f_2(x+d). \qquad (9)$$

The estimation of distance **d** can be done by minimisation of the least mean square deviation:

$$\sum_{(edge)} [\alpha + \beta * f_2(x_\nu + d) - f_1(x_\nu)]^2 ==> Min. \qquad (10)$$

This method is useful in more complex images as shown in Fig. 4 too. There may be used combinations of edges in a section plane for calculation of distances according Eq. (10).

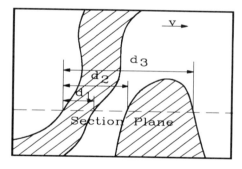

Fig. 4: General binary image with motion blur.

EXPERIMENTAL RESULTS FOR APPROXIMATION

The solution of Eq. (8) does not give correct results for distance **d** in all cases. This depends on the time behaviour the motion. The cause is a different sharpnes of Min. in Eq. (10).

Fig. 5 shows some experimental results for the approximation error σ^2 if the motion is a sinusoidal vibration. We can distinguish roughly two different situations:

1. If the object is moving with a steady velocity the left and right edges are nearly straight lines. Therefore the minimum has only small changes depending on distance **d**.

44

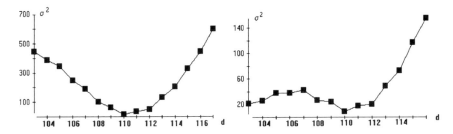

Fig. 5: Dependence of approximation error from time behavior of motion
        left: acceleration   right: steady velocity (zero crossing)

2. If the edges have an important curvature the minimum strongly depends on distance **d**. This case occurs for accelerated motion.

ADAPTATION OF THRESHOLD

From the presented results follows that the estimation of **d** according Eq. (10) for general conditions is not applicable. Additional a corresponding processing capacity is needed for fulfilling real time conditions. Avoiding the mentioned difficulties the block diagramm in Fig. 6 is proposed.

In the case of a swinging object the estimation of the measured quantity takes place by threshold decision in real time. The adaptation of the threshold using Eq. (10) and averaging algorithm occurs in the background and presupposes only slow changes of industrial conditions. If there is nearly a steady velocity of image the proposed method can be used for adjustation (calibration) of threshold causing a suitable motion. For adaptation of threshold the theory of learning systems may be used [11].

The approximation according Eq. (10) at suitable sampling points results in nearly exact distances **d**.

Assuming slowly changing distances **d** there can be used an exponential averaging of **d**:

$$\overline{d}_{i+1} = \overline{d}_i + \delta * (d_{i+1} - \overline{d}_i) \tag{11}$$

In Eq. (11) i is the number of the computed cycle and d_i the averaged distance.

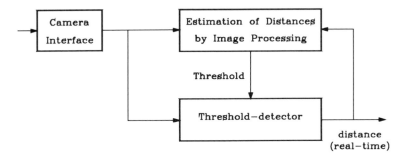

Fig. 6: Adaptive adjustation of threshold

The averaged distance $\overline{d}_i$ is applicated for checking the individual quantities are within given boundaries. The distances d_i following from Eq. (10) are used for adjustation of threshold voltage $V_{s,i}$. (In this example we presuppose only one locus-independent threshold and one distance.)

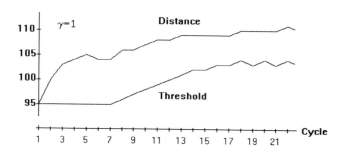

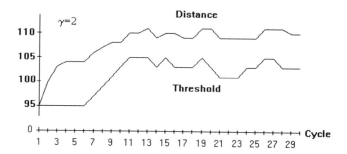

Applying a simple learning rule [11] the adaptation of threshold voltage is described by

$$V_{s,i+1} = V_{s,i} + \gamma^* R^* (d_{s,i} - d_{i+1}) \qquad (12).$$

In Eq. (12) $d_{s,i}$ is the distance estimated by threshold decision, R a constant and γ a factor influencing the adaptation speed.

Some experimental results are given in Fig. 7 for different factors γ. The delayed change of threshold is caused by checking the instantaneous distances with the aid of the averaged distance d. The adaptation of threshold is started after the distances are within the given boundaries.

Modified learning rules are tested too. But the advantages and disadvantages cannot be discussed in this paper.

The presented results confirm with the theoretical considerations above.

CONCLUSIONS

In this paper is shown that with the aid of an adaptive threshold operation the original shape of an binary image can be reconstructed. Such a learning system is useful if shutter cameras, pulsed ligth sources and other possibilities does not give the desired result. The adaptation process can be used for adjustation of (locus-dependend) threshold or occurs in the background combining flexibility with real time processing.

46

REFERENCES

[1] Michaelis, B.; Maaß, R.: Meßwerterfassung mit CCD-Sensoren. Mikroprozessortechnik 1 (1987) 2, S. 41-43.

[2] Michaelis, B.; Maaß, R.: Signal Processor for Optical Length Measurement. In: Kemeny, T. (Ed.) Signal Processing in Measurement. IMEKO TC No.16, Nova Science Publishers, S. 245-248.

[3] Seifart, M.; Michaelis, B.; Rauchhaupt, L.: Knowledge Based Systems used in Instrumentation with Process Coupling Modules. In: Knowledge based measurement, VDI Berichte 856, Düsseldorf, 1990, S. 377-384.

[4] Michaelis, B.; Heimburger, T.: Adaptive Bildauswertung bei schwingendem Meßgut. Wiss. Z. Techn. Univ. Magdeburg 35 (1991) 2, S. 78-82.

[5] PROXICAM Restlichtkameras, PROXITRONIK, Firmenschrift.

[6] TM-745/TM-765 high Resolution CCD Shutter Camera. PULNIX America Inc., Firmenschrift

[7] Lehnert, R.; Michaelis, B.; Wartini, Chr.: Kalibrieren einer optoelektronischen Meßeinrichtung. Materialien des 33. IWK, Ilmenau, 24.-28.10.1988, H. 2, S. 59-62.

[8] Riemann, M.; Kießling, B.; Wystup, P.: Optoelektronische Meßanordnung. Wirtschaftspatent Nr. 258347 A3.

[9] Wartini, Chr.: Abbildungs- und Beleuchtungsprobleme bei der Anwendung von CCD-Sensoren. Wiss. Z. Techn. Univ. Magdeburg 32 (1988) 8, S. 47-50.

[10] Maaß, R.: Hardwarestrukturen opto-elektronischer Meßsysteme für industrielle Fertigungsanlagen. Dissertation A, Techn. Univ. Magdeburg 1990.

[11] Zypkin, Ja. S.: Grundlagen der Theorie lernender Systeme. VEB Verlag Technik, Berlin 1972.

STEREO MATCHING USING A NEW LOCAL DISPARITY LIMIT

Andreas Koschan[1]

Abstract

A new solution to the correspondence problem in stereo images using a local disparity limit is presented. The local disparity limit will be estimated by applying the Block Matching technique to the stereo image. Line segments can be matched easily using the estimated values mentioned above. The results achieved with this new method are, in most cases, more precise than the results achieved with methods which require much more computational time.

Introduction

In general, a lot of data can be handled very fast and very reliable with computers. In contrast, the known stereo vision algorithms require too much computational time and are imperfect. The main problem in stereo vision is how to match corresponding features in both images, referred to as the correspondence problem. A new solution to this problem will be presented in this paper.

Simple features (line segments) are extracted in both images and are matched using a new local disparity limit [2] [4]. If the parameters influencing the image acquisition process are known, a global maximum disparity limit can be easily estimated for the stereo image. With respect to a particular selected feature this means that a maximum value can be fixed for the possible disparity in the stereo image. This paper proposes to determine a more precise local disparity limit for each feature. This value is always less than or equal to the global maximum disparity limit.

The local disparity limit can be estimated with the help of Block Matching in the stereo image [3] [5] and there are three good reasons to use Block Matching for the estimation of this local value:

- Block Matching is independent of feature extraction in the stereo image.
- Block Matching can be executed parallel to low level vision tasks.
- A special processor for Block Matching already exists [1] for real time applications.

Line segments instead of pixels are matched using the method presented in this paper. The features in the stereo image are extracted by calculating the zero crossings of the Laplacian of the stereo image. Zero crossings (ZCs) and spaces (not greater than 1 pixel) between two ZCs are linked to a line segment.

First, the Block Matching technique for the determination of the local disparity limit will be detailed below. Afterwards, the new method for stereo matching using this local disparity limit and the computed results will be presented.

---

[1] This work has been carried out at the Technische Universität Berlin, Institut f. Technische Informatik, W - 1000 Berlin 10, Franklinstr. 28-29, Germany.

The Block Matching technique

A common technique for image sequence coding is based on motion analysis. Here, the actual image is determined from the temporal preceding image using motion vectors for the pixels. A motion vector is defined by the change of location of a pixel in two temporally successive images. The temporal change between the images corresponds to the different viewpoints of the two cameras if this technique is applied for stereo matching. In this way the disparity between both images instead of the motion vector is determined. Assuming that the optical axes of the cameras are in parallel (standard stereo geometry), the motion vectors or the disparities, respectively, have to be computed only in the horizontal direction (i.e. in one row).

The main idea of Block Matching is based on a similarity check between the intensity distributions in two equal sized blocks (nxm matrices) in the left and the right image (area based stereo). The same disparity value is assumed for all pixels of one block. Therefore, only one disparity value has to be estimated for every block. This technique can be devided into several processing steps. One of the images (e.g. the left) is segmented into a constant number of equal sized blocks during the first processing step. The search for a corresponding block in the right image is only carried out for the segmented blocks in the left image. The mean square error MSE between the intensity values of the pixels inside the respective blocks is used as measure for the similarity of two blocks.

The disparity D between the blocks in both images is defined by the distance between the positions (the difference in the columns) of the blocks, showing the minimum mean square error in both images while the block (of size $n \times m$) is shifted point by point inside the search area. With regard to the definition above, the disparity value is only well defined if there is only one minimum of the MSE-function in the search area. In case there exists more than one minimum, all disparity values determined by a minimum in the MSE-function are compared with the values of the neighbouring blocks. The disparity with the smallest difference to the disparity of the neighbouring block is then selected.

Correct stereo matching using the similarity measure mentioned above is restricted for images containing regular textures and/or areas with only small intensity changes (homogeneous regions). The selection of a suitable block size is very important for the quality of the results. So far, the best results are achieved with the square block size of $n = m = 8$ pixels. A further improvement in the results is reached using the pixel selection method suggested by Reuter [5]. An explicit disparity value can be computed for every pixel, using this method.

The right stereo image has been reconstructed from the left stereo image and the disparity matrix to evaluate the results of the method. The reconstructed image has been compared with the original right image. Additionally, a statistical analysis of the results has been carried out. The difference image between the reconstructed right image and the original right image has been computed. Furthermore, a histogram of the differences between the computed and the exact disparities has been computed as well as the mean error. The investigation has been carried out for a series of monochrome stereo images representing natural opaque objects of different complexity [2] [4].

Most of the false matches have been detected for pixels representing the image background. This could be expected because the background in the image is generally represented by a homogeneous intensity distribution. A value of 1 or 2 pixels has been computed for the most frequently occuring difference between the estimated disparity and the exact disparity (for about 50% of all pixels and a block size of 8 x 8 pixels). A maximum difference of about 10 pixels occurred for about 0,5% of all pixels. About 20% of all pixels are matched exactly (difference equal to zero). It has to be emphasized that the average error occurring with the determination of the disparity values along the edges is 1 or 2 pixels.

The results do not fulfill the accuracy requirements for stereo vision methods, but they are very suitable to determine search intervals for continuing stereo vision methods. This idea will be extended into a new method for stereo matching and will be described below.

Stereo matching using a local disparity limit

Line segments instead of pixels are matched in the stereo image when this method is applied. To achieve this, the line segments have to be estimated in both images in a first processing step, i.e. it has to be determined which ZC lies on a respective line segment. Therefore, an interval for the gradient orientations will be defined. The size w of that interval defines the maximum value for the permissible difference between the orientations of the gradients along the line segments (e.g. $w = 10°$). Line segments are generated with regard to the following three processing steps.

a) Determination of the beginning of a line segment.

All rows and columns of the zero crossing image are checked from left to right and from top to bottom. The local 4-neighbours (see illustration opposite) are examined for a neighbouring ZC, if a ZC is found. A line segment consisting of only 1 pixel is not permitted. The central pixel is regarded as the beginning of a line segment if a second ZC has been detected in the local neighbourhood and the orientation of the gradient at this location differs less than w degrees (e.g. $w = 10°$) from the orientation of the gradient at the central location $\star$.

b) Selecting the successor from the neighbouring ZCs.

The ZC, having the minimum difference between the orientation of the gradient and the orientation of the gradient at the central location, is selected as successor from all neighbouring ZCs where the orientation of the gradient at that location differs less than w degrees from the orientation of the gradient at the central location. The successor is called ZC1. Example: The orientation of the gradient at the central location is 17° and the orientation of the gradient at the location ZC1 is 20°. The difference between both orientations is in this case less than $w = 10°$.

c) Selecting an additional pixel of the line segment.

The bounds of the interval for the gradient orientation are modified based on the gradient orientation of the first element of the line segment and the gradient orientation of the successor ZC1. The lower bound of the interval is given by the minimum of both values and the upper bound is given by the maximum of both values. An additional pixel lies on the line segment if its gradient orientation is in the (modified) interval. With regard to the example mentioned above, the lower bound of the interval is min $= 17°$ and the upper bound is max $= 20°$. From two additional candidates ZCa and ZCb (see illustration opposite) with for example the gradient orientations 19° and 23° the candidate is selected successor having a gradient orientation within the (modified) interval. ZCa with a gradient orientation of 19° is the selected candidate in the example mentioned above.

Line segments are detected in both images using the method mentioned above, and the results are stored in separate lists. A line segment is characterized by the following attributes:

a) by its length L,

b) by its center of gravity (x_m, y_m), given by the mean value of the x-coordinates and the mean value of the y-coordinates of all pixels belonging to the same line segment,

c) by its "mean orientation" R, given by the mean value of the orientation of the intensity gradients along the line segment (and a rotation of 90°), and

d) by its initial "mean disparity" D, determined by the mean value of the disparities estimated for all pixels along the line segment using the Block Matching technique.

An estimated disparity value for the pixels on the line segment has already been computed using the Block Matching technique. Therefore, the search area for corresponding line segments is considerably restricted. A specific search area in the right image is determined for every single line segment in the left image with regard to its length and position in the image. The determination of the search area will be explained using the following example.

Let K_L be a line segment in the left image with the length L_L, the center of gravity (x_{mL}, y_{mL}), the "mean orientation" R_L and the "mean disparity" D_L. Furthermore, x_{L_max} is the largest value and x_{L_min} is the smallest value of all x-coordinates of the pixels belonging to the line segment K_L. y_{L_max} and y_{L_min} are defined analogously for the y-coordinates and the line segment K_L. Now the centre (a,b) of the smallest rectangle covering the line segment has to be determined. The center is defined by $a = (x_{L\_max} - x_{L\_min})/2$ and $b = (y_{L\_max} - y_{L\_min})/2$. A minimum value of 4 is fixed for a and b to guarantee a minimum size of the search area. The upper left corner of the search area is set to $(x_{mL} + D_L - a, y_{mL} - b)$ and the lower right corner is set to $(x_{mL} + D_L + a, y_{mL} + b)$. The search area and its computation is outlined in Fig. 1.

Two line segments in the left and the right image are regarded as candidates for stereo matching if the following three conditions are fulfilled:

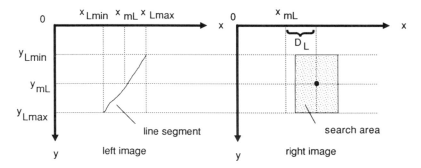

Fig. 1: Computation of the search area in the right image.

1) The center of gravity of the line segment in the right image lies inside the corresponding search area.

2) The lenghts of both line segments differ not more than factor 3 from each other, i.e. $1/3L_L < L_R < 3L_L$ holds.

3) The "mean orientations" of both line segments differ not more than v degrees from each other, i.e. $\mid R_L - R_R \mid < v$ holds.

The candidate in the right image, having the minimum difference between its "mean orientation" and the "mean orientation" of the line segment in the left image and also having the minimum difference between the lengths of both line segments, is matched. Let Ω be the set of corresponding candidates K_{Ri} ($i = 1,...,n$) in the right image for a line segment K_L in the left image and let R_{Ri} be the "mean orientation" and L_{Ri} the length of the line segment K_{Ri}. Now a line segment $K_{Rj} \in \Omega$ with a minimum difference of $\mid R_L - R_{Rj} \mid$ and a minimum difference of $\mid L_L - L_{Rj} \mid$ is searched for. If there does not exist a special line segment with a minimum in both differences the one line segment K_{Rj}, having the smallest difference between its disparity and the "mean disparity" of the left line segment, is selected. The line segment K_{Rj} is matched to the line segment K_L.

The results of stereo matching using this method depend on the suitable selection of the interval for the gradient orientation, i.e. they depend on the parameters w and v. The number of selected line segments is influenced by these parameters and the number of matches as well. Dependent on the selected stereo image the best results have been reached with values between 12 and 25 for w and v during the evaluation of the results with our test images. The number of detected line segments is reverse proportional to the size of w. The larger the value for w is selected the less line segments are detected and can be matched. The number of detected line segments increases if a small value is used for w. In contrast, the number of matches does not increase. Good results have always been reached with fixed parameters w = v = 20 for all investigated test images. The results have been verified manually for the matched line segments.

The results of stereo matching are visualized by example for two selected stereo images. A detailed overview of the results can be found in [4]. Furthermore, the results have been compared

52

to the results achieved with 8 other selected methods. Unfortunately, due to space limitation the comparison of the results can not be presented in this paper. A detailed representation can be found in [2].

In summary, I believe that precise results in stereo matching can be obtained more easily using this simple new method. This work was carried out within SFB 203 at the Technische Universität Berlin and was funded by the Deutsche Forschungsgemeinschaft (DFG).

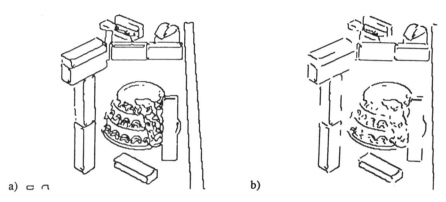

Fig. 2: Matched line segments in the stereo image SZENE1 (with w = v = 25).
a) All 616 detected line segments in the left image are shown.
b) The matched line segments in the left image having a length of more than 3 pixels are shown (228 of 333).

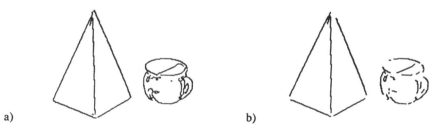

Fig. 3: Matched line segments in the stereo image SZENE2 (with w = v = 12).
a) All 123 detected line segments in the left image are shown.
b) The matched line segments in the left image having a length of more than 3 pixels are shown (56 of 73).

References

[1] Considine, V., A.S. Bhandal, and J.N. Gooding: Single Chip Motion Estimator for Video Codec Applications. Proc. 3rd Int. Conf. on Image Processing and its Applications, University of Warwick, GB (1989), 285-289.

[2] Koschan, A.: Eine Methodenbank zur Evaluierung von Stereo-Vision-Verfahren. Dissertation, TU Berlin, Fachbereich Informatik (1991).

[3] Musmann, H.G., P. Pirsch, and H.-J. Grollert: Advances in picture coding. Proc. of the IEEE 73 (1985) 4, 523-548.

[4] Ohnesorge, K.: Ein Verfahren zur Korrespondenzanalyse in Stereobildern unter Verwendung eines maximalen lokalen Disparitätslimits. Diplomarbeit, TU Berlin, Fachbereich Informatik (1990).

[5] Reuter, T.: HDTV standards conversion. IEEE-ASSP & EURASIP 5th Workshop on Multidimensional Signal Processing, Nordwijkerhouth, the Netherlands (1987), (reprint).

A Gestalt Model for Textur

Dinu Scheppelmann[1], Ansgar Springup[1],
Uwe Engelmann[1], Hans-Peter Meinzer[1]

Abstract

Textur is a comprehension for all features of a pattern. The texture anlysis is the quantitative description of that pattern by numbers, the so called texture parameters. In image processing hundreds of texture parameters have been invented so far, but there exists neither a theory of texture nor a true definition.

The article provides two definitions of texture, the semantic one formulated by VanGool et al. and a heuristic definition based on digital geometry. Those two definitons are linked by an explicit texture model, that is based on concepts of the gestalt theory of Wertheimer and others. While the gestalt theory is formulated in a rather fuzzy way, which is not suitable for a formular description or processing algorithm, the model of the 'cognitive texture parameters' is supported by a digital numeric concept, providing texture measures for some of the visual effects.

In the first step of the model, the resolution is seperated as an independent property of a texture. In the second step different texture effects, which may appear at any resolution, are described: homogenous, amorphous, anisotropic and symmetric behavior of a texture. All of these features can by quantified without detection of single textons. Therefor this approach is a gestalt model.

The last clue to a texture gestalt description is the combination of the cognitive texture parameters through the scale space: a texture may have only homogenous features at high resolution, some amorphous aspects at medium resolution, which are themselves arranged in a symmetric way at a coarse level. This is a way humans **and** machines may describe a texture.

Keywords: gestalt theory, texture model, moments, semantic of texture, cognitive texture parameters

Introduction

Although a lot of papers have been published in this field, none of them give a precise definition of texture. As already stated by Haralick [HARA, p.786], there is only little correlation between the semantic meaning of texture and the hundreds of texture measures developed so far.

While the form of a closed region can be described by mathematical morphology, no such easy and consistent approach exists for the description of the inner part of the region, the texture. So texture analysis is typically performed by using all of the known texture

---

[1]   German Cancer Research Center, Dep. Medical and Biological Informatics. Im Neuenheimer Feld 280, D-6900 Heidelberg.

parameters (appr. 500) and finding the significant ones by some statistics. This approach has a lot of disadvantages:

- You never can say if the used parameters, even they are so many, are sufficiant.
- The parameters are strongly correlated. A very unimportant measure can be decisive.
- You don't know, if your selected texture parameters quantify the real texture or some artefacts correlated with that texture.
- Since it is not clear which effect is measured by which parameter, no semantic information can be achieved.

The main problem with such an approach arises, when you try to use symbolic processing methods (e.g. expert systems). It is impossible to set up a knowledge base, if no semantic knowledge about the image can be extracted. The classical texture parameters have been derived from the question 'what can be calculated' rather than from the question 'what can be seen'.

The real main philosophic problem in this field is, that there is no definition of texture and no model, that makes it possible to describe texture by some mathematics or some algorithms.

This paper sketches a theory for texture, that I proposed in my dissertation [SCHP]. My intend here is to open the discussion. The suggested gestalt model is a very primitive and basic one, only offering measures for very global effects of texture. The texture parameters are called 'cognitive', because they are related to human impressions while looking on a textured image. The idea is, that a textured image may be described by an 'expert' (where every one who can see is an expert) following the described model, but also may be quantified using the appropriate measures.

A brief review

In 1979 Haralick [HARA] suggested to differentiate texture analysis approaches into the following classes, a taxonomy, which has not been changed or expanded up today:

A) **Statistical approaches (microtexture):** autocorrelation methods, optical processing methods, digital transform methods, texture edgeness, mathematical morphology, cooccurrence, textural transform, generalized gray-tone spatial dependence, run length, autoregressive models, mosaic texture models.

B) **Structural approaches (macrotexture):** define primitives, spatial relationships, weak texture measures, strong texture measures (generalized cooccurrence).

The above scheme does not describe any texture model, it just demonstrate the confuseness in the field. Four years later Van Gool et al. [VGO] still uses the same terms, but some important insigths have been achieved meanwhile:

- Many authors work on **normalized images**, thus indicating that grayvalue properties can be handled independently.
- Van Gool shows some approaches how to get **rotation invariant texture parameters**, since most of the existing ones depend on the choice of the coordinate system.

- The dependecy of the scale space is stated and the **pyramid concept** of Larkin and Burt [BURT] influences image processing.
- The improovement of texture analysis by **multispektral and 3D analysis** is suggested, but unfortunately rejected by Rosenfeld [ROS].

In the same time, some important works have been done to texture analysis. For example the statistical approach from Laws [LAWS], which is one of the very first pure digital theories, or the description with markov fields [KIND, HASS] and the Gibbs distribution [ISIN, DERI, GEMA]. All of these theories have in common, that they do not support a semantic texture model, although many of them have been denoted so. They are just a mathematical description of one special feature of texture. Of course we can interpret the mathematical description as being the realization of an underlying model, which leads to the following six classes of texture description provided in literature so far (examples in parentheses):

1) **Transforms** (Cooccurrence, run length, fourier spectrum)
2) **Analytical functions** (Gabor functions, Legendre polynomial, Wigner distribution)
3) **Digital filters** (Laws masks)
4) **Statistical description** (Markov fields, Gibbs distribution, the moments of Hu [HU])
5) **Textonal models** (Voorhees and Poggio [POGG], Vistness [VIST], mathematical morphology [SERA])
6) **Syntactical description** (Carlucci [CARL], Lu and Fu [LUFU])

Except of the textonal models and the syntactical approach of Lu and Fu, all of these 'models' have no semantic meaning. The real problem of texture analysis (and sometimes image processing in general) was stated by Haralick:

'Unfortunately, few experiments have been done attempting to map semantic meaning into precise properties of tonal primitives and their spatial distributional properties.' [HARA, p.786]

As always in scientifics, a model is based on observations and some hypotheses. Concerning texture, there is even a lack of a true definition, that helps us defining what a human thinks that texture is. Ravishankar Rao in 1990: 'Interestingly, most researchers in computer vision do not attempt to define texture in their work.' [RAO, p.2]

Concepts of a texture model, definitions

The only usefull definition of texture was given by Van Gool [VGO] in 1983. He carefully used the subjunctive mood:

'Texture could be defined as a structure composed of a large number of more or less ordered similar elements or patterns without one of these drawing special attention.'

And he continues: 'So a global unitary impression is offered to the observer'. But this definition contains all problems in analysing texture:

- What is the difference between 'texture' and 'structure' ?
- What is a large number ?
- What is ordered, and what means 'more or less' ?
- The most difficult question: What is 'similar' ?
- What is the element of a texture ?
- What is the difference of texture and pattern ?
- How can we avoid drawing special attention to the single element ?

Besides the semantic definition of Van Gool, we may construct a heuristic definition, in the sense of digital geometry [VOSS]. The fact, that each closed region in an image is a finite set of pixels, is rather important to the theory of texture parameters. It gives us an upper limit of parameters, that fully describes the texture. Please refer to [SCHP] for a more detailed derivation of the simple definition:

> 'Textur is the global appearance of a closed region, that is independand of the form (morphology describes the form). The texture is described by a set of numbers, called texture parameters. Texture analysis is the transformation from a closed region to a vector.'

To satisfy both definitions, we need a **texture model**. This model must be close to 'what wee see' but also must be calculatable.

Already in 1958 Max Wertheimer [WERT] postulated a human visual perception of gestalt that is not based on the conscious recognition of primitives. According to this we have can set up two different types of models: A **textonal model** or a **gestalt model**.

Also we can base our theory on an image function defined over the **continuum**, or we may construct a pure **digital theory**.

Furthermore we can try to find texture parameters, that give a **complete** description of the textured region, or we may be satisfied with a smaller set of parameters, which offers a good **abstraction** of the texture.

Finally we may use (or not) the texture measures for segmentation. In this case we need some information about the locality of a texture. But this is always a deal of **accuracy in the feature space against resolution in the real space** - the uncertainty principle of image processing (stated by many researchers in many different ways, e.g. [CANY]).

A gestalt model

According to the above scheme, the following concept is a gestalt model, based on digital geometry, that gives an abstract description of the texture in the real space. Van Gool states two major characteristics of a texture: coarseness and directionality. But this is not enough. True is, that we can split the **resolution** of the texture from the rest of it's 'behaviour'. The texture of D27, D28 and D29 from [BROD] can be interpreted as the same basic texture type viewed at different resolution levels. The remaining problem is to find features of a texture, which can be described independantly from resolution effects:

1) Homogenous texture

The most primitive features of a texture are the grayvalue properties, providing no structural infomation at all. Since the locality of a single pixel is irrelevant, the grayvalue histogram is a complete description of those effects! The problem of quantification reduces to the parameterisation of a histogram, which can be done in many different ways. The one, that is very close to the human impressions of 'brightness' and 'contrast' is simply the use of the statistical moments.

With this choice of parameters we implicitly go for an abstract decription, since the higher order moments are not independant and therefore only a limited set is usefull (typically the first three moments). We can't get a complete description with this. But for me it seems like a philosophical law. Similarity - without giving any definition - lives from the uncertainty of the parameters, while independant features may give a complete description, but are useless for comparsion of similar objects.

2) Amorphous textures

We would call a texture 'amorphous' if it exhibits some structure, that has no law of special ordering (see next types). All significant textures are at least of this type - if no amorphous features can be seen, we have a simple noise image. The transition of 'noise' to 'structure' is of course very unsharp and depends on the resolution, that we consider seperatly. The amorphous features of a texture can be quantified by the gradient and the higher order structural moments as they where decribed by Hu [HU]. Originally I derived the measures in analogy to the inertia moments from theoretical physics, but they figured out to be formal identical to what Hu derived with completely different mathematics.

3) Anisotropic textures

Some more special arrangement of the textons may appear globally as an oriented texture. This behavior can also be seen by the theory of the structural moments. The second moments with respect to the coordinate system form a so called 'structural tensor', whose eigenvector is parallel to the direction of the oriented texture. The degree of orientation can be quantified by the quotient of the eigenvalues (the principal moments of inertia). For isotropic textures both eigenvalues are equal. As the examples below will show, only with this primitive measures in combination with the resolution effects, a lot of textures can be easily classified.

4) Symmetries

'Without drawing special attention' to the textons, the human being is able to see all of the above stated effects. A much more complex behavior of a set of textons is the symmetry of their organisation, which also can be seen without detection of single elements. We can split this group into **axial**, **rotational** and **grid symmetries**. For the later, autocorrelation texture measures may be the appropriate tool.

Axial or rational symmetry have not been object of research so far. They can be quantified by an approach similar to the structural tensor, but with different antisymmetric convolution masks. Again the symmetry moments for the coordinate axes are calculated and the eigenvectors of the resulting matrix give the direction of the axial symmetry. For rotational symmetry there is yet no direct way, and transformation into a polar coordinate system is only a loophole. Another problem with symmetry is the definition of higher order moments.

5) Multitextonal textures

Symmetries exhibit the most complexity you can achieve with identical elements. A further distinction of two textures, which seem to be equal in all of the above features, can be done only by the inspection of **different textons**. But this is no more a gestalt model. As shown in my work, with only two different textons a tremendous amount of complex texture situations can be constructed. But in some cases, even the human being has problems seeing the difference, because no global gestalt feature can be used.

Texture analysis

A real texture can have all of these properties simultaneously, but each feature may be expressed differently on each resolution level. Although the above features are pretty simple, they offer a lot of information if applied on different scales. But the basic idea of scale space may be extended to a generalized pyramid approach, not only using one type of pyramid (e.g. Gaussian or Laplacian) but instead using every texture parameter at each level of resolution, and combining them through the scale space.

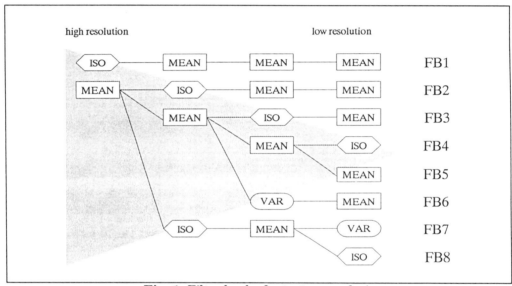

Fig. 1 Filter banks for texture analysis

This job can be easily performed, if the texture analysis is implemented as convolution. Figure 1 illustrates this idea, with two homogenous texture parameters, the mean (MEAN) and the variance (VAR), and one amorphous parameter, the isotropic structural moment (ISO). At the left we have the full resolution image. After each convolution the image is scaled down, reducing the resolution one level. The example shows eigth different filter banks (FB1 to FB8), which perform the following tasks:

- FB1 to FB4 analyse the fine, medium fine, medium coarse and coarse structure.
- FB5 is simply the gaussian pyramid as a special case, offering the mean brightness of the texture.
- FB6 shows the medium coarse contrast.

- FB7 first analyses the medium fine structure, and looks if this exhibits any fluctuations at coarse resolution.
- FB8 does the same, but measures the spatial fluctuation ('the structure of the structure').

Examples

The examples demonstrate the use of the isotropic structural moment. Figure 2 shows the structure of noise at different resolutions (1/2, 1/4 and 1/8 of the original image size, achieved by gaussian scaling). The plot shows the mean response of the texture measure. The striped area is the range of one standard deviation. Typically for noise, we find a very strong fine structure (high pixel value changes at high frequency). The structural contents drops rapidly, when the resolution is lowered.

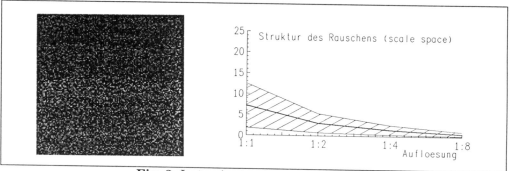

Fig. 2 Isotropic structure of white noise

Figure 3 shows three strong structures, D103 and D104 from [BROD] and a hand drawing. The plot of the isotropic structural moment shows a strong structure (compare the ordinate with figure 2) with a typical maximum. The three textures are 'similar', although they have different orientation and different contrast (one is a 'negative'). The isotropic structural moment of D103 and D104 is almost the same, while my hand drawing shows up to be not quite correct at the resolution of 1:2.

Conclusions

The suggested texture model has important advantages compared to the classical approach of trial and error. It offers an explicit semantic model, which facilitates the formulation of expert knowledge about texture. Since the features are correlated to human feelings about texture, the effect of a texture measure can be judged objectivly and subjectivly.

The seperation of resolution effects through the suggested filter bank approach offers a huge set of texture parameters, by combining the primitive measures for homogenous, amorphous, anisotropic and symmetric behavior through the scale space.

60

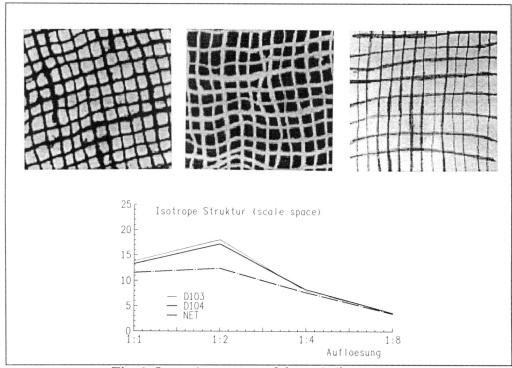

Fig. 3 Isotropic structure of three similar textures

References

[BROD]   Brodatz, P.: Textures. New York: Dover Publications 1966.

[BURT]   Larkin, L.I.; Burt, P.J.: Multi-resolution texture energy measures. Proceedings of the Conference on Computer Vision and Pattern Recognition, Washington D.C., (Jun.1983) 519-520.

[CANY]   Canny, J.F.: Finding Edges and Lines in Images. Massachusetts: Massachusetts Institute of Technology 1983 (Technical Report 720).

[CARL]   Carlucci, L.: A formal system for texture languages. Pattern Recognition, vol.4, (1972) 53-72.

[DERI]   Derin, H.; Elliott, H.: Modeling and segmentation of noisy and textured images using Gibbs random fields. IEEE Transactions on Pattern Analysis and Machine Intelligence, Vol.PAMI-9, 1 (Jan.1987) 39-55.

[GEMA]   Geman, S.; Geman, G.: Stochastic Relaxation, Gibbs Distributions, and the Bayesian Restauration of Images. IEEE Transactions on Pattern Analysis and Machine Intelligence, Vol.PAMI-6, 6 (Nov.1984) 721-741.

[HARA]   Haralik, R.M.: Statistical and Structural Approaches to Texture. Proceedings of the IEEE, vol.67, 5 (1979) 786-804.

[HASS]   Hassner, M.; Sklansky, J.: The use of Markov random fields as models of texture. Computer Graphics and Image Processing, Vol.12, (1980) 357-370.

[HU]   Hu, M.-K.: Visual pattern recognition by moment invariants. IRE Transactions on Information Theory, Vol.IT-8, (Feb.1962) 179-187.

[ISIN]   Ising, E.: Zeitschrift Physik, Vol.31, (1925) 253.

[KIND]   Kindermann, R.; Snell, J.L.: Markov Random Fields and Their Applications. American Mathematical Society, Providence, R.I., 1980.

[LAWS]   Laws, K.: Textured Image Segmentation. Technical Report, Jan 1980, USCIPI Report 940. Los Angeles, CA 90007: Image Processing Institute, University of Southern California.

[LUFU]   Lu, S.Y.; Fu, K.S.: A syntactic approach to texture analysis.Computer Graphics and Image Processing, Vol.7, (1978)303-330.

[POGG]   Voorhees, H.; Poggio, T.: Detecting textons and texture boundaries in natural images. Proceedings of the First International Conference on Computer Vision, (1987) 250-258.

[RAO]   Rao, A.R.: A taxonomy for texture description and identification. Berlin: Springer-Verlag 1990.

[ROS]   Rosenfeld, A.; Thurston, M.: Edge and curve detection for visual scene analysis. IEEE Transactions on Computing, Vol.C-20, (1971) 562-569.

[SCHP]   Scheppelmann, D.: Analyse von Texturen in digitalen Bildern. Universität Heidelberg, Fakultät für theoretische Medizin, Dissertation 1990.

[SERA]   Serra, J.: Theoretical bases of the Leitz texture analysis system. Leitz Sci. Tech. Inform., Supplement 1, 4, p.125-136. Wetzlar: Leitz Wetzlar GmbH (Apr.1974).

[VGO]   Van Gool, L.; Dewaele, P.; Oosterlinck, A.: Texture Analysis Anno 1983. Computer Vision, Graphics and Image Processing 29 (1985) 336-357.

[VIST]   Vistnes, R.: Texture Models and Image Measures for Texture Discrimination. International Journal of Computer Vision 3 (1989) 313-336.

[VOSS]   Voss, K.: Discrete integral geometry. Proceedings of the CAIP'87, Wismar, (Sept.1987).

[WERT]   Wertheimer, M.: Principles of perceptual organization. In Beardslee, D.C.; Wertheimer, W: (eds.): Readings in Perception. 115-135. Princeton: Van Nostrand, 1958.

GENERATION AND DISPLAY OF AN EXTENDED CELL ENUMERATION REPRESENTATION

Klaus D. Toennies, Christian Daunis[1]

Abstract

The purpose of an extended cell enumeration (XCE) representation is the integration of three-dimensional functions from medical imaging devices and from results of analysis and manipulation of these images. It is based on a simple patient model $P = \{f_i, r_j\}$ of a set of functions and a set of relations. Functions f_i represent anatomically or physiologically significant parameters, such as the X-ray absorption coefficient, an object class membership or a treatment plan. Relations may exist either between function names representing dependencies known in advance or they may exist between values of a function describing dependencies between segments computed during data analysis.

The XCE representation is a discrete-space description of that model based on a cell enumeration representation being capable of representing different functions. The number of functions, their range and the resolution, with which function values can be represented, may vary. The representation consists of a data cube of cells and two graphs associated with it. Nodes of the first graph, which is called the *description graph*, describe for each function its type and range as well as its position in the cells of the data cube (additional information can be added). Arcs between the nodes stand for relations between the set of function names. The second graph, which is called the *structure graph*, is designed to represent relations between values of a function.

We report on preliminary results of a realization of a XCE representation. This implementation requires access mechanisms for efficient information retrieval from the data cube *through* the description graph. We propose an approach, where information on how to access values of a certain function is located in the function nodes of the description graph and we present results of using this mechanism for visualization purposes.

Introduction

The usefulness of information presented to the physician from medical images can be increased if results from all examinations, evaluations and treatment plans on the patient are represented in an integrated fashion. In this case, information from sources as different as an anatomic atlas and a radiation treatment plan contribute to an integrated view of the current state of a patient. Such a representation should be based on digital slice data from medical imaging devices and it should be easy to create and modify.

Existing representations to describe information from medical images can be characterized as *analysis* or *synthesis* representations. An analysis representation is designed to interpret patient-

---

[1]Fachgruppe Computer Graphics, Institut für Technische Informatik, Fachbereich Informatik, Technische Universität Berlin, Sekr. FR 3-3, Franklinstr. 28-29, W-1000 Berlin 10, Germany

specific information which describes the context of objects within a certain class of objects. Analytical representations are used for analysis of medical image data[17] or the description of natural phenomena[15]. For the purpose of interactive diagnosis and therapy, however, a synthesis representation is more suited. Early synthesis representations have focused on the description of analysed objects from the images as surface [3], [5], [16] or volume representations [8], [12]. This was mainly caused by lack of storage capacity and computation speed requiring a maximum of data reduction. Research has concentrated on storage efficient representation schemes, on algorithms to create the representation, and on the development of fast visualization and manipulation methods. A major disadvantage of this kind of description is that information, which has been discarded once, cannot be retrieved from the representation.

Though these kinds of representation continue to play an important role [4], [19] (for speed is an important issue in evaluation and treatment planning), improvements in computer technology offer the chance to keep all the information needed in a common representation, being available at any time. Thus, since the late 80s, the emphasis has been on the investigation of representation schemes to handle multispectral and multidimensional data. Two different research directions can be identified:

- The development of visualization and manipulation algorithms to handle multidimensional data arrays [2], [6], [9], [10], [11], [18].

- The research towards integrated representation and manipulation of data from varying sources [14], [20], [21], [22], [24].

The objective is to handle the vast amount of different information from imaging devices, analysis modules and treatment plans in an efficient, consistent, and unified fashion.

The XCE representation

In the field of medical imaging there will always be a necessity to represent more than one function at a time, since information from different sources complement one another. Knowledge related to medical images can be differentiated into prototype and patient-specific information which can be further subdivided into geometrical and functional information. Prototypes are needed to interpret actual findings in the patient. They usually consist of global descriptions of anatomical or physiological phenomena. Such information may include spatial relationships between parts of anatomical objects, the number and approximative size of objects, the expected position, or an expected change of parameters over time. Functional information of a prototype describes the expected normal or abnormal behaviour in objects.

From the point of developing a representation, information can be classified as

- global information *on* objects (anatomical, physiological or artificial entities) describing these objects and the way they behave.

- local information *from* objects describing perceived behaviour (not necessarily containing an object membership information).

Many applications require only the second type of knowledge to be described, since analysis or evaluation is done prior or after creating the representation, and the associated information is kept in the algorithms but not in the representation itself.

An important feature of a representation will be the means of visualizing patient-specific information from it, because inspection of the data is computationally inexpensive as compared to an evaluation by other means of computer assisted analysis. In order to facilitate visualization there should be a common, simple structure to keep patient-specific information. If imaging devices are the source of information this structure will obviously be a discrete space representation. The underlying model is a set of functions which are represented by their values at evenly spread locations in space and time. Such a description is a special form of a cell enumeration (CE) representation as presented, e.g., by Höhne et al. [7]. However, some problems remain:

- The representation can be inefficient for the description of artificial objects.

- Global information (e.g., blood pressure or class membership to a class of organs) must be represented on a local level and is not easily retrieved as a global entity.

- Prototype knowledge cannot be integrated and accessed easily, since it also needs to be represented locally.

The points listed above play an important role, if more than just inspection of the data is needed, and thus, extensions of the base representation to describe other kinds of knowledge are necessary.

A simple extension, the so-called extended cell enumeration (XCE) representation, is the addition of a description graph and structure graphs to the CE representation (see Figure 1). A description graph consists of nodes describing functions in the CE representation and of arcs representing relationships between the functions. Information in a function node consists of global information on the function (type of function, range, etc.) and of information on how to access function values in the underlying CE representation. The link to the CE representation may be omitted, if the XCE representation shall be used as a prototype description. Information from the CE representation can only be accessed through the description graph. A structure graph represents relations between function values. The nodes of the structure graph contain global information on all elements of the CE representation related to the corresponding structure. This information may later be interpreted by comparison with a prototype structure in the description graph of another representation.

A first implementation of the XCE representation assumed a fixed division of the cells of the data cube [20], [23]. Each cell contained the following three functions:

- an imaging function f_{RCT} (12 bit) to represent the x-ray absorption coefficient.

- a segmentation function $f_{segment}$ (6 bit) to represent enumerated class membership combinations (the structure graph was used to define the classes, since cells could be members of more than one class).

- an auxiliary imaging function f_{aux} (7 bit) to represent a second imaging source, e.g., data from a magnetic resonance imaging system.

The representation was developed to test applications for the planning of radiation therapy and neuro-stereotactic operations (see [24] for details). The implementation of the description graph was omitted and function values in the data cube were accessed directly.

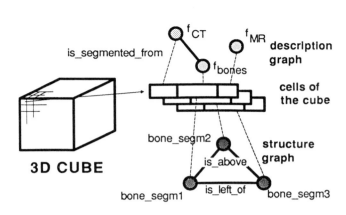

Figure 1: The XCE representation: Each cell of the cube represents several functions (three in this example) which are described in the nodes of the description graph. Relations in this graph describe relationships (conceptual or spatial) between function names. The structure graph can be used to establish relationships between values of a function.

However, this implementation is not sufficient to assess the usefulness of the application-independent XCE framework and, therefore, a second implementation was created using the description graph (see [1] for details). Access to information in the 3D data cube has to take place through that graph, as only there the information is available on how the data is structured within the cells. Our representation consists of the following three parts:

(1) General information on the representation is kept in a global descriptor of the representation. The descriptor contains information on the space allocated for the cube, the dimensionality of the cube, the number of functions represented, and the number of bits reserved for each cell.

(2) Information on the functions within the cube is located in the description graph. This information consists of the name of the function, its range and discretization, the location of the function values in the cube cells, as well as of the relations between functions.

(3) Values of the functions are located in the elements of the cube.

The size allocated for all function values of a cell can only be increaesed bytewise, in order to minimize access overhead. Procedures to append, read, modify and delete functions of the cube were implemented and tested. These procedures interpret that node of the description graph which is associated to the function to be accessed prior to accessing the function values themselves. The 'read' and 'modify' procedures can be applied to single cells or all cells of the cube. The other two procedures can only access the complete function.

A volume rendering algorithm was implemented to visualize functions of the XCE representation. Data access for the rendering algorithm was carried out in two different ways. Functions are either read from the cube, completely creating a separate 3D data cube prior to

66

subjecting it to the visualization algorithm, or function values are accessed at the time they are needed for computation by the rendering procedure. While the former requires additional storage the latter leads to longer computation times when - as is the case here - a function value needs to be read more than once.

Visualization of the data

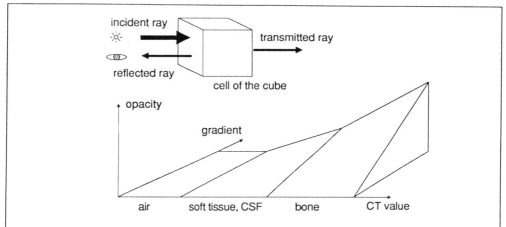

Figure 2:   Computing transparency and reflection: Transparency is inversely proportional to the opacity, and the reflection is the result of an application of Phong's illumination model to the reflected portion of the incident ray which is proportional to opacity.

For visualization we used a rendering algorithm presented by Levoy[9] which was developed to render volume data with a maximum of output information on a 2D screen. Output information is coded as follows:

- Probability of class membership to a certain object class is displayed as transparency. It is assumed that there is a linear relationship between this probability and the function values of the image function. This is an appropriate approximation for X-ray CT and class memberships to the classes 'bone', 'soft tissue', 'cerebrospinal fluid' and 'air' (another algorithm which is based on arbitrary but known probabilities was presented by Drebin et al. [2]).

- Probability of a surface is transformed into strength of reflection. That probability is assumed to be linearly related to the length of the gradient vector approximated by local differences of the discrete function. This again is an appropriate assumption, if the above assumption holds.

For each volume element a transparency and reflection component can be computed as shown in Figure 2. Rays are sent through the data cube from the point of an assumed light source. For each ray and each cell there is computed how much of the incoming light intensity is reflected towards the viewer and how much is transmitted towards the next cell. On the reflected portion the

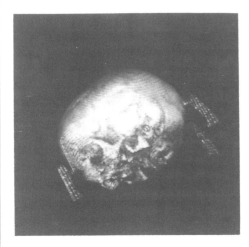

Figure 3:   Visualization of a sequence of X-ray CTs in the XCE representation. The left
image shows low opacity for skin (soft tissue), thus highlighting the bone
structure whereas the right image shows high opacity for skin.

illumination model by Phong[13] is applied using the normalized gradient as surface normal. If the position of the viewer equals that of the light source the reflected portion of the light towards the viewer passes the same cells as the ones passed by the incident ray.

The result of the rendering algorithm is a semi-transparent visualization of the function, where a surface can be seen at a change between different object class memberships (see Figure 3). The amount of transparency for a certain object class can be changed interactively, allowing that from the same data set different objects can be highlighted.

Results

The access mechanisms of the XCE representation underwent a preliminary evaluation. Our objective was to test, whether for realistic situations access times were short enough to allow practical use in a clinical environment. For a data set with 250·250 picture elements in each of 40 slices, computation times were measured on a SUN 4/330 for appending, modifying, reading and deleting function values in the XCE representation.

Access times to the function are shown in table 1. Further tests revealed linear increase in computation times with the number of cells of the underlying CE representation. In the case of the append function computation times increased with the number of already existing functions in the representation, since these had to be copied into the newly sized data cube prior to appending the new function. An increase by factor 4 to 5 was observed, if instead of accessing the complete function at the same time, the access was carried out cell by cell. This is due to the fact, that the

number of bits per function value	8	16	24	32
append	7.8 sec	9.5 sec	11.3 sec	12.9 sec
delete	15.4 sec	20.4 sec	17.9 sec	19.9 sec
read	5.7 sec	7.4 sec	8.8 sec	10.3 sec
modify	9.6 sec	12.0 sec	12.9 sec	15.0 sec

assignment of the function to variables: 3.6 sec

Table 1:   Access times on a SUN 4/330 for different functions ($250 \cdot 250 \cdot 40$ cells each) in the XCE representation. Computation times for the append function are for appending the first function.

address computation cannot be optimized using an incremental address scheme. However, the size of representation of a function value did not play an important role (the increase was less than linear with the number of bits per element).

The results show that computation times to access the XCE representation are considerably higher than the access by simple assignment of function values to variables. Thus the implemention of algorithms to manipulate image data for the purpose of diagnosis or treatment planning is noticeably influenced by the fact that data is stored in the XCE representation. This can be observed when comparing the two different data access mechanisms for volume rendering of a function. If the complete function was extracted from the XCE representation prior to visualization, then computation times for a $165 \cdot 140 \cdot 110$-cell representation were 7 minutes per image as compared to 10 minutes, if cells were accessed on the fly. This difference in computation times resulted mainly from the fact, that each function value needs to be accessed 7 times for volume rendering (6 times as a neighbor element for the approximation of the gradient and once to read the grey level for classification) and the type of access was cell-by-cell. This may not be very important, if the rendering algorithm is slow, but for applications in near-real-time rendering methods, e.g. in surgical planning, the structure of the XCE representation may constitute a serious disadvantage for algorithm development.

Conclusions

We presented a new representation to describe multispectral and multidimensional data from medical images. The test implementation of the XCE representation showed high versatility of the representation to different applications, but also a low efficiency for access to the information. The latter was caused by the requirement for physical representation of function values at the same location in a single element. Currently, we are testing an alternative representation, where the description graph is used as a meta-representation, specifying in each node the representation form which is used. Thus, we are maintaining the concept of an integrated representation of different functions at a virtual level while enabling different forms of actual representation. It is expected, that this will facilitate access to single functions. On the other hand it is expected that the combined access to a set of function values at a certain location in space will be slower than it is the case in our current version of the XCE representation.

Our ongoing research will concentrate on implementing an initial representation to be used within a medical research environment to test the acceptance of the representation. Although we believe that our approach is appropriate to represent multispectral data in an integrated form there remain some questions to be answered within that project:

(1)   The diversity of different sub-representations calls for an object-oriented approach to access and manipulate data efficiently. Investigations are needed to define appropriate objects (that is, sub-representations).

(2)   The wealth of different functions to be represented requires research for the combined visualization of a multitude of functions.

(3)   Mechanisms to guarantee consistency of information have to be developed and integrated in the representation, since information in the representation is created and changed at various times by various persons or machines (radiologists, therapists imaging devices, ...).

The final goal is to define a patient-centered description scheme combining all the information from medical examinations. This does not just include images or representation of images but also other information currently contained in a conventional patient folder.

Bibliography

[1]   Daunis, C., *Erzeugung und graphische Darstellung einer XCE (Extended Cell Enumeration) Repräsentation*, Studienarbeit, Technische Universität Berlin, FB Informatik, Berlin 1991.

[2]   Drebin, R.A., Carpenter, L. and Hanrahan, P., 'Volume rendering', *Computer Graphics*, Vol.22, No.4, 1988, pp. 65-74.

[3]   Fuchs, H., Kedem, Z.M. and Uselton, S.P., 'Optimal surface reconstruction from planar contours', *Communications of the ACM*, Vol.20, No.10, 1977, pp.693-702.

[4]   Gordon, D. and Udupa, J.K., 'Fast surface tracking in three-dimensional binary images', *Computer Vision, Graphics and Image Processing*, Vol.45, 1988, pp.196-214.

[5]   Herman, G.T. and Liu, H.K., 'Three-Dimensional Display of Human Organs from Computed Tomography', *Computer Graphics and Image Processing*, Vol.9, No.1, 1979, pp.1-21.

[6]   Höhne, K.H. und Bernstein, R., 'Shading 3D-Images from CT Using Gray Level Gradients', *IEEE Transactions on Medical Imaging*, Vol. MI-5, No.1, 1986, pp.45-47.

[7]   Höhne, K.H., Riemer, M. and Tiede, U., 'Viewing operations for 3-D-tomographic gray level data', *Computer Assisted Radiology, Proceedings of the International Symposium CAR'87*, H.U.Lemke et al. (eds.), Berlin 1987, pp.599-609.

[8]   Jackins, C.L. and Tanimoto, S.L., 'Oct-trees and their use in representing three-dimensional objects', *Computer Graphics and Image Processing*, Vol.14, pp.249-270, 1980.

[9]   Levoy, M., 'Display of surfaces from volume data', *IEEE Computer Graphics and Applications*, Vol.8, No.3, 1988, pp. 29-37.

[10]   Levoy, M., 'Efficient ray tracing of volume data', *ACM Transactions on Computer Graphics*, Vol.9, No.3, 1990, pp.245-261.

[11]   Lorensen, WE. and Cline, H.E., 'Marching cubes: a high resolution 3D surface construction algorithm', *Computer Graphics*, Vol.21, No.4, 1987, pp.163-169.

[12]   Meagher, D., 'Geometric modeling using octree encoding', *Computer Graphics and Image Processing*, Vol. 19, 1982, pp.129-147.

[13]   Phong, B.T., 'Illumination for computer generated pictures', *Communications of the ACM*, Vol.18, No.6, 1975, pp.311-317.

[14]   Pizer, S.M., Levoy, M., Fuchs, H. and Rosenman, J.G., 'Volume rendering for display of multiple organs, treatment objects, and image intensities', *Science and Engineering of Medical Imaging, Proceedings of the SPIE*, Vol.1137, Paris 1989, pp.92-97.

[15]   Prusinkiewicz, P., Lindemayer, A. and Hanan, J., 'Developmental model of herbaceous plants for computer imagery purposes', *Computer Graphics*, Vol.22, No.4, pp.141-150, 1988.

[16]   Scharnweber, H. and Toennies, K.D., 'Three-dimensional reconstruction and display of complex anatomical objects', *Proceedings of the 1984 International Joint Alpine Symposium*, Innsbruck, February 1984, pp.7-10.

[17]   Stiehl, H.S. and Jackél, D., 'On a framework for processing and visualization of spatial images', *Computer Assisted Radiology, Proceedings of the International Symposium CAR'87*, H.U.Lemke et al. (eds.), Berlin 1987, pp. 665-670.

[18]   Tiede, U.,Höhne, K.H., Bomans, M., Pommert, A., Riemer, M., and Wiebecke, G., 'Investigations of medical 3D-rendering algorithms', *IEEE Computer Graphics and Applications*, Vol.10, No.2, 1990, pp.33-40.

[19]   Toennies, K.D., 'Surface triangulation by linear interpolation in intersecting planes', *Science and Engineering in Medical Imaging, Proceedings of the SPIE*, Vol.1137, Paris 1989, pp.98-105.

[20]   Toennies, K.D. and Tronnier, U., '3D modelling using an extended cell enumeration representation', *Computer Graphics*, Vol.24, No.5, 1990, pp.13-20.

[21]   Toennies, K.D. and Tronnier, U., 'Application of a discrete-space representation to three-dimensional medical imaging', *Medical Imaging V, Proceedings of the SPIE*, Vol.1444, San José 1991, to appear.

[22]   Toennies, K.D., 'Modeling of medical imagery', *Computer Assisted Radiology, Proceedings of the Interantional Symposium CAR'91*, H.U.Lemke et al. (eds.), Berlin 1991, to appear.

[23]   Tronnier, U., Wolff, K.D. and Trittmacher, S., 'A 3-D surgical planning system and its clinical applications', *Computer Assisted Radiology, Proceedings of the International Symposium CAR'89*, H.U.Lemke et al. (eds.), Berlin 1989, pp. 403-407.

[24]   Tronnier, U., Hasenbrinck, F. and Wittich, A., 'An experimental environment for true 3D surgical planning by simulation - methods and first experimental results', *Computer Applications to Assist Radiology, Proceedings of the S/CAR'90*, R.L.Arenson et al. (eds.), Anaheim 1990, pp. 594-601.

ROBUST CURVE DETECTION BY TEMPORAL GEODESICS

D. Gutfinger, R. Nishimura, H. Doi and J. Sklansky

University of California, Irvine, California 92717, U.S.A.

Abstract

The formation of temporal geodesics (i.e., fast routes) in a velocity field seems to offer a means of detecting curves by parallel hardware in a wide range of images with little *a priori* design information. We tested this hypothesis by devising and constructing a dotted-curve detector based on it, and applying the detector to several synthetic dotted images covering a wide range of dotted curves and dotted partially coherent noise. The results were encouraging.

The dotted-curve detector searches for fast routes in a velocity field determined locally by the approximate collinearity or cocircularity of clusters of dots, and globally by the tortuosity of the route and the uniformity of the spacing of dots along the route. The routes are found by a parallel adaptive classification of the dots into curve dots and noise dots, followed by a parallel merging and splitting of graphs spanning temporally close dots or subgraphs at successively higher levels of abstraction. The classification is carried out by "mixed adaptation" — a mixture of supervised and unsupervised training.

1   Introduction

We show that *temporal geodesics* (i.e., fast routes visiting many dots) can be useful for detecting a wide variety of dotted curves in dotted 2-D images (i.e., arrays of dots in 2-space) with little *a priori* information. The curves have no restrictions other than they are piecewise gentle, i.e., they have mostly low curvature. The noise too may be quite diverse. Although all of the images considered in this paper are dotted and 2-dimensional, we believe the principal concepts of our approach to curve detection can be extended to continuous-tone and 3-dimensional images.

The detection of curves in 2-D images (and surfaces in 3-D images) impacts on segmentation, parallelism and robustness, all of which are major issues in computer vision. In this paper we simplify this problem, while retaining these impacts, by restricting our attention to 2-D dotted images.

We present an algorithm for detecting dotted curves in dotted images based on temporal geodesics and adaptive cluster-finding. This algorithm has several attractive attributes: It is inherently parallel. It does not require *a priori* specification of the curves to be detected, except that they are gentle, with no more than a few sharp changes in local direction. It is adaptive, in that it adjusts its parameters in response to a set of examples (i.e., a "design set") of arrays of dots belonging to the same class. It is robust, in that it accommodates a wide range of classes of arrays of dots beyond those in the design set.

Consider a 2- or 3-dimensional space containing an array of dots some of which lie on one or a few gentle curves $\{K_i\}$. We refer to these as *curve dots*, and to the remaining dots as *noise dots*. Our objective is to find routes which visit all of the curve dots and which lie on or near $\{K_i\}$.

Toward this end imagine a tiny spaceship (the size of a dot) that travels along a route P. Its velocity along P is determined by a *velocity field*. This field is produced positively by the collinearity or co-circularity of nearby dots, and negatively by the tortuosity or the degree of curvature along the route. By parallel merging and splitting of graphs spanning temporally close dots or subgraphs at successively higher levels of abstraction, our algorithm finds routes that visit large numbers of dots in a short time. (Thus our algorithm provides solutions to a generalized form of the traveling salesman problem: to visit a large number of cities, but not necessarily all cities, in a short time.) We refer to these routes as *temporal geodesics*. Our hypothesis, which is supported by our preliminary experiments, is that these temporal geodesics will usually lie on or near the curves $\{K_i\}$.

2   Temporal Spanning Graphs in 2-Space

Let $\mathcal{D} = \{D_i\}$ denote an array of dots in 2-space.

A *temporal geodesic* from dot D_i to dot D_j is the route along which the time to travel from D_i to D_j is minimized. The traveling time along any route is determined by a *velocity field* created by all of the dots in $\mathcal{D}$. The velocity at any point P in this space depends on the approximately collinearity or cocircularity of P with nearby dots. As a result the average velocity on a route joining dots that lie on a gentle curve is relatively large. On other routes the average velocity is relatively small. We search for a route that enables visits to a large number of dots N in a short time T, maximizing a figure of merit such as N/T. Our hypothesis is that the best routes with respect to this figure of merit lie along the images of dotted gentle curves.

To help us find such best routes, we define a velocity V_{ij} for every pair of dots (D_i, D_j). The time T_{ij} for traveling between D_i and D_j is d_{ij}/V_{ij}, where d_{ij} is the distance between D_i and D_j. In Section 4 we define a set of features that are used to estimate the value and direction of the velocity field at each dot.

The detection of dotted curves in $\mathcal{D}$ is carried out at successively higher levels of abstraction $L_0, L_1, \ldots$. $\mathcal{D}$ is partitioned into clusters in feature space by a mixture of supervised and unsupervised training using a "mixed adaptation" technique recently developed at the Pattern Recognition Project of the University of California, Irvine [1]. One of these clusters represents an initial determination of the noise dots; the remaining clusters represent an initial segmentation of the curve dots. At level L_1 each cluster obtained in L_0 is mapped into a set of temporal spanning graphs (TSGs). Let $\mathcal{G}^1$ denote the union of these sets of TSGs. At level L_k groups of TSGs that represent portions of the same curve or closely related curves are mapped into a new set of TSGs $\mathcal{G}^{k+1}$, such that each node in $\mathcal{G}^{k+1}$ denotes a TSG in $\mathcal{G}^k$ ($k = 1, 2, \ldots$).

Our motivation in breaking the analysis into multiple levels $\{L_k\}$ is to estimate temporal geodesics at high levels of abstraction (i.e., over a large neighborhood of dots), while maintaining the parallel nature of the curve-finding algorithm.

3 Comparison to Other Methods

Most of the earlier algorithms for curve detection are inherently sequential [2] or require *a priori* knowledge of the shapes of the curves [3,4]. Two earlier techniques do not require this knowledge: those of Zucker *et al.* [5] and Ahuja *et al.* [6]. The technique of Zucker *et al.* is restricted to multiple-gray-level images, while that of Ahuja *et al.* is restricted to dotted images.

The technique of Zucker *et al.* finds curves by applying the principle of least action to the dissipation of the kinetic energy produced by deformable splines in a tangent field potential function. In the sense that this technique is parallel and minimizes a global criterion, it is similar to ours. However, it requires interactive determination of design parameters for each application [5]. Hence it is unlikely to be fully automatic.

The technique of Ahuja *et al.* analyzes dot patterns by applying relaxation labeling to an initial labeling that is based on features extracted from a Voronoi diagram. This procedure classifies dots into four classes: interior, border, curve and isolated. The curves that it identifies cannot be embedded within a heavy background of noise dots, because dots on such curves will be classified as interior dots. In our procedure only two classes are considered (curve dots and noise dots), and curves can be extracted from a heavy background of noise dots.

Our approach to curve detection breaks curve detection into classification by mixed adaptation, classifying the dots into curve dots and noise dots, followed by finding of temporal spanning graphs (TSGs). The classification process is adaptive and robust as a result of the exploitation of statistically scene invariant features and clustering features in a mixture of supervised and unsupervised training. This process can use a wide variety of features, depending on the application — the tangent field in [5] is one example, and the set of nearest neighbor directions in this paper is another. The TSG finding process provides additional robustness as a result of its ability to find temporal geodesics at several levels of abstraction. A preliminary test of the robustness of this approach to curve detection was carried out on six images (discussed in Section 5 of this paper), with encouraging results.

Both the Zucker and the Ahuja techniques achieve robustness through the use of relaxation labeling. Our technique achieves robustness through the use of mixed adaptation (supervised training on scene invariant features and unsupervised training on scene variant features) followed by the finding of temporal geodesics. Our technique seems to offer an improved organization of the design — in particular, improved insights into the design of features and the adaptation process.

4 Features for Classification of Dots

We distinguish between features that are *statistically scene invariant* (or *scene invariant*, for short) and features that are *statistically scene variant* (or *scene variant*, for short) [1]. A *scene invariant feature* of a dot is a feature whose statistical distribution over the range of scenes of interest does not depend on the scene in which the dot appears. A *scene variant feature* of a dot is a feature whose statistical distribution over the range of scenes of interest depends on the scene in which the dot appears.

The following scene invariant characteristics allowed us to distinguish between curve dots and noise dots.

- The slope of a line is the same at all points along the line.

- Let l denote the slope of the line joining points A and B. Suppose A and B lie on a curve Γ. Let $L(A)$ and $L(B)$ denote the slopes of Γ at A and B, respectively. Let

$$\Delta(A, B) = \Big| |L(A) - l| - |L(B) - l| \Big|. \quad (4-1)$$

We refer to $\Delta(A, B)$ as the *cocircularity* [5] of A and B with respect to Γ. Note that if Γ is a circle then $\Delta(A, B) = 0$.

- In dotted image data, the spacing between points along a curve is usually similar.

A set of scene invariant features based on these characteristics were devised, along with several scene variant features. These features are listed in Table 1. Mathematical definitions of these features appear in [1].

We define the *velocity* at D_i as a vector quantity $\mathbf{v}_i$, such that the magnitude and angle associated with $\mathbf{v}_i$ are defined as follows:

$$|\mathbf{v}_i| = P_M(i) \qquad \angle \mathbf{v}_i = \theta_M(i). \quad (4-2)$$

The time T_{ij} for traveling between a pair of dots D_i and D_j is defined as follows,

$$T_{ij} = \frac{1}{2}\left(\frac{d_{ij}}{|\mathbf{v}_i|\cos(\theta^i(j) - \angle \mathbf{v}_i)} + \frac{d_{ij}}{|\mathbf{v}_j|\cos(\theta^i(j) - \angle \mathbf{v}_j)} \right). \quad (4-3)$$

In this definition the projections of $\mathbf{v}_i$ and $\mathbf{v}_j$ along the line segment joining D_i and D_j are used in computing the traveling time between D_i and D_j. Although it is not clear whether this definition is the best choice, our experiments indicate that this definition produces satisfactory results.

Table 1: Definitions of Dot Pattern Features

SYMBOL	DEFINITION
Scene Invariant Features	
$U(i)$	uncertainty of $\theta_M(i)$
$P_M(i)$	probability of $\theta_M(i)$
$\sigma(\theta_M(i))$	standard deviation of $\theta_M(i)$
$\kappa(i)$	$|\theta_M(i) - \mu(\theta_M(i))|$
$\sigma(R_N(i))$	standard deviation of $R_N(i)$
$\mu(\gamma(i))$	mean cocircularity
$\sigma(\gamma(i))$	standard deviation of cocircularity
Scene Variant Features	
$\theta_M(i)$	angle of most likely line segment
$y_{255}(i)$	y-intercept of most likely line
$R_N(i)$	distance to nearest neighbor
$\mu(\theta_M(i))$	mean angle of most likely line
$\mu(R_N(i))$	mean spacing of dots along line

5   Experiments

We tested our algorithm on twelve dotted images: six *a priori* design images and six *a posteriori* field images. The six *a priori* design images $\mathcal{I}_1^D$ through $\mathcal{I}_6^D$ are shown in Figure 1. The six *a posteriori* field images $\mathcal{I}_1^F$ through $\mathcal{I}_6^F$ are shown in Figure 2. The images forming the design set depict one type of scene, and the images forming the field set depict other types of scenes. The design set was selected so that it will provide adequate statistics for the scene invariant features of a class of dotted curves embedded in dotted noise.

From the *a priori* design images the sample mean vector and covariance matrix of all the scene invariant features were estimated for the curve dots and noise dots separately. These statistics were used in estimating the class-conditional probability densities and in constructing the initial classifier by supervised training.

Next, unsupervised training (cluster analysis) was applied to the initial classifier using both the scene invariant features and scene variant features defined in Table 1, yielding a revised classifier. Table 2 summarizes the classification errors produced by the initial and revised classifiers for the a posteriori field data $\mathcal{I}_1^F$ through $\mathcal{I}_6^F$. The classification results of the revised classifier reflect the results of the analysis carried out in L_0. For all six field images the error rate of the revised classifier was less than that of the initial classifier.

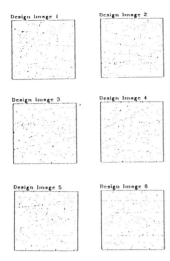

Figure 1: A priori design images

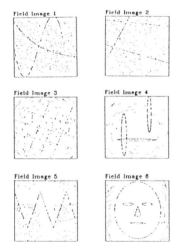

Figure 2: A posteriori field images

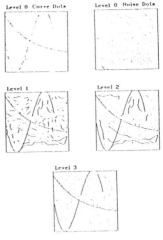

Figure 3: Multilevel graph analysis for image $\mathcal{I}_1^F$

Table 2: Classification Errors for Field Sets			
Field Set	Initial Classifier	Level L_0	Level L_3
$\mathcal{I}_1^F$	26.0 %	13.8 %	9.0 %
$\mathcal{I}_2^F$	19.5 %	6.8 %	5.8 %
$\mathcal{I}_3^F$	24.3 %	10.0 %	6.3 %
$\mathcal{I}_4^F$	10.9 %	6.6 %	6.6 %
$\mathcal{I}_5^F$	21.8 %	7.5 %	5.2 %
$\mathcal{I}_6^F$	34.5 %	26.9 %	26.4 %

In our experiments TSGs were constructed at levels L_1, L_2 and L_3. Figure 3 shows the TSGs produced at the various levels for field image $\mathcal{I}_1^F$. The results shown at levels L_2 and L_3 correspond to the results after TSG classification and route smoothing. To distinguish TSGs of curves from TSGs of noise, the TSGs of curves are displayed as connected curves in levels L_2 and L_3; the TSGs of the detected noise are shown as isolated nodes. Figure 4 shows the final results for field images $\mathcal{I}_2^F$ through $\mathcal{I}_6^F$. Using the results obtained at L_3, we classified the dots as being either curve dots or noise dots. The error rates corresponding to this classification are summarized in Table 2. These results suggest that the graph analysis at levels L_k ($k \geq 2$) produces a slight improvement in classification accuracy. The major benefit of our multilevel graph analysis is that it specifies the number of curves found, along with the ordered sequence of dots forming each curve.

A close examination of the results in Figure 4 shows minor imperfections in the formed TSGs. These imper-

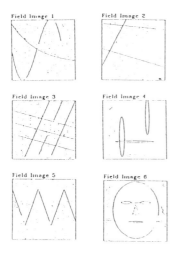

Figure 4: Results of multilevel graph analysis

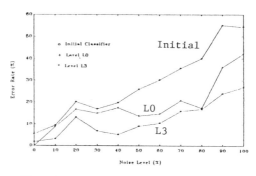

Figure 5: Error rate versus noise level for image $\mathcal{I}_1^F$

fections occur: 1) near curve segments with high curvature; 2) near the end points of curve segments; and 3) when noise is present near a gap of a curve segment.

We also tested the sensitivity of our curve detection technique to the *noise level*, i.e. the percentage of noise dots in the image. Figure 5 shows the error rates of the initial classifier, the revised classifier (level L_0), and the multilevel graph analysis (level L_3) as functions of the noise level in field image $\mathcal{I}_1^F$. The results in L_0 show an improvement over the results of the initial classifier. The results in L_3 show that the multilevel graph analysis produces an improvement over the classification in L_0. The results in L_3 demonstrate that our curve detection technique has low sensitivity to the noise level.

6 Summary

Our example in Section 5 illustrates the ability of our curve detection technique to detect a wide variety of dotted curves embedded in a wide variety of dotted noise with very little *a priori* information and no interactive determination of design parameters. Our current algorithm exhibited weakness on curves having high curvature. Our experiments indicate that estimating velocity fields at multiple levels of abstraction is effective for constructing temporal geodesics that span the dotted curves.

Acknowledgements

This research was supported by the Army Research Office under grant DAAL03-88-K-0117, the University of California Microelectronics Innovation and Computer Research Opportunities (MICRO) Program, Hitachi Ltd., and Nippon Telegraph and Telephone Corporation.

References

[1] D. Gutfinger and J. Sklansky, "Robust classifiers and mixed adaptation," Technical Report TP-90-7, Machine Vision and Pattern Recognition Project, University of California, Irvine, 1990.

[2] A. Rosenfeld, A. C. Kak, *Digital Picture Processing*, second edition, Academic Press, Orlando, Florida, 1982.

[3] J. Sklansky, "On the Hough technique for curve detection," *IEEE Trans. Comput.*, Vol. C27, 1978, pp. 923–926.

[4] D. H. Ballard, "Generalizing the Hough transform to detect arbitrary shapes," *Pattern Recognition*, Vol. 13, No. 2, 1981, pp. 111–122.

[5] P. Parent, S. W. Zucker "Trace inference, curvature consistency, and curve detection," *IEEE Transactions on Pattern Analysis and Machine Intelligence*, Vol. PAMI-11, No. 8, 1989, pp. 823–839.

[6] N. Ahuja and M. Tuceryan, "Extraction of Early Perceptual Structure in Dot Patterns: Integrating Region, Boundary, and Component Gestalt," *Computer Vision, Graphics, and Image Processing*, Volume 48, pp 304-356 (1989).

STABLE SEGMENTATION USING COLOR INFORMATION

LENA BONSIEPEN & WOLFGANG COY[*]

An environmental application of image processing

Measuring biological entities generates insights in the quality.of environmental conditions like air, water, soil etc. Lichens (*Lichenes*) have proven to be inexpensive though highly responsive air indicators [1]. Irregularities in shape, growth and color are interpreted as quantitative and qualitative measures of stress factors, where combinational effects are better observable than in any analytical approach.

The technical base for these environmental measurements is computer supported image analysis [2]. Image processing in this project includes:

- Digitization, storage and retrieval of high quality color images of a large number of lichens in time series;
- Automatic measurement and interpretation of shape and growth;
- Automatic measurement and interpretation of change of colors.

The *Lichenes* species *Parmelia sulcata* and *Hypogymnia physodes*, which are investigated in the project, grow mainly flat. This allows a quite stable interpretation of their growth as a two-dimensional problem — a welcome constraint for image analysis.

The segmentation problem

In general, the aim of image segmentation is the identification of segments denoting significant objects or part of objects within an image, which are subsequently grouped together and eventually supplied to higher-level image interpretation processes. Segments are usually identified by their boundaries or their region. The main types of segmentation algorithms are thresholding by histogram analysis, clustering techniques, line-oriented and region-oriented methods [4].

Use of color information can significantly improve the correct recognition of meaningful segments compared with purely intensity based methods. Several segmentation algorithms for color images have been proposed, mainly recursive thresholding by histogram analysis [7, 8]. Algorithms based on color difference metrics [3, 6] have generated better segmentations for color images, but they are only applicable under controlled conditions.

Special requirements of the application under view

The basic problem of processing images of the lichens is the segmentation of the lichen's thallus from its dark background. The lichens change color from green to grays, browns and even reds, where low intensities dominate. Any binary segmentation and even gray-valued

---

[*] Authors' address: Universität Bremen Informatik, Postfach 330440, D-2800 Bremen 33

segmentation will lead necessarily to some quite artificial decisions on the exact border of the lichen's thallus. The growth and change of shape of a lichen within the standard time curve of seven days is quite small: the species under consideration change only 10 to 20 % p. a. in area; therefore an exact segmentation is highly recommended to enable reliable interpretations. This is the point where color segmentation is a useful enhancement of mere intensity-based processing. With the growth of a lichen there is also a change of shape, which has to be treated separately for an automatic interpretation of the lichen's condition.

On the other hand, the application offers some favourable a priori knowledge: In general there is only one single object in the analysed image; the background of the image changes only slightly in color and texture; and finally, we are dealing with time series of images, that means we have a lot of similar images, for which a special segmentation method can be designed.

The choice of the method depends on the characteristics of the specific application. Lichens are no simple objects with welldefined line orientations: the shape of the lichen's outline may change in unforeseeable ways. So line- or region-oriented methods based on models of the objects are of no use. The a priori knowledge about the pictures suggests the application of a simple thresholding algorithm. The parameters of the algorithm — color feature and threshold — must hold for a class of pictures, at least for one species of lichens. Therefore data driven methods where the parameters vary depending on the specific picture under view are out of question. Color feature and threshold have to be computed in advance for a whole class of pictures for which they have to keep validity.

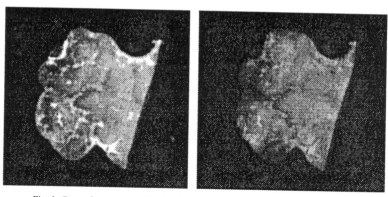

Fig. 1: *Parmelia sulcata* at the first (left) and last (right) day of the test period

Comparison with other approaches to color segmentation

Since the color features supplied to the segmentation algorithm described here resemble those applied by Ohta, Kanade and Sakai [8], we will shortly describe their results.

A color feature is defined as a linear or nonlinear transformation of the primary color components R, G and B into one dimension. Intensity for example is the average of the components R, G and B; the components of alternative color spaces HSI, HSV, CMY, CIE-XYZ, YIQ etc. each represent color features in this sense. Ohta et al. analyzed the usefulness of 100 different color features by segmenting eight color images with a recursive thresholding algorithm. The set of the three color features (R+G+B)/3, (R-B) and (2G-R-B)/2 proved to be effective compared with other sets of color features commonly used in color image analysis.

We applied the above set of color features to the lichen images. The pictures were taken from a test set of several *Parmelia sulcata* and *Hypogymnia physodes* which were photographed daily during a time period of one week. Fig. 1 shows pictures of a *Parmelia sulcata* from the first and last day of the test period. The changes of size and color of the lichen are significant. Fig. 2 shows histograms of the two pictures after transforming them according to the proposed color features. It is obvious, that the features (R-B) and (2G-R-B)/2 are useless for the segmentation of the lichen pictures.

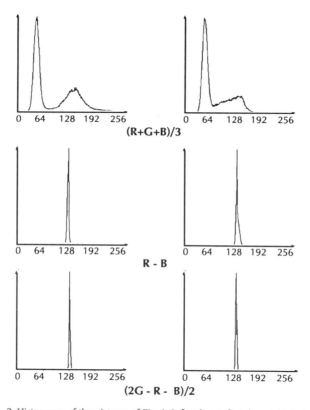

Fig. 2: Histograms of the pictures of Fig. 1. Left column: first day, right: last day

Determination of effective color features

The relative uniformity of the pictures gives rise to the hope, that a thresholding method with a single color feature will produce sufficiently stable segmentation results. Images are digitized 24 bit RGB color pictures taken by a CCD matrix camera. A NuVista digitizer is connected to a Macintosh IIfx. A circular neon tube calibrated with a neutral cold light source is used as light source. The lichen is approximately 6 mm^2 in area supported by a black solid plate which is usually fixed to some outdoor tree.

Segmentation is by no means unique, changing from color to color. In order to generate reliable results about the changes of a lichens area and color, the segmentation method must use fixed color features for a whole class of lichen images, at least for all pictures of a time series. Therefore a calibration process for a stable color segmentation was designed. Pictures of 24 lichens of the species *Parmelia sulcata* and *Hypogymnia physodes* were taken daily during a time period of one week. Each lichen was photographed under dry and moist condition. From the resulting test set of 336 pictures, two classes of artificial images were composed manually, one class containing background sections, the other object-colors. These pictures were supplied to an algorithm which tested the separating quality of about 1000 different linear color features [9].

A linear color feature κ is defined as weighted and normalized transformation of the RGB-values into one dimension:

$$\kappa_{\alpha\beta\gamma}(x,y,z) = \frac{\alpha \cdot x + \beta \cdot y + \gamma \cdot z}{|\alpha| + |\beta| + |\gamma|}$$

where x, y and z denote the R, G and B values of a pixel respectively. Different color features are obtained by varying the parameters α, β and γ. A color feature is considered to be *effective* for a specific class of images, if the histograms of the transformed background and object images do not overlap. The test set of the lichen images produced no effective color features but several *semi-effective* ones, that means, the overlapping regions — denoting incorrect classified pixels — of the histograms of background and object images are below 0.5 %. For each effective or semi-effective color feature, the thresholding level is set to that intensity value where a minimal number of misclassifications is obtained.

In Figure 3, one of the semi-effective color features (0.25R+4G-B)/5 was applied to the pictures of Fig. 1. The histograms of the transformed images are shown on the left. For illustration purposes, the corresponding linear plane in the RGB space for the color feature with threshold level 148 is shown on the right.

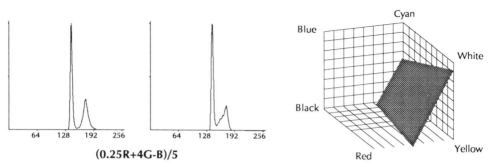

Fig. 3: Histograms of the images of Fig. 1 after transformation using weighted and normalized RGB values and the corresponding linear thresholding plane in the RGB-space. The left peaks of the histograms represent background, the right ones object pixels. The local minimum of the histograms at 148 is chosen as thresholding level.

80

Evaluation of the segmentation method

The precalculated color feature produced stable segmentation results for whole classes of lichen images which were not contained in the original test set. Fig. 4 shows three segmented pictures of a time series of a *Parmelia sulcata*. The superiority of color segmentation to intensity based methods is demonstrated in Figure 5, where the same image was segmented using the color feature (R+G+B)/3 (equivalent to intensity) and the predetermined color feature (0.25R+4G-B)/5.

Fig. 4: Segmented versions of three images of a time series (1st, 3rd and 7th day) using color feature (0.25R+4G-B)/5 and thresholding level 148.

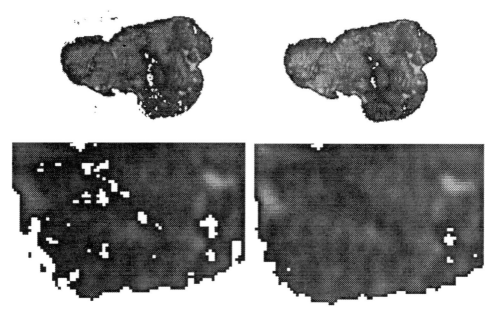

Fig. 5: Comparison of segmentation results of a lichen picture. Upper left: Segmentation by intensity; Upper right: Segmentation using color feature (0.25R+4G-B)/5; Below: blow-ups of a section from the lower part of the images.

The algorithms for predetermining effective color features and for segmentation are integrated into an image analysis system for environmental biologists. The system provides several other functions such as filtering, histogram calculation, computation of the center of gravity and of the axes of inertia. In addition, the user may interactively pick certain colors as a base for further smoothing the colors of a pictures. These colors separate the 24-bit RGB-space in subspaces. Figure 6 shows the smoothed versions of the three pictures of Fig. 4, where the base colors are approximated by their intensities. This further processing of the lichen images has proven to be useful for monitoring color changes of the lichens as an indication for environmental stress factors. The system is in everyday use by environmental biologists.

Fig. 6: Lichens of Fig. 4, color-smoothed by four interactively chosen colors.

Fig. 7: A well-known hard to segment black and white image

Fig. 8: Picture of dog in front of speckled meadow (left). Segmented picture of dog (right). Parts of the background — shadow of the dog and some speckles of the meadow — cannot be removed by linear color features.

Other objects of any size may be segmented by the same technique. Figure 7 shows a wellknown, difficult to segment image. In fact, it raised the question whether low level segmentation must be supported by high level model-based segmentation methods. The black and white image is in fact highly artificial. Picture 8 and its automatic segmentation demonstrate that the level between low-level and high-level image segmentation may be shifted using color information. The method has also been applied successfully to various other pictures including test tables for human eye red-green insufficiency (Fig. 9) and arbitrary scenes (Fig. 10).

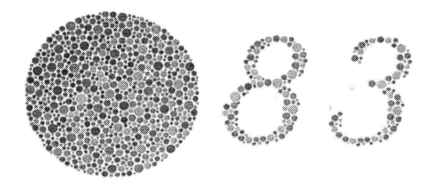

Fig. 9: Test table for human eye red-green insufficiency. Left: original image; middle: identification of the hidden number; right: artificial identification of parts of the hidden number demonstrating the effect of red-green weakness.

Fig 10: Left: Solid green color object (a tea pot) hidden behind a plant. Right: Total removal of the plant.

Outlook

Using color information for the segmentation of images can enhance the segmentation results substantially. It seems that fast thresholding algorithms can be applied, where low-level intensity based methods fail.

Actually we are investigating the usefulness of nonlinear color features for the demonstrated segmentation method. To keep the computational costs for the precalculation of effective color features in reasonable bounds, a rule-based approach is investigated. Furthermore, experiments are made to combine measurements of a lichen's area with measurements of its three-dimensional growth using range image data [5].

Acknowledgements

The environmental department of the Senate of Bremen supports the project BREMA, part of which is communicated here. We thank Dr. Tielong Chen for teaching us basics of the lichens' biology, and Uwe Pirr for transforming our ideas into running programs.

References

[1]   *Bioindikation.* VDI-Bericht 609. Düsseldorf: VDI-Verlag 1987,

[2]   Bonsiepen, L. & W. Coy: Rechnergestützte optische Vermessung des Bioindikators *Parmelia sulcata*, in: Informatik für den Umweltschutz IFB 256, (Berlin et al.) : Springer 1990

[3]   Daily, M. J.: Color Image Segmentation Using Markov Random Fields, in: Computer Vision and Pattern Recognition 89 (San Diego), 304-312, IEEE Computer Society 1989

[4]   Haralick, R. M. & L. G. Shapiro: Survey: Image Segmentation Techniques. Computer Vision Graphics and Image Processing *29*, 100-132 (1985)

[5]   Hönisch, U. & W. Coy: Zur Extraktion von Kanten in Distanzbildern. Bild und Ton *7*, Sept. 1990

[6]   Kanade, T.: Computer Vision: From Ad Hocs to Sciences, in: Proceedings of AAAI 88 (Minneapolis) 1988

[7]   Ohlander, R., K. Proce & D. R. Reddy: Picture Segmentation Using a Recursive Region Splitting Method. Computer Graphics and Image Processing *8*, 313-333 (1978)

[8]   Ohta, Y., T. Kanade & T. Sakai: Color Information for Region Segments. Computer Graphics and Image Processing *10*, 222-241 (1980)

[9]   Pirr, U.: Segmentierung von Farbbildern. Diplomarbeit, Univ. Bremen Informatik 1991

FAST SPECTRAL ALGORITHMS FOR INVARIANT PATTERN RECOGNITION AND IMAGE MATCHING

R. Creutzburg

V. G. Labunets & E. V. Labunets

University of Karlsruhe
Institute of Algorithms and Cognitive Systems
Am Fasanengarten 5, P. O. Box 6980
D-7500 Karlsruhe 1
(Phone: +49-721-608 4325)
(Fax: +49-721-696 893)

Ural Polytechnical Institute
Faculty of Radioelectronics
Department of Automatics and Telemechanics
SU-620002 Sverdlovsk
Soviet Union
(Phone: +7-3432-449 779)
(Fax: +7-3432-562 417)

June 24, 1991

1 Introduction

Nowadays great attention is paid to the problem of video sensor systems development. These systems are intended for robot sensibilization. One of the main tasks here is the controlled recognition of details and their shift estimation in the field of view of the robot. The consideration of all possible geometrical distortions of a given image is one of the most difficult problems in pattern recognition. These distortions combine scaling, translation, rotation and others. So, algorithms of recognition and image shift estimation must be invariant with respect to the corresponding geometrical transforms group, acting on a given image. One of the effective approaches to the development of such algorithms is based on the correlation of image invariants [AP83], [Hu62], [Tea80].

The aim of this paper is to introduce a new fast algorithm for the computation of affin-invariant moments for pattern recognition and image matching applications. The introduced algorithm uses modular moments that can be computed efficiently without roundoff errors compared to the standard ordinary moments..

Let $\mathcal{G}$ be the group of affine transforms of the two-dimensional space $\mathbb{R}^2$ and let $g(\alpha, \varphi, x_0, y_0)$ denote an arbitrary group element $g \in \mathcal{G}$, where α is a scaling coefficient, φ is a rotation angle and x_0, y_0 are the current image displacements with respect of the template image to be estimated.

Denote as $f(x, y)$ the brightness function of arbitrary image which satisfies the following conditions:

$$1) \quad f(x, y) \neq 0, \quad (x, y) \in \Pi \subseteq \mathbb{R}^2;$$

$$2) \quad \int_{(x,y) \in \Pi} \int |f(x, y)| \, dx \, dy < \infty,$$

where Π is a bounded subset of $\mathbb{R}^2$.

Furthermore, $f(x, y)$ denotes the brightness function of an arbitrary image, where $(x, y) \in \Pi \subseteq \mathbb{R}^2$. The space of functions $f(x, y)$ is denoted as $L(\Pi)$.

Definition 1 *The functional $\mathcal{J} : L(\Pi) \to \mathbb{R}$ is called the $\mathcal{G}$-invariant of the image $f(x, y)$, if*

$$\mathcal{J}(f[g \circ (x, y)]) = A(g)\mathcal{J}(f[(x, y)]), \qquad \forall g \in \mathcal{G},$$

where the symbol $g \circ (x, y)$ denotes the action of an element $g(\alpha, \varphi, x_0, y_0)$ of the group $\mathcal{G}$ on the point (x, y), $A(g)$ is a constant, depending only on the element g. If $A(g) \equiv 1$ then the $\mathcal{G}$-invariant $\mathcal{J}$ is called absolute and is denoted by I.

Invariants of an image $f(x,y)$ are constructed usually in two steps [Hu62], [AMP83]. In the first step two-dimensional moments of the image $f(x,y)$ are computed:

$$m_{pq} = \sum_{x=0}^{A-1} \sum_{y=0}^{B-1} f(x,y)x^p y^q, \qquad p,q \in \mathbf{Z}^+,$$

where $\mathbf{Z}^+$ denotes the set of positive integers. In the second step the direct computation of invariants values is performed by substitution of m_{pq} into quite definite algebraic expressions. The form of the latter depends on the view of the group $\mathcal{G}$ (see for example [Hu62], [Tea80], [AMP83], where these expressions are given).

There are two drawbacks of the algorithm of invariants computation. Firstly, fast procedures of moments computations - the most difficult part of the algorithm - are not known. Secondly, it is not possible to estimate the moments of higher order on a standard fixed-point computer, because the dynamic range is often exceeded for larger moment orders. These moments and the corresponding invariants will be called (in terms of quantum-mechanics) unobservable by a fixed-point computer (FiP).

It is only partially possible to avoid this problem and to increase the order of observable moments a little bit and thus to increase the number of invariants when a standard floating-point computer is used. Indeed, if L is the binary wordlength of the processor and $L = l_1 + l_2$, where l_1 and l_2 are the numbers of mantissa and order bits, respectively, then for a fixed-point computer the maximal number of observed moments is directly proportional to L : $\max(p+q) \propto L$, while for floating-point computers this value increases to $\max(p+q) \propto 2^{l_2} - 1$. Hence the increase of l_2 allows to observe moments of higher order. But increasing on one side the number of bits l_2 results in an estimation error increase, which is defined by the mantissa length l_1 and equals 2^{k-l_1}, $2^{-2^{l_2}-1} \le k \le 2^{2^{l_2}-1}$, for every dynamic range. To preserve admittable computation precision a doubling of the mantissa bits number is necessary for an increase of l_2 by 1. If this rule is not considered, the errors in the higher order moments computation would grow extremely and the values of these moments wouldn't contain any useful information. So, the increase of the number of observable moments with preserving of admittable computation precision is only possible by an extremely increase of the processors word length, both for the fixed-point and the floating-point computer.

The task of this paper is to introduce a new class of invariants, for which the computational algorithm is free of such drawbacks.

2 Modular moments

When processed on a computer two-dimensional arrays are sampled on space coordinates and samples are quantized. That's why one can think, that intermediate and final results are expressed as integers on FiP-computers. This allows to introduce new invariants $\tilde{I}_{p,q}$, connected with the old by the relation $\tilde{I}_{p,r} \equiv I_{p,r} \bmod Q$, where Q is a prime number.

Definition 2 *The functionals $\tilde{I}_{p,r} \equiv I_{p,r} \bmod Q$ will be called modular $\mathcal{G}$-invariants.*

As the residue operation for computing $\tilde{I}_{p,r}$ is commutative according to the addition, multiplication and exponentiation operation, the invariants $\tilde{I}_{p,r}$ can be estimated with the help of modular moments, which are defined by

$$\tilde{m}_{pq} = \sum_{x=0}^{A-1} \sum_{y=0}^{B-1} f(x,y)x^p y^q \bmod Q. \tag{1}$$

Note that in a Galois field $\mathbf{GF}(Q)$ the congruence $x^{Q-1} \equiv 1 \bmod Q$ holds for any element

86

$x \not\equiv 0$ and the equation $A = B = Q$ follows. Hence the maximal order of invariants $\check{I}_{p,r}$, which can be estimated on modular arithmetic computer (MA computer), equals to Q, and the total number of observed invariant equals

$$N_{\mathrm{mod}Q} = ((Q-1)(Q+4)/2) - 1.$$

As $x^{Q-1} \equiv 1 \bmod Q$ the maximal order of invariants $\tilde{I}_{p,r}$, which can be estimated on a modular arithmetic computer, equals Q (where $Q = A = B$) and the total number of observed invariants is

$$N \bmod Q = ((Q-1)(Q+4)/2) - 1 > N_{(float)} > N_{(fixed)}.$$

The dynamic range of the modular invariants doesn't exceed Q. The latter is chosen from the condition $Q < 2^n$, where n is the processor wordlength. Hence the processor wordlength defines both the maximal number $N_{modular}$ of observed modular invariants and their dynamic range.

Traditionally, invariants $I_{p,r}$ are used for the solution of two problems: pattern recognition and image matching.

3   Pattern recognition

The problem of pattern recognition is formulated as follows. Let the set of M images $\{f_i(x,y) \mid i = 1, 2, \ldots, M\}$ which will be called template, be given and let the group $\mathbb{G}$ of their transforms be known. For any image $f_i(x,y)$ corresponds the set $\mathbb{O}_i$, containing all images, which can be obtained from template $f_i(x,y)$ under the action of transforms $g \in \mathbb{G}$:

$$\mathbb{O}_i = \{f_i[g * (x,y)] \mid \forall g \in \mathbb{G}\}.$$

The set $\mathbb{O}_i$ is called the orbit of template image $f_i(x,y)$. The problem of pattern recognition consists of the determination of such $i = 1, \ldots, M$ that for current image $f^c(x,y)$ the inclusion $f^c(x,y) \in \mathbb{O}_i$ is fulfilled.

Definition 3 *The set of functionals $I_k[f(x,y)]$ is called the complete invariants system, if every functional is constant on the orbit [SS76]*

$$I_k\left(f_i\left[g * (x,y)\right]\right) = I_k\left(f_i\left[(x,y)\right]\right), \qquad \forall g \in \mathbb{G}; \; \forall k = 1, 2, \ldots$$

and has different values at least on two different orbits

$$\forall k \forall i \exists j \left(\mathbf{I}_k\left(\mathbb{O}_i\right) \neq I_k\left(\mathbb{O}_j\right)\right).$$

Invariants system completeness means that all functionals in totality "distinguish" between all orbits.

The finite set of invariants

$$I_k f_i[(x,y)], \qquad k = 1, \ldots, M,$$

determines the image with some precision. Let us clarify this fact. Let's introduce in the space $L(\Pi)$ of images $f(x,y)$ among the orbits $\mathbb{O}_i$ ϵ-eroded orbits as

$$\mathbb{O}_i(\epsilon) = \{f_i[g * (x,y)] \mid \int_{(x,y) \in \Pi} \int \mid f_i[g * (x,y)] - f[g * (x,y)] \mid dx \, dy < \epsilon, \quad \forall g \in \mathbb{G}\}.$$

Let's introduce N-dimensional vector space of invariants $\mathbf{V}_N$; spanned on orthonormal basis $\{e_k \mid k = 1, \ldots, N-1\}$. We'll put the value of the corresponding invariant I_k along every vector e_k. Then the point (vector) $\mathbf{I} = (I_0, I_1, \ldots, I_{N-1})$ will correspond to the set $(I_0, I_1, \ldots, I_{N-1})$. If one introduces the measure

$$d[\mathbf{I}, \mathbf{I}'] = N^{-1} \sum_{k=0}^{N-1} \mid I_k - I_{k'} \mid$$

then $\mathbf{V}_N$ is transformed into metric space.

Definition 4 *We'll say that with given N function $f(x, y)$ belongs to orbit $\mathbb{O}_i$ with some $[\delta(N), \epsilon(N)]$-precision, depending on N, if such an element $g \in \mathbb{G}$ exists that for $d(\mathbf{I}^i, \mathbf{I}(f(x, y)))$ $< \delta(N)$ we have*

$$\int_{(x,y) \in \Pi} \int \mid f_i[g * (x, y)] - f[g * (x, y)] \mid dx\, dy < \epsilon(N)$$

that is $f(x, y) \in \mathbb{O}_i(\epsilon)$.

The latter definition gives that the sphere $S_i(\delta)$ of radii δ and center $\mathbf{I}^i$ corresponds to every ϵ-eroded orbit $\mathbb{O}_i(\epsilon)$ for some N in the space $\mathbf{V}_N$.

Definition 5 *It is said that function $f(x, y)$ belongs to orbit $\mathbb{O}_i$ with the given $[\delta_0, \epsilon_0]$-precision (that is, $f(x, y) \in \mathbb{O}_i(\epsilon_0)$), if there exists such number $N = N(\delta_0, \epsilon_0)$, depending on δ_0 and ϵ_0, and such element $g_0 \in \mathbb{G}$, that for $d(\mathbf{I}^i, \mathbf{I}(f(x, y))) < \delta_0$ we have*

$$\int_{(x,y) \in \Pi} \int \mid f_i[g * (x, y)] - f[g * (x, y)] \mid dx\, dy < \epsilon_0.$$

So if limited technical means allow to evaluate some limited number of N invariants, then it is this number that defines $[\delta, \epsilon]$-precision of the description of the orbit $\mathbb{O}(\epsilon)$, that is, it's ϵ-erodicity and radius δ of its representing sphere $S_i(\delta)$. The problem of pattern recognition in this case can be solved only if ϵ-eroded orbits and spheres don't intersect pairwise $\mathbb{O}_i[\epsilon(N)] \cap \mathbb{O}_i[\epsilon(N)] = \emptyset$, $S_i(\delta) \cap S_j(\delta) = \emptyset$. Otherwise (which can be with small values of N, for with the decreasing of N the numbers δ, ϵ will increase) the problem will not be solved. To solve it is necessary to turn to other technical means which allow computation (observation) of a larger number of N invariants, with which the earlier mentioned objects do not intersect. Then the problem of recognition is solved as follows.

First, centers $\mathbf{I}^i$ of the spheres $S_i(\delta)$ in the space of invariants v_N are evaluated for M images $f_i(x, y)$. Coordinates I_k^i, $k = 0, 1, \ldots N-1$ of these centers are stored in the computer's memory. When current image $f^c(x, y)$ is brought to the system, the set of N of its invariants

$$I_k^c = I_k(f^c(x, y))$$

is estimated, that is, the point $\mathbf{I}^c$ is determined in $\mathbf{V}_N$. Then M distances are computed

$$d_i = d_i(\mathbf{I}_i, \mathbf{I}^c) = N^{-1} \sum_{k=0}^{N-1} \mid I_k^i - I_k^c \mid . \tag{2}$$

The least distance $d_{i0} = \min_i(d_i)$ is found among them, which indicates that the current image $f^c(x, y)$ lies nearest to the i_0-th orbit $\mathbb{O}_{i_0}$. One can consider that current image is a distorted version of the i_0-th image $f_{i0}(x, y)$.

Transition from arithmetic moments to modular ones asks for metric (3) changing, that we'll define as follows:

$$d(\tilde{\mathbf{I}}, \tilde{\mathbf{I}}') = \sum_{k=0}^{N-1} \left[\mid \tilde{I}_k - \tilde{I}' \mid, Q - \mid \tilde{I}_k - \tilde{I}'_k \mid \right].$$

With such metric the space $\mathbf{V}_N$ changes into an N-dimensional torus $\tilde{\mathbf{V}}_N$ with period Q of all its coordinates k.

This effect is tightly connected with the geometrical interpretation of invariants computation processes on FP computers on one hand and on MA computers on the other hand.

Let the needed number N of invariants be determined and N-dimensional space $\mathbf{V}_N$ be formed, starting with the $[\delta_0, \epsilon_0]$-precision of orbit $\mathbf{0}_i$ description. Let the limited bit set of FiP-computer allows to evaluate invariants of the order up to $p(FiP)$ (including $p(FiP)$), that is

$$N(FiP) = [p(FiP) - 1][p(FiP) + 4/2] - 1$$

invariants (usually $p(FiP)$ lies in the range $2\ldots4$ and so $N(FiP) = 2\ldots11$). With these assumptions a FP-computer is equivalent to projective linear operator, which gives the projection of N-dimensional space on subspace $\mathbf{V}_{N}(FiP)$. Obviously, the transition to subspace is provided with decrease of distance d between the spheres $S_i(\delta_0)$. If inequality $\delta < 2\delta_0$ is yet preserved, then the recognition system with the given precision will separate template images $f_i(x, y)$, $i = 1, \ldots, M$ orbits. Note that non-observed invariants are gathered in subspaces $\mathbf{V}_{N-N(FiP)} = \mathbf{V}_N - \mathbf{V}_{N(FiP)}$.

Let's pass over to the second arithmetic analysis. According to (2), if the former computer word length is preserved then it helps to observe $N(M) = [(Q-1)(Q+4)/2] - 1$ invariants already, where prime number Q is chosen so way that $Q \approx 2^n >> p$, and n is the computer word length. Let with such Q the first $N(FiP)$ invariants satisfy unequality $I_k < Q$ and the values of the other $N(M) - N(FiP)$ invariants exceed Q and hence exceed the computers number range. On FP-computer such invariants are non-observable. MA-computer makes their remainders modulo Q observable, that is, it allows to observe the values $\tilde{I}_k \equiv I_k \bmod Q$, $k > N(FiP)$. Accordingly, $N(M)$-dimensional subspace $\tilde{\mathbf{V}}_{N(M)}$ of modulo observable invariants be broken into two subspaces $\tilde{\mathbf{V}}_{N(M)}$ and $\mathbf{V}_{N(M)-N(FiP)}$. The former subspace $\tilde{\mathbf{V}}_{N(FP)}$ is spanned on invariants the values of which are not destroyed by modular arithmetics. The latter one $\tilde{\mathbf{V}}_{N(M)-N(FiP)}$ is spanned on the remainders of their invariants the values of which exceed Q. It is clear that

$$\tilde{\mathbf{V}}_N = \tilde{\mathbf{V}}_{N(M)} \oplus \tilde{\mathbf{V}}_{N-N(M)} = \tilde{\mathbf{V}}_{N(FiP)} \oplus \tilde{\mathbf{V}}_{N(M)-N(FiP)} \oplus \tilde{\mathbf{V}}_{N-N(M)}.$$

If FP-computer is a projector on $\mathbf{V}_{N(FP)} \subset \mathbf{V}_{N(M)}$ then MA-computer is a projector on $\tilde{\mathbf{V}}_{N(M)}$. Geometrical considerations show that in the second case the distance between the spheres is more then in the first one, and this is always followed by an increase of correct pattern recognition probability on MA-computers as compared with FiP-computers.

4 Fast algorithms of modular invariant evaluation

Now we show that less arithmetic operations are needed to compute modular moments as compared to the

$$0.5Q^2(3Q + 1) \text{ multiplications and } 0.5Q(Q - 1)(3Q + 1) \text{ additions,}$$

necessary to compute $Q(Q + 1)/2$ ordinary moments.

Let ϵ be a primitive root of the field $GF(Q)$, that is an element x for which an arbitrary element $x \neq 0$ can be represented as $x = \epsilon^{t_x}$, where $t_x = \text{ind}_\epsilon x \bmod (Q - 1)$. Let $y = \epsilon^{t_y}$. Then we have

$$\tilde{m}_{pq} = \sum_{t_x=0}^{Q-2} \sum_{t_y=0}^{Q-2} f(\epsilon^{t_x}, \epsilon^{t_y}) \epsilon^{t_x p} \epsilon^{t_y q} \bmod Q \tag{3}$$

instead of (1). So, modular moments $\tilde{m}_{pq}$ as a matter of fact are the spectral values of the image $f(x,y)$ in a number-theoretical basis $\{\epsilon^{t_x p}, \epsilon^{t_y q}\}$, for which fast and highly efficient algorithms have been considered in [Lab84], [Cre89]. The computational amount of these algorithms can be significantly reduced by a careful selection of the transform parameters as the primitive root of unity. Indeed, if $\epsilon = 2$ then (2) reduces to the computation of a 2-dimensional fast Rader-transform, which can be performed without multiplications.

There is an analogeous possibility in the computation of complex moments too [ABM83]:

$$\dot{m}_{pq} = \sum_{x=0}^{A-1} \sum_{y=0}^{B-1} (x + iy)^p (x - iy)^q f(x,y). \tag{4}$$

As in the case of real moments all computations in (4) can be made modulo Q, if the polynomial $p(z) = z^2 - 1$ is irreducible over $\mathbf{GF}(Q)$

$$\dot{\tilde{m}}_{pq} = \sum_{x=0}^{A-1} \sum_{y=0}^{B-1} (x + iy)^p (x - iy)^q f(x,y) \bmod Q. \tag{5}$$

So, when $\dot{\tilde{m}}_{pq}$ is evaluated all operations are made according to the laws of the field $\mathbf{GF}(Q^2)$.

As $(x + iq)^Q \equiv (x - iy) \bmod Q$ then (5) can be rewritten in the form

$$\dot{\tilde{m}}_{pq} \equiv \sum_{x=0}^{Q-1} \sum_{y=0}^{Q-1} (x + iy)^{p+Qq} f(x,y) \bmod Q. \tag{6}$$

Let $r = p + Qq = (p, q)$ be a two bit number, which is written in radix-Q number system, then

$$\dot{\tilde{m}}_{pq} \equiv \sum_{x=0}^{Q-1} \sum_{y=0}^{Q-1} (x + iy)^r f(x,y) \bmod Q. \tag{7}$$

Consider a primitive root $\dot{\epsilon}$ in the field $\mathbf{GF}(Q^2)$, such that with some $\dot{\epsilon}^t = x + iy = (x, y)$. Substituting the last equation into (7), we get

$$\dot{\tilde{m}}_{pq} = \sum_{t=0}^{Q^2-2} \dot{\epsilon}^{tr} f(\dot{\epsilon}^t) \bmod Q, \qquad r = 0, \ldots, Q^2 - 1. \tag{8}$$

As the result, the computation of complex moments is reduced to complex Gaussian NTT [Lab84] of length $Q^2 - 1$.

As it was mentioned earlier, usage of modular arithmetic puts hard limitations of the form of the modulus Q. Number Q had to be chosen prime in order to cover all the spatial window $\Pi = A \times B$ (exclusively 0, null column and null line) by the power $x^p y^q \bmod Q$. This brought us to proportional dependence among A, B and $Q : A = B = Q - 1 \simeq 2^n$, where n is the wordlength of the MA computer. This fact essentially limits the choice of the numbers A and B, for the given computer's cardinality, on one hand. On the other hand, if A and B are fixed then one would like to have an opportunity to select the maximal Q (in the limits of technical possibility).

One gets such possibility if the chinese theorem is used. Let modulo Q equals to the product of two prime multiplies r_1 and $r_2 : Q = r_1 r_2$, where $\gcd(r_1, r_2) = 1$. According to the Chinese remainder theorem an arbitrary number $0 \leq x \leq Q - 1$ can be represented in the form of two residues: $x_1 \equiv x \bmod r_1$ and $x_2 \equiv x \bmod r_2$, i.e. is written in the number system of residue classes: $x = (x_1, x_2)$. By remainders x_1 and x_2 the number x is restored uniquely according to the following expression

$$x = s_1 x_1 + s_2 x_2 \bmod Q, \tag{9}$$

where numbers s_1, s_2 satisfy the comparisons $s_i \equiv \delta_{ij} \bmod r_j$; $s_i^2 \equiv s_i \bmod r_i$; $s_i \cdot s_j \equiv 0 \bmod r_i$ and are defined as $s_1 \equiv r_1 (r_1 \bmod r_2)^{-1} (\bmod r_2)$; $s_2 \equiv r_2 (r_2 \bmod r_1)^{-1} (\bmod r_1)$.

Theorem 1 *The equations* $x^t = s_1 x_1^t + s_2 x_2^t = (x_1^t, x_2^t) = (x_1^t, 1)(x_2^t, 1) \bmod Q$, *are fulfilled in the ring* $\mathbb{Z}/Q$.

Proof. Let's rise both sides of the equation (9) to the t-th power

$$x^t = (s_1 x_1 + s_2 x_2)^t = \sum_{l=0}^{t} C_t^l s_1^l s_2^{t-l} x_1^l x_2^{t-l}. \tag{10}$$

As $s_1^k \equiv s_1 \bmod Q$ and $s_2^k \equiv s_2 \bmod Q$ and $s_1 \cdot s_2 = 0$, only the first and latter terms in (10) are remained.

We'll consider only the case when the power t changes from 0 to $Q - (r_1 + r_2) + 1$. Then the number t can be written in two number systems $< r_1 - 1, r_2 - 1 >$ and $< r_2 - 1, r_1 - 1 >$:

$$t = \begin{cases} p + (r_1 - 1)q, & \text{where} \quad p \equiv t \bmod (r_1 - 1), \\ q + (r_2 - 1)q, & \text{where} \quad q \equiv t \bmod (r_2 - 1), \end{cases}$$

and $p = 1, \ldots, r_1 - 1$; $q = 1, \ldots, r_2 - 2$.

That's why

$$(x_1^t, x_2^t) = (x^{p+(r_1-1)q}, x^{q+(r_2-1)p}) = (x_1^p, x_2^q) =$$

$$(x_1, 1)^p (x_2, 1)^q, \text{ as } x_1^{r_1-1} \equiv 1 \bmod r_1, \ x_2^{r_2-1} \equiv 1 \bmod r_2.$$

Hence we get an expression for real modular moments

$$m_t = \sum_{x=0}^{Q-1} x^t f(x) \text{ or } m_{pq} = \sum_{x_1=0}^{r_1-1} \sum_{x_2=0}^{r_2-1} (x_1, 1)^p (x_2, 1)^q f(x_1, x_2). \tag{11}$$

Let ϵ_1 and ϵ_2 be primitive roots in the fields $\mathbf{GF}(r_1)$ and $\mathbf{GF}(r_2)$, respectively, then there exist such numbers t_1 and t_2 that $(x_1, 1) = \epsilon_1^t 1$ and $(1, x_2) = \epsilon_2^t 2$. Substituting the latter equations into (11), we'll get two-dimensional NTT

$$m_{pq} = \sum_{x_1=0}^{r_1-2} \sum_{x_2=0}^{r_2-2} \epsilon^{t_1 r_1} \epsilon^{t_2 r_2} f(x_1^{t_1}, x_2^{t_2}). \tag{12}$$

Summation limits in the latter expression show that $A = r_1 - 1$, $B = r_2 - 1$. If $r_1 \approx r_2$ then $A \approx B \approx \sqrt{2^n}$, where n is the word length of the MA computer.

So, if the Chinese theorem used then linear sizes of spatial window are directly proportional to $\sqrt{2^n}$, but not to 2^n as in the case of moments, evaluated according to (5).

$$\tilde{m} = \sum_{t=0}^{Q^2-2} \dot{\epsilon}^{tr} f(\dot{\epsilon}^t) \bmod Q, \qquad r = 0, 1, \ldots, Q^2 - 1.$$

As the result the computation of the complex moments is reduced to a complex Gaussian number-theoretic transform [Lab84], [Cre89] of length $Q^2 - 1$.

A lot of experiments was done to study the classification robustness of the new algorithms. In particular Hu-invariants [Hu62] and modular invariants have been used as objects specifiers. Moreover, in the case of modular invariants, computations have been carried out for different values for the modulus $Q : Q_1 = 17$ and $Q_2 = 65537$ and with a different number of invariants: $N(M)_1 = 7$, $N(M)_2 = 51$.

The experiments showed a lot of interesting results. Modular invariants allow a better object classification in a larger range of distortions than Hu-invariants. Surprisingly, for example a 5-bit (!) special purpose processor which realizes modular arithmetics with $Q = 17$ performs as good as a 32-bit floating-point processor that computes standard Hu-invariants. Further it is necessary to underline the minimal hardware amount needed for the modular invariants computation.

5   Image matching with the help of modular invariants

Let $f(x, y)$ describe a digitized optical $(M \times M)$-image of some observable scene. Let's pick out an $(N \times N)$-part of the image $f_N^t(x - x_t, y - y_t)$ (one of the brightest), where x_t, y_t are the coordinates of the upper left corner of this part. We'll call this part a template. Let's mark its absolute modular invariants as $\{I_k^t\}$, $k = 1, \ldots, M$, and the current image of the observable scene as $f^c(x, y)$. It can differ from $f_N^t(x - x_t, y - y_t)$ by various geometrical distortions. We'll consider that $f^c(x, y) = f^t[g * (x, y)]$, where $g = g(\alpha, \varphi, x_0, y_0)$ is some element of the 2-M affine transforms group.

To estimate parameters x_0, y_0 of $f^c(x, y)$ displacement with respect to $f^t(x, y)$ we'll modify a known search algorithm for modular invariants. The image $f^c(z, y)$ we'll call search region. Let this region be scanned by $(N \times N)$-window

$$\Pi(x, y) = \begin{cases} 1, & \text{if } 0 \leq x, y \leq N - 1, \\ 0, & \text{otherwise.} \end{cases}$$

The window will take $(M - N + 1)^2$ positions while scanning: $\Pi(x + i\Delta x, y + j\Delta y)$. We'll compute m absolute modular invariants $I_k(i\Delta x, j\Delta y)$, $i, j = 0, \ldots, M - N$; $k = 1, \ldots, m$ of the selected part $\Pi(x + i\Delta x, y + j\Delta y) f^c(x, y)$ of the search region in every position of spatial window. Then we'll evaluate the distance $d[\mathbf{I}^t, \mathbf{I}^c(x, y)]$ between template $\mathbf{I}^t = (I_1^t, I_2^t, \ldots, I_m^t)$ and current $\mathbf{I}^c = (I_1^c, I_2^c, \ldots, I_m^c)$ invariant vectors. The position of spatial window for which $d(i\Delta x, j\Delta y)$ is achieved, gives the estimate of image $f^c(x, y)$ displacement with respect to $f^t(x, y)$.

The profit of this method as compared to the traditional one, based on classical invariants, is the following: it is not necessary to use even fast NTT in every spatial window position , as the sliding algorithm is more useful and asks for less arithmetic operations in $(\log_2 A)(\log_2 B)$ times as compared to fast NTT.

Note that classical moments computation methods are less efficient then fast algorithms as for computational expenditures. So, they are less efficient as compared to "sliding" algorithms.

6   Experimental results on pattern recognition

To get experimental estimates of exact results frequency of object classification process (P_{cr}) a model has been constructed. This model imitates the work of a pattern recognition system and it was implemented on a computer. To compare the characteristics of the classificators functioning realized on FP-computer and MA-computer, Hu invariants [Hu62] and modular invariants have been used as objects specifiers. Moreover, in the case of modular invariants, simulations of a classificator work have been carried out for different values of moduli $Q : Q_1 = 17$ and $Q_2 = 65537$, and with different number of invariant speers: $N(M)_1 = 7, N(M)_2 = 51$.

The functions $R(x, y) = A - d[\mathbf{I}^t, \mathbf{I}^c(x, y)]$, which characterize the tightness between $\mathbf{I}^t$ and $\mathbf{I}^c(x, y)$, where $A = \max_{x,y} d[\mathbf{I}^t, \mathbf{I}^c(x, y)]$, have been constructed in order to illustrate the work of this image matching algorithm for the two binary images of differently printed letters "A". Their images differ by the scale only: $\alpha_1 = I$, $\alpha_2 = 0.77$. $R(x, y)$ is used instead of $d(x, y)$ because of it's more vivid. In Fig. 1 the functions $R(x, y)$, constructed for three values of $Q: Q_1 = 17$, $Q_2 = 257$ and $Q_3 = 65537$, and for two values of $N(M): N(M)_1 = 7$ and $N(M)_2 = 51$, are depicted. These images while showing the tightness measure of invariants $\mathbf{I}^t$ and $\mathbf{I}^c(x, y)$, gives the opportunity to estimate visually the algorithm stability to scale distortions in relation to Q and $N(M)$. For an analogous estimate with respect to the image rotation angle and to the joint influence of the scale and rotation Fig. 2 depicts $R(x, y)$, were obtained for the same values of Q and $N(M)$ and with template image of the letter "A" rotated by the angle $\varphi = 30^0$.

Twelve images of the four letters "A", "K", "M", "Y" printed differently were used in the task of image recognition. Each letter was printed in 3 different ways. One image was chosen as template. The dimensions of the images were 64×64 and the lines were 6 pixel thick. When organizing imitation simulation clutter situation is formed as follows. In the block of geometrical distortions affine transforms of the plane coordinates are fulfilled: $f^c(x, y) = f^t[g * (x, y)], g = g(\alpha, \varphi, x_0, y_0), g \in \mathbf{G}$, in object form distortion block segmentation mistakes on the border of two regions are reproduced.

Segmentation noise quantity was considered equal to the deviation $\Delta S = S_c - S_t$ of the letter distortion from the template S_t, and the value of noise-to-signal ratio $q = \Delta S/S_t$.

The main results of simulation are represented in the form of objects correct classification probability dependence on the value of noise-to-signal ratio q (Fig. 3), rotation angle φ and scale coefficient change $\Delta\alpha$ (Fig. 4).

The adduced dependencies show that modular invariants allow correct object classification in the larger range of distortions then Hu invariants with $Q = 17$ specifiers $\tilde{I}_{pr}$ are worse then I_{pr}. But the opportunity of objects classification is retained. And it is necessary to underline minimal hardware expenditures asked needed modular invariants computation (5-bit special purpose processor which realizes modular arithmetics with $Q = 17$) as compared to Hu invariants (48-bit processor).

References

[AP83]   ABU-MUSTAFA, Y.; PSALTIS, D.: *Image normalization by complex moments.* IEEE Computer Society Conference on Computer Vision and Pattern Recognition, 1983, pp. 114 - 120

[Cre89] CREUTZBURG, R.: *Parameter determination for complex number-theoretic transforms using cyclotomic polynomials.* Mathematics of Computation **52** (1989) No. 185, pp. 189-200

[Hu62]   HU, M. K.: *Visual pattern recognition by moment invariants.* IRE Trans. Inform. Theory. **8** (1962), pp. 179-187

[Lab84] LABUNETS, V. G.: *Algebraic Theory of Signals and Systems (in Russian).* Krasnojarsk: Krasnojarsk State University Press 1984

[SS76]   SCHVEDOV, A. M.; SCHMIDT, A. A.: *Zadatha uznavanij (in Russian).* Preprint DVNZ AN SSSR (1976), pp. 12

[Tea80] TEAQUE, M.: *Image analysis via the general theory of moments.* J. Opt. Soc. Am. **7** (1980), pp. 70-80

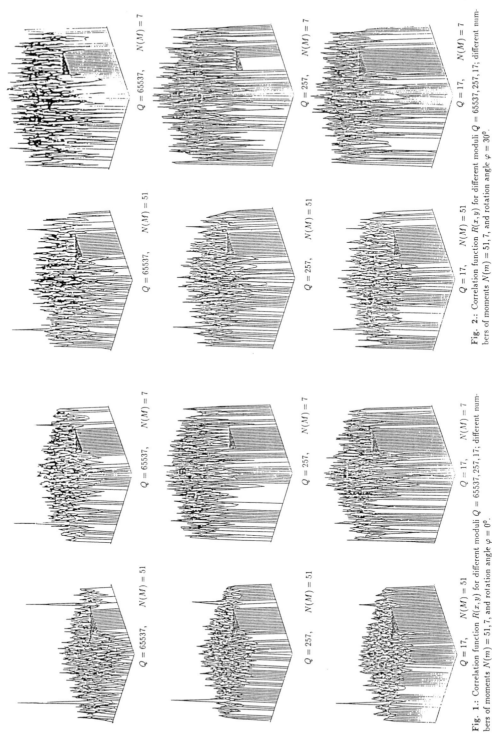

$Q = 65537, \quad N(M) = 7$

$Q = 257, \quad N(M) = 7$

$Q = 17, \quad N(M) = 7$

$Q = 65537, \quad N(M) = 51$

$Q = 257, \quad N(M) = 51$

$Q = 17, \quad N(M) = 51$

Fig. 2.: Correlation function $R(x,y)$ for different moduli $Q = 65537, 257, 17$; different numbers of moments $N(m) = 51, 7$, and rotation angle $\varphi = 30^0$.

$Q = 65537, \quad N(M) = 7$

$Q = 257, \quad N(M) = 7$

$Q = 17, \quad N(M) = 7$

$Q = 65537, \quad N(M) = 51$

$Q = 257, \quad N(M) = 51$

$Q = 17, \quad N(M) = 51$

Fig. 1.: Correlation function $R(x,y)$ for different moduli $Q = 65537, 257, 17$; different numbers of moments $N(m) = 51, 7$, and rotation angle $\varphi = 0^0$.

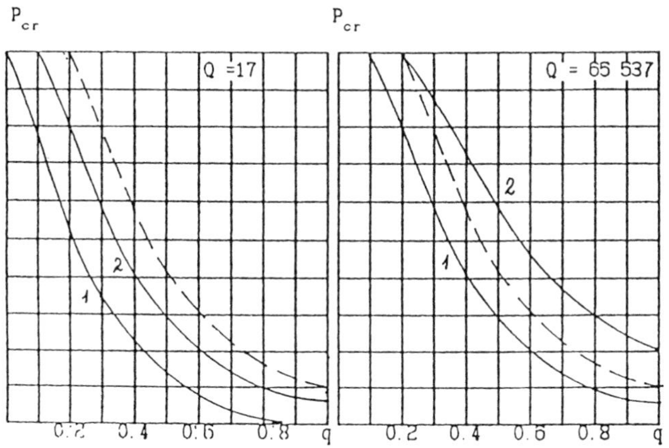

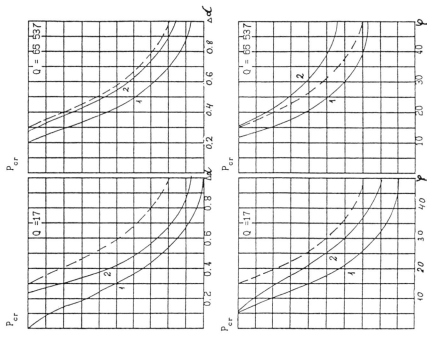

Fig. 4.: Dependence of correct recognition probability of the letter "A" on the scaling ratio $\Delta \alpha = 1 - \alpha$ and the rotation angle φ for Hu invariants (dotted lines) and modular invariants: 1 - $N(M) = 7$; 2 - $N(M) = 51$.

Fig. 3.: Dependence of correct recognition probability of the letter "A" on the signal-to-noise ratio q for Hu invariants (dotted lines) and modular invariants: 1 - $N(M) = 7$; 2 - $N(M) = 51$.

EDGE PRESERVING SMOOTHING BASED ON A NEW IMAGE MODEL

H. Jahn, R. Reulke [1]

Introduction

Edge preserving smoothing filters for image preprocessing have been investigated intensively in recent years. It has become obvious that linear filters always blur edges to a certain amount and that nonlinear ones are necessary for edge preserving smoothing, therefore. The use of nonlinear smoothing filters means that the probability distribution of the signal and or the noise are not Gaussian ones. For instance, median filters are optimal if the noise has a double exponential distribution (see Justusson [1]) which has wider tails than the Gaussian distribution.

The success of such filters depends on the quality of the implicitly underlain models and they may fail to work satisfactorily if the model is violated by the image data. Therefore, the choice of a proper scene (and noise) model is essential for the quality of the smoothing filter. Of course, there is a large variety of different classes of images which cannot be described by an unique image model. But many outdoor scenes may be divided into some almost homogeneous parts (regions, segments) which are limited by discontinuities or edges. A cut through such a scene shows intervals of smoothly varying intensity which are separated by jumps of intensity or gradient. The number and extents of the intervals and the heights of the jumps are different and cannot be forecasted without additional prior knowledge. Therefore, it is adequate to describe such scene cuts (rows or columns of nonblurred images) by random models and especially by certain Non-Gaussian Vector Wiener Models (NGVWM). If one chooses the transition probability density as a mixture of two different Gaussian densities, then the NGVWM properly fits the above mentioned class of scenes.

If the model is overlain by additive white Gaussian noise then the smoothing problem is reduced to an estimation problem. A useful guide to its solution is the Bayesian estimation method which provides a new class of smoothing filters after some necessary approximations. For the most simple NGVWM the filter requires the calculation of arithmetic means in windows of

---

[1]Institute of Space Research, Federal Republic of Germany, O-1199 Berlin, Rudower Chaussee 5

different extents and the choice of the optimal window according to a certain criterion. So an algorithm with variable window size is obtained, which resembles that derived by Pomalaza-Raez and McGillem [2], but with another criterion for the optimization of window size. The filter presented here can also be derived by least mean square estimation, which shows us the way to a generalization of the filter to more adequate image models. There is also a close connection to edge detection in the sense of Leclerc and Zucker [3] (see also Jahn [4]) which will be discussed shortly.

In principle the derived smoothing filter may be generalized to 2D-windows. But in this case the computational effort is too high because of the great variety of possible image structures and adequate (non-rectangular) windows needed for the calculation of local means. Therefore, it seems to be adequate to use 2D-windows for image restoration, i.e. for the reduction of the blur caused by the imaging camera, but 1D-windows (possibly of different orientations) for edge preserving smoothing and edge detection.

Non-Gaussian Vector Wiener Models

In order to describe the intensity values in an image row or column we consider the following stochastic model

$$x_i = x_{i-1} + \zeta_i \tag{1}$$

The ζ_i are statistically independent random variables with the probability density

$$p(\zeta) = P_0 \cdot \delta(\zeta) + \frac{(1-P_0)}{\kappa \cdot \sqrt{2 \cdot \pi}} \cdot \exp\left(-\frac{\zeta^2}{2 \kappa^2}\right) \tag{2}$$

where $\delta(\zeta)$ is the Dirac Delta function. $p(\zeta)$ is a mixture of two distributions which will be chosen randomly with the probability P_0. If P_0 is near to unity (e.g. $P_0 = 0.9$) then with high probability in each step of the recursion (1) the value $\zeta_i = 0$ is chosen which results in $x_i = x_{i-1}$. But with the small probability $1-P_0$ a value $\zeta_i \neq 0$, which obeys a Gaussian distribution with dispersion κ, is generated. Then x_i essentially deviates from x_{i-1}. Therefore the scene consists of large regions of constant intensity which are separated by step edges (figure 1). The equation (1) defines a

Fig.1 Example for NGVWM

Non-Gaussian Wiener Process. A more realistic scene model can be obtained if one considers the following generalization of (1)

$$x_i = x_{i-1} + v_{i-1} + \zeta_i$$
$$v_i = v_{i-1} + \eta_i \qquad (3)$$

which constitutes a Non-Gaussian Vector Wiener Process with the state vector $\mathbf{z} = (x,v)^T$. In (3) the η_i are random variables like the ζ_i with

$$\langle \eta_i, \zeta_i \rangle = 0 \quad , \quad \langle \eta_i, \eta_j \rangle = 0 \quad (i \neq j)$$
$$p(\eta) = Q_0 \cdot \delta(\eta) + \frac{(1-Q_0)}{\rho \cdot \sqrt{2 \cdot \pi}} \cdot \exp(-\frac{\eta^2}{2 \cdot \rho^2}) \qquad (5)$$

Now regions with increasing or decreasing intensity are separated by a more general edge type, containing step and roof edges as special cases.
To be still more realistic the δ - functions in (2) and (4) can be replaced by Gaussian distributions with small dispersions (compared with κ, ρ). The observed grey values y_i of an image row or column are given by

$$y_i = x_i + \xi_i \qquad (6)$$

where ξ_i is additive Gaussian noise with

$$\langle \xi_i \rangle = 0 \quad , \quad \langle \xi_i, \xi_j \rangle = \sigma^2 \cdot \delta_{i,j} \qquad (7)$$

(5) together with (1) or (3) is a quite realistic image model, if blur caused by the point spread function of the recording system can be neglected or if the blur already has been removed

by an image restoration filter. This model is the basis for the estimation of the scene values x_i, which will be considered in the next section.

Derivation of the Smoothing Filter

In this section the estimation of the wanted intensity values x_i is demonstrated at the model (1), (2), (5), (6) using the Bayesian estimation method (van Trees [5]). If the grey values y_i ($i = n, n\pm1, \ldots, n\pm N$) are used for the estimation of the value x_n, then one needs the posterior probability density $p(x_n|y_{n-N} \ldots y_{n+N})$ to apply the method. According to the Bayes theorem it is given by

$$p(x_n|y_{n-N}, \ldots, y_{n+N}) = C p(x_n) \cdot p(y_{n-N}, \ldots, y_{n+N}|x_n)$$

$$= C \cdot \int_{-\infty}^{\infty} dx_{n-N} \cdots \int_{-\infty}^{\infty} dx_{n-1} \int_{-\infty}^{\infty} dx_{n+1} \cdots \int_{-\infty}^{\infty} dx_{n+N} \, p(x_{n-N} \cdots x_{n+N}) \cdot p(y_{n-N} \cdots y_{n+N}|x_{n-N} \cdots x_{n+N})$$

(8)

where C is a normalization constant.
Taking into account (5) and (6) the likelihood is given by

$$p(y_{n-N} \cdots y_{n+N}|x_{n-N} \cdots x_{n+N}) = C \cdot \exp\left[-\frac{1}{2 \cdot \sigma^2} \sum_{k=-N}^{N} (y_{n+k} - x_{n+k})^2\right]$$

(9)

The prior probability density $p(x_{n-N} \ldots x_{n+N})$ can be written as

$$p(x_{n-N} \cdots x_{n+N}) = p(x_{n-N}) \cdot p(x_{n-N+1}|x_{n-N}) \cdots p(x_{n+N}|x_{n+N-1}) =$$

$$p(x_{n-N}) \prod_{k=1}^{2N} p(x_{n-N+k}|x_{n-N+k-1})$$

(10)

because of the Markovian behavior of the process $\{x_i\}$. According to (1) and (2) the transition probability density $p(x_{n-N+k}|x_{n-N+k-1})$ is given by

$$p(x_{n-N+k}|x_{n-N+k-1}) = P_0 \cdot \delta(x_{n-N+k} - x_{n-N+k-1}) +$$

$$+ \frac{(1-P_0)}{\kappa \cdot \sqrt{2 \cdot \pi}} \cdot \exp\left[-\frac{x_{n-N+k} - x_{n-N+k-1})^2}{2 \cdot \kappa^2}\right]$$

(11)

We don't use any information on the "initial" state x_{n-N}, which means that all values of x_{n-N} are equally probable ($p(x_{n-N}) \to C$). Now, in principle, the posterior density (7) may be calculated.

But the evaluation of (7) is complicated because of the calculations of the product (9) of the transition densities (10). Therefore, we neglect all terms $[(1-P_0)/P_0]^m$ with m>1, which is justified if P_0 is near to unity. Because of the relation

$$\int dx \, \delta(x-x_0) \cdot f(x) = f(x_0)$$

most of the integrals of (7) can be calculated easily, and the following result is obtained:

$$
\begin{aligned}
p(x_n | y_{n-N} \cdots y_{n+N}) = C \cdot \Bigg\{ & \exp\left[-\frac{1}{2\sigma^2} \sum_{k=-N}^{N} (y_{n+k}-x_n)^2 \right] \\
& + Q \sum_{l=1}^{N} \exp\left[-\frac{1}{2\sigma^2} \sum_{k=-l+1}^{N} (y_{n+k}-x_n)^2 \right] \cdot J_-(l) \\
& + Q \sum_{l=1}^{N} \exp\left[-\frac{1}{2\sigma^2} \sum_{k=-l+1}^{N} (y_{n-k}-x_n)^2 \right] \cdot J_+(l) \Bigg\}
\end{aligned}
\tag{11}
$$

Here again C is a normalization constant; further

$$Q = \frac{1-P_0}{P_0} \cdot \frac{1}{\kappa\sqrt{2\pi}}$$

and

$$J_\pm(l) = \int_{-\infty}^{+\infty} d\xi \cdot \exp\left[-\frac{(\xi-x_n)^2}{2\kappa^2} \right] \cdot \exp\left[-\frac{1}{2\sigma^2} \sum_{k=1}^{N} (y_{n\pm k}-\xi)^2 \right]$$

Introducing the quantities

$$
\begin{aligned}
\overline{y}_\pm(l) &= \frac{1}{N+1} \cdot \sum_{k=-l+1}^{N} y_{n\pm k} \\
\overline{y^2}_\pm(l) &= \frac{1}{N+1} \cdot \sum_{k=-l+1}^{N} y_{n\pm k}^2
\end{aligned}
\tag{12}
$$

we obtain

$$
\begin{aligned}
J_\pm(l) = \sqrt{2\pi} \cdot \frac{\dfrac{\sigma}{\sqrt{N-l+1}} \cdot \kappa}{\sqrt{\dfrac{\sigma^2}{N-l+1} + \kappa}} \cdot & \exp\left[-\frac{N-l+1}{2\sigma^2} \left(\overline{y^2}_\pm(-l+1) - \overline{y}_\pm^2(-l+1) \right) \right] \cdot \\
& \cdot \exp\left[-\frac{(x_n - \overline{y}_\pm(-l+1))^2}{2\left(\dfrac{\sigma^2}{N-l+1} + \kappa^2 \right)} \right]
\end{aligned}
\tag{13}
$$

To simplify the expression for the posterior density we consider low noise with $\sigma^2 \ll \kappa^2$. Then we obtain from (11) – (13)

100

$$p(x_n|y_{n-N}\cdots y_{n+N}) = C \cdot \left\{ \exp\left[-\frac{2N+1}{2\sigma^2}(x_n-\bar{y})^2\right] + \right.$$

(14)

$$+\sum_{l=1}^{N} R_l \exp\left[\frac{(2N+1)(N-l+1)}{2\sigma^2(n+1)}(\bar{y}-\bar{y}_-(-l+1))^2\right]\exp\left[-\frac{N+1}{2\sigma^2}(x_n-\bar{y}_+(1))^2\right]$$

$$\left. +\sum_{l=1}^{N} R_l \exp\left[\frac{(2N+1)(N-l+1)}{2\sigma^2(N+1)}(\bar{y}-\bar{y}_+(-l+1))^2\right]\exp\left[-\frac{N+1}{2\sigma^2}(x_n-\bar{y}_-(1))^2\right]\right\}$$

with

$$\bar{y} = \frac{1}{2N+1}\sum_{k=-N}^{N} y_{n+k}$$

and

$$R_l = \frac{1-P_0}{P_0}\cdot\frac{\sigma}{\kappa\sqrt{N-l+1}}$$

Now the normalization constant C can be determined from the condition

$$\int dx_n\, p(x_n|y_{n-N}\cdots y_{n+N}) = 1$$

Then it is easy to obtain the Bayes estimate

$$\hat{x}_n = \int dx_n\, x_n\cdot p(x_n|y_{n-N}\cdots y_{n+N})$$

The result is

$$\hat{x}_n = \frac{\bar{y}+\dfrac{1-P_0}{P_0}\dfrac{\sigma}{\kappa}\sqrt{2N+1}\displaystyle\sum_{l=1}^{N}\dfrac{1}{\sqrt{(n+1)(N-l+1)}}[\bar{y}_+(1)\cdot A_+ + \bar{y}_-(1)\cdot A_-]}{1+\dfrac{1-P_0}{P_0}\dfrac{\sigma}{\kappa}\sqrt{2N+1}\displaystyle\sum_{l=1}^{N}\dfrac{1}{\sqrt{(N+1)(N-l+1)}}[A_+ + A_-]}$$

$$A_\pm = \exp\left[\frac{(2N+1)(N+1)}{2\sigma^2(N-l+1)}\cdot(\bar{y}-\bar{y}_\pm(1))^2\right]$$

Of course, this result can only be applied, if the parameters P_0, σ, κ are known. Because this is not realistic in most cases we seek an expression which doesn't depend on these parameters. Therefore, the limit $\sigma \to 0$ is considered. For $\sigma \to 0$ only that term $\exp(A/\sigma^2)$ in the expression (16) survives for which A is maximum. Therefore, we have to calculate

$$M = \underset{l=1\ldots N}{MAX}\left[\frac{N+1}{N-l+1}(\bar{y} - \bar{y}_+(l))^2 \; ; \; \frac{N+1}{N-l+1}(\bar{y} - \bar{y}_-(l))^2\right] \qquad (17)$$

and we obtain

$$\frac{N+l_0}{N-l_0+1}[\bar{y}-\bar{y}_+(l_0)]^2 = M > 0 \quad or \quad \frac{N+l_0}{N-l_0+1}[\bar{y}-\bar{y}_-(l_0)]^2 = M > 0 \qquad (19)$$

For M = 0 the result is

$$\hat{x}_n = \bar{y} \qquad (20)$$

This means that we must calculate 2N+1 arithmetic means (12), (15) in different sub-windows of the window $n-N \leq k \leq n+N$ and that we have to choose the best one according to (19). The condition (19) guarantees that the best sub-window never crosses an edge (if there is at most one edge in the window $n-N \leq k \leq n+N+m$, which in most cases is fulfilled because of small $(1-P_0)/P_0$). The result (18) - (20) may be interpreted in terms of least mean square error (LMSE) estimation. If we assume that there is only one edge in the window $n-N\ldots n+N$, i.e.

$$x_{n+k} = \begin{cases} a & ; \; k \leq i-1 \\ b & ; \; k \geq i \end{cases} \qquad (21)$$

where the position i is unknown $(-N \leq i \leq N)$, then we can minimize

$$J(a,b;i) = \sum_{k=-N}^{i-1} (y_{n+k} -a)^2 + \sum_{k=1}^{N} (y_{n+k} - b)^2 \qquad (22)$$

in order to obtain

$$\hat{a}_i = \frac{1}{N+i} \sum_{k=-N}^{i-1} y_{n+k} = \frac{1}{N+i} \sum_{k=-i+1}^{N} y_{n-k} = \hat{y}_-(i),$$

$$\hat{b}_i = \frac{1}{N-i+1} \sum_{k=i}^{N} y_{n+k} = \bar{y}_+(-i+1) \qquad (23)$$

If we put these estimates into J(a,b;i) (22) then we obtain the result

$$J_i = J(\hat{a}_i,\hat{b}_i;i) = \sum_{k=-N}^{N}\left[(y_{n+k}-\bar{y})^2 - (2N+1)\frac{N+i}{N-i+1}(\bar{y} - \hat{a}_i)^2\right]$$

The minimization of J_i in order to obtain the optimum position i is equivalent to the maximization of

102

$$\frac{N+i}{N-i+1}(\overline{y} - \hat{a}_i)^2 \quad (i = -N...N) \qquad (24)$$

Then, if the best position i is obtained, we choose

$$\hat{x}_n = \begin{cases} \hat{a}_i & ; \ if \ i \geq 1 \\ \\ \hat{b}_i & ; \ if \ i < 1 \end{cases}$$

Therefore, this LMSE-procedure leads to the same result as (18)-(20). This shows us the direction of the investigation of more complicated models such as (3) and of cases, where more edges than a single one are contained in the window n-N...n+N. But such generalizations of the method are not considered in this paper.

The developed method of edge preserving smoothing is closely related to edge detection. The estimated value x_n is the left-hand limit of the intensity, if the edge is between n and n+1 or the right-hand limit, if the edge is located between n and n-1. Then in the sense of references [3] and [4] an edge will be detected, if $|x_n - x_{n+1}| > T$. But the new approach has the advantage, that the peak of the edge operator $|x_n - x_{n+1}|$ is very sharp because the windows, which are chosen by the algorithm for the estimation of x_n and x_{n+1}, never cross the edge. Of course, the disadvantage of the method is the greater amount of calculation.

Results and Conclusions

Some results of the application of the derived smoothing algorithm are presented in figures 2,3 and 4. Figure 2a shows a sample of a Non-Goussion Wiener Process with $P_0 = 0.96$, $\kappa = 1.0$, which is superposed by white Gaussian noise with $\sigma = 0.5$.

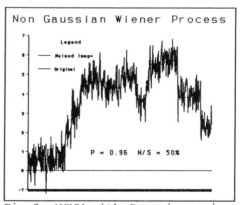

Fig.2a NGWM with Gaussian noise

The noise-to-signal ratio is defined here by $N/S = \sigma/\kappa$. The result of the application of the edge preserving smoothing filter is presented in figure

2b. The noise-supression is
better then a factor 3. Edges
are preserved. The filter size
encompassed 11 measurement
points. Structures within this
order of magnitude will be
smoothed out by the algorithm
applied. The quality of the
smoothing, especially in
regard to the preservation of
the edges, depends on the
amplitude of the noise to be

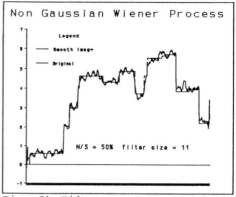

Fig. 2b Filter output

suppressed and on the instantaneous edge height. If they are
comparable, then in addition to the noise also these structures
will be smoothed.

These filters are also effective as edge detectors. It is
possible for multispectral images to derive the information
about edges from less noisy spectral channels in order to smooth
edge preserving more noisy spectral channels.

In figure 3 an IR-image of the Elbe river (blue) is shown. In
green colors is characterised the flow of the warmer Saale river
into the Elbe. In order to remove the noise in image 3a the
above mentioned filter has been utilized (Fig 3b). Because of
the one-dimensionality of the filter, the direction of smoothing
for each measurement point has been chosen by means of a random-
generator. After the smoothing process cooler structures become
visible wihin the upstream part of river Elbe (darker blue
regions).

In figure 4a the aerodrom Oberpfaffenhofen is shown in an image
taken with the Daedalus Scanner (channel 1). Figure 4b gives the
smoothed image. This image has been processed by means of the
image processing system DIBIAS (DLR Oberpfaffenhofen) with our
algorithm implemented. Especially in homogeneous parts of the
scene the noise supression is obvious and structures are easily
to be identified. A higher resolution of figure 4b would show
that smaller structures are smoothed out.

Other noise models such as salt-and-pepper-noise should be
studied too. This can be done by the use of

$$J(a,b;i) = \sum_{k=-N}^{i-1} |y_{n+k} - a| + \sum_{k=i}^{N} |y_{n+k} - b|$$

104

instead of (22), which results in the calculation of medians in different sub-windows.

After these generalizations the following preprocessing scheme should be applied: First the blur cause by the imaging device has

to be removed or diminished by the use of a local linear restoration filter (see Jahn [6]). This filter must be a two-dimensional one because of the 2D-character of the point spread function. After this, one-dimensional edge preserving filters of different orientations are be to applied for noise reduction and edge detection. Finally the result of this well-founded preprocessing scheme should be compared with that of other preprocessing algorithms.

Acknowledgements

The authors are thankful to Dr. Schroeder (Institute for Optoelectronics, DLR, Oberpfaffenhofen) for the Daedalus images. A part of the numerical work was performed on the image processing system DIBIAS. Thanks for support go to Dr. Kritikos at the same institute.

References

1. Justusson, B. I., 1981, in: "Two-Dimensional Digital Signal Processing " (Ed. T. S. Huang): Springer-Verlag, Berlin, pp. 161 - 196

2. Pomalaza-Reaz, C. A.; and McGillemm, C. D., 1984 IEEE-Transactions, ASSP-32, 571 - 576

3. Leclerc, Y. G., and Zucker, S. W., 1987, IEEE-Transactions, PAMI-9, 341 - 355

4. Jahn, H., 1987, in: "Computer Analysis of Images and Patterns" (Ed. L. P. Yaroslavskii, A. Rosenfeld, W. Wilhelmi), Akademie-Verlag, Berlin, 23 - 33

5. Van Trees, H. L., 1968, "Detection, Estimation, and Modulation Theory", Part 1, J. Wiley, New York

6. Jahn, H., and Reulke, R., Proceedings of CAIP '89, Akademie-Verlag, Berlin ,88-96

Fig 3a Temperature distribution at the outflow of river Saale
flow into the Elbe (the Elbe flows from left to right)

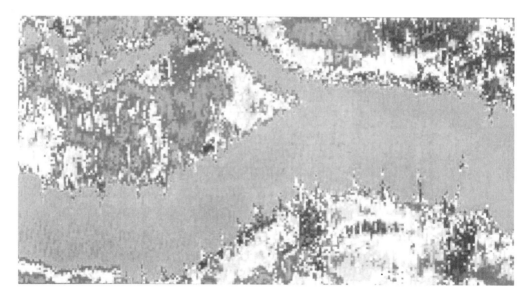

Fig 3b After smoothing with the edge preserving smoothing filter

106

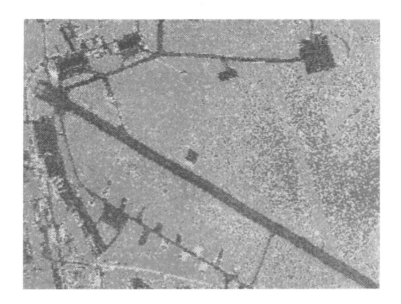

Fig 4a Aerodrome Oberpfaffenhofen taken with
Daedalus Scanner

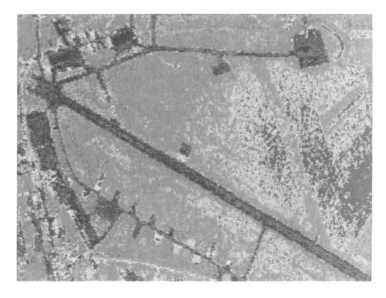

Fig 4b Smoothed image

GREY LEVEL CONTROLLED RANK ORDER FILTERING
(for smoothing of plateaus and sharpening of edges)

G.Stanke [1]

1. Introduction

Rank order filtering is a well known type of nonlinear filtering, in general used for removal of noise and image smoothing, whereby edges are preserved. The chosen rank is fixed over the whole image and influences the position of edges. A thinning or a thicking of lines can be accomplished but no improvement of the slope of edges is done. A new type of Rank Order Filter **(ROF)** described below allows to control the rank separately for each operator window position. The procedure to carry out is a very simple one, it is contents depending. As the result a sharpening of the slope of edges can be reached, whereby the noise smoothing feature of ROF is preserved. This type of filter gives a impressiv result for one dimensional operator windows and is usable for free chosen window shapes.

2. Properties of rank order filters

Rank order filters represent a widely used class of local nonlinear operators. The median is the best known. A detailed description of their properties is found in [1]. Some important features are :

- ROF smooth noise; exeption to this: the minimal or the maximal rank are chosen

- The application of ROF changes the mean image intensity; exeption: median to images with symmetrical noise distribution

- No new intensity values are generated by application of ROF; this property can be explicitly used for effective implementations especially for parallel machines.

---

[1] Institut of Image Processing in the CICIP, Kurstr.33, Berlin, O-1086, Tel.(0372) 20372314, Fax: (0372) 20372310

108

- The application of ROF shifts the position of edges; exeption: the median is selected.

- ROF preserve the shape of edges (also of corners if 1-dimensional windows are used). Small lines can be bloted out, what is useful for shading correction.

- Using ROF the image algebra can be simulated (binary images/ programmable windows).

- ROF for programmable windows provide the possibility to detect and to label "features" in images.

- The difference of two rank order images gives a gradient like result.

For implementations of ROF it seems to be a disadvantage that ordering procedures are neccessary. Nevertheless it is shown, that ROF can be implemented in a very effective manner for parallel machines [2] as well as for serial machines [3], [4] and [5]. Moreover, integrated circuits which accomplish the filtering nearly in real time are on the market.

3. Controlling the rank

An interesting approach for a controlled ROF, the Adaptive Median Filter (AMF), is found in [6]. The parameters underlying the control are window size and window shape. If the original signal contains peaks small in respect to the operator window size errors occur because filter cannot distinguish peaks from noise. That's why parts of the signal of interest can be cut of. The AMF avoids this effect. Before the median is taken, size and shape of the operator window are adapted to the local signal statistics, but the rank is fixed - it is the median.

As mentioned above in ROF's known the rank is fixed over the whole image. We learned in the "properties" that a thickening of dark lines (areas) can be done when a low rank in the ordered operator window (accumulator) is chosen and that a thickening of bright lines (areas) can be done when a hight rank is chosen. By combination of these

properties we design the Controlled Rank Order Filter (CROF). That
means the CROF does not work with a fixed rank but with a flexible
one. Thus we get the advantage to strengthen the stepness of edges
and therefor to sharpen blurred images. This effect occures due to
contents depending using of different rank positions during the
movement of the operator window over the image. A special procedure
watches if at the window position in the signal a plateau, an
increasing slope or a decreasing slope are found. To simulate a kind
of inertia for plateau signal levels the rank will be changed from
the median (or from a value near to the median) in the directions of
the extremes (not neccessarely to the extremes in order to preserve
the noise smoothing property of ROF) if a slope (a step in the first
derivation) is detected. The rank will jump back to the median when
the first derivation is again at a constant level (second derivation
near to zero).

In detail the following steps are carried out. The rank position is
shifted from the median to the higher end of the ordered operator
window (in an accumulator, comp. [4]) when a decrease of the grey
levels of the new comming pixels in the operator window is detected
(decreasing slope/negativ step in the first derivation). The higher
rank is chosen up to a constant level of the first derivation. If a
constant level of the first derivation is reached the higher rank
jumps back to the median. When the lower end of the decreasing slope
is detected (positiv step in the first derivation) the rank switches
to a lower rank positions. When an increasing slope after a plateau
in the signal is detected a similar procedure will be carried out,
but in this case first the rank will be shifted to the lower end of
the ordered operator window (accumulator), etc. As the result slopes
will be transformed to more step like functions. An edge sharpening
will be performed whereby the noise smoothing features are maintained
(if no extreme rank positions are chosen). The actually reached
sharpening of edges depends on the window parameters in the relation
to the signal parameters.

The rank position can be controlled also in a more simple way if some
information on the relations of basic signal levels in the image is
available. It means, the rank will be a direct function of the grey
level at the window pixel position. For higher grey levels a higher
rank and for lower grey levels a lower rank will be taken. Clearly,
it works only for grey scale images with two basic signal plateaus.

110

Figure 1 gives an example for an one-dimensional signal (1a) filtered by a ROF (median, window size 7 pixels, new pixel values are denoted by "n",1(b)) and by a CROF (lower rank 2, higher rank 6, window size 7, new pixel values are denoted by "c", 1(c)).

```
                *
* * * * *   * *   *
          *     . *
          .   *           1.(a) Original   image
          .      *
          .        *
          .          *       *
          .            * *   *   * * * *
          .              .       *
          .              .
          .              .
          .              .
* * * * * n * * n *      .
          . *            .
          .   *          .     1.(b) Image filtered by a
          .     *        .           Normal Rank Order
          .       *      .           Filter (Median)
          .         * .
          .           * * n * n * * * *
          .              .
          .              .
          .              .
          .              .
* * * * * c * * c * c c      .
          .     .        .
          .              .     1.(c) Image filtered by a
          .        c     .           Controlled Rank
          .       .      .           Order Filter
          .         .    .
          .           c c * * c * c * * * *
```

Figure 1.(a) - 1.(c)   Comparison of controlled and uncontrolled
                       ROF for a one-dimensional signal

4. Conclusion

The CROF gives on the base of a very simple procedure a further
possibility for image enhancement. It smooths images and
simultaneously sharpens edges. The procedure works without a-priori
information. In some cases (two level images) a-priori information
can leed to a further simplification. The sharpening of edges can be
combined with an edge shifting but to get this effect the parameters
in the control procedure must be changed. The Controlled Rank Order
Filter (CROF) is easy to implement and doesn't want any complicated
procedures. Using one-dimensional or two-dimensional updating for the
ordering of the values of the operator window in an accumulator time
consume remains in reasonable limits also for serial machines. The
usefulness of this new non-linear filtering operator can be
demonstrated by its application to different blurred images, e.g.
second or third copies of typewriter written documents as well as
other pictures containing different signal areas with unsharp
borders.

5. Literature

[1] Hodgeson, R.M.; Bailey, D.G.; Naylor, M.J.; McNeil, S.J.:
    Properties, Implementations and Applications of Rank Filters.
    Image and Vision Computing, Vol. 3(1985)1., S. 3-14.
[2] Stanke, G.; Osten, W.: Rangordnungsoperatoren auf einem paralle-
    len Prozessor. Bild und Ton 42(1989)3, S. 84-88.
[3] Ataman, E.; Aatre, V.K.; Wong, K.M.: A Fast Method for Realtime
    Median Filtering, IEEE Trans. on Acoust. Speach. Signal
    Processing 28(1980)7/8. - S. 343-354.
[4] Stanke, G.; Osten, W.: Rank-order filters - algorithms for
    effective implementation on serial and parallel machines, in:
    Proceedings International Fair Conference (CAIP'89), Computer
    Analysis of Images and Patterns, KdT-WGMA, Leipzig, Sept. 1989
[5] Pitas, I.: Fast Running Ordering and Max/Min Selection
    Algorithms, in: Mathematical Research (vol. 55), Computer
    Analysis of Images and Patterns, ed. by K. Voss, D. Chetverikov,
    G. Sommer, Akademieverlag, Berlin, 1989
[6] Bundschuh,B.: Adaptive Medianfilter zur Glättung Ein- und Zwei-
    dimensionaler Signale, OPTO 7, 1. Intern. Messe und Kongress,
    Nürnberg, 16.-18. Oct. 1990

MORPHOLOGICAL FILTERS AND IMAGE SYMMETRIES

P.A.Zalesskii, A.V.Tuzikov [1]

Mathematical morphology is widely used in image processing and pattern recognition [2]. It based on main transformations dilation, erosion, opening, closing and gives good possibilities in getting geometrical characteristics of images.

Here we investigate the following problem: which symmetries of the image are preserved by morphological transformations. We also construct transformations which preserve symmetries of the image. Here we consider morphological transformations on complete lattices like Serra [3] and Heijmans, Ronse [4,5].

Note that a partially ordered set L is called a complete lattice if every nonvoid subset K of L has a supremum and an infimum. Further we consider a complete lattice L with the order relation $\leq$, the supremum $\vee$, the infimum $\wedge$, the greatest element I and the least element O. Elements of L are written as capital letters A,B,C,D etc.

Let * be an operation of a complete lattice L, i.e. a function * :L x L $\longrightarrow$ L. Then we say that:
- * is dilation if for every $\mathfrak{I} \subseteq L$, $C \in L$, $(\vee\mathfrak{I})*C = \vee_{X \in \mathfrak{I}}(X*C)$,
- * is erosion if for every $\mathfrak{I} \subseteq L$, $C \in L$, $(\wedge\mathfrak{I})*C = \wedge_{X \in \mathfrak{I}}(X*C)$.

Here $\vee\mathfrak{I}$ and $\wedge\mathfrak{I}$ denote the supremum and the infimum of the set $\mathfrak{I}$ in the lattice L, respectively.

Definition 1. Operations * and x are called adjoint operations and the pair (*,x) is an adjunction when for every A,B,C $\in$ L

$$A * B \leq C \quad iff \quad A \leq C \times B.$$

By analogy with [4] it is easy to show that:

a) if (*,x) is an adjunction then * is dilation and x is erosion,

b) for any dilation there exists unique adjoint erosion and vice versa.

c) dilation and erosion are increasing operations on the first argument.

Further we shall use $\oplus$, $\ominus$ for dilation and erosion, respectively.

---

[1] Institute of Engineering Cybernetics of the Byelorussian Academy of Sciences, Surganova 6, Minsk, 220072, USSR

Let $A, B \in L$. Operations $\circ$ and $\bullet$ defined as
$A \circ B = (A \ominus B) \oplus B$ and $A \bullet B = (A \oplus B) \ominus B$ are called morphological opening and closing, respectively. Morphological opening and closing are antiextensive and extensive operations, respectively

Let and be dilation and erosion defined on a complete lattice L. The triplet $(L, \oplus, \ominus)$ is called a morphological space. An automorphism of the morphological space $(L, ,)$ is a bijective lattice morphism $f: L \longrightarrow L$ with $f(A \oplus B) = f(A) \oplus f(B)$, $f(A \ominus B) = f(A) \ominus f(B)$ for every $A, B \in L$.

1. Let $(L, \oplus, \ominus)$ be a morphological space and $A, B \in L$ be an image and a structuring element, respectively.

Definition 2. An automorphism g of a morphological space $(L, \oplus, \ominus)$ is called a symmetry of an image $A \in L$ if $g(A) = A$.

Let $S(A)$ denote the set of all symmetries of A. It is obvious that $S(A)$ is a group.

A composition $f(A, B_1, B_2, \ldots, B_n)$ of suprema, infima and morphological operations (i.e., dilation, erosion) with structuring elements $B_1, B_2, \ldots, B_n$ is called a morphological transformation of the image $A \in L$.

Let A, $B_i \in L$, $i = 1, 2, \ldots, n$. Then, for example, the following transformations $\bigwedge_i (A \oplus B_i)$, $\bigvee_i (A \ominus B_i)$, $\bigwedge_i (A \circ B_i)$, $\bigvee_i (A \bullet B_i)$ are morphological ones.

Proposition 1. Let $f(A, B_1, B_2, \ldots, B_n)$ be a morphological transformation and $S = S(A) \cap S(B_1) \cap S(B_2) \cap \ldots \cap S(B_n)$. Then f preserves the symmetries from the group S, i.e., for every $g \in S$.
$$g(f(A, B_1, B_2, \ldots, B_n)) = (A, B_1, B_2, \ldots, B_n).$$

To prove this proposition it is just necessary to take into consideration that g commutes with suprema, infima and morphological operations since g is an automorphism of the morphological space.

2. Skeleton

2.1. Let us suppose further that that dilation $\oplus$ is an associative operation, i.e., for any elements $A, B, C \in L$ holds
$$A \oplus (B \oplus C) = (A \oplus B) \oplus C$$

Then taking into account that dilation and erosion are adjoint operations we could show that
$$A \ominus (B \oplus C) = (A \ominus C) \ominus B$$
Naturally, we have for any elements A, B, C, D L the following

relations

$$D \oplus (B \oplus C) \leqq A \quad \text{iff} \quad D \leqq A \ominus (B \oplus C)$$

$$(D \oplus B) \oplus C \leqq A \quad \text{iff} \quad D \oplus B \leqq A \ominus C \quad \text{iff} \quad D \leqq (A \ominus C) \ominus B$$

So it is true

$$D \leqq A \ominus (B \oplus C) \quad \text{iff} \quad D \leqq (A \ominus C) \ominus B$$

Now we can conclude that

$$A \ominus (B \oplus C) = (A \ominus C) \ominus B$$

Further in this section we will suppose that in L an infinite distributivity law is fulfilled [1], i.e.,

$$A \vee \left(\bigwedge_{i \in I} X_i \right) = \bigwedge_{i \in I} (A \vee X_i)$$

2.2. Now we denote the notion of skeleton and investigate which symmetries of the original image preserves this transformation. Let $A, B \in L$ and A, B are the original image and the structuring element, respectively. Define the element $n B$ for any $n > 0$ as follows $B = B \oplus B \oplus \overset{n \text{ times}}{\ldots} \oplus B$. We shall suppose that OB is the minimal element O of the lattice L.

Define the n-th skeleton component $SK_n(A, B)$ of A as follows. If $n = 0$, then

$$SK_0(A, B) = \bigwedge_i \{ X_i, \text{ such that } X_i \vee (A \circ B) = A \}$$

If $n > 0$, then

$$SK_n(A, B) = \bigwedge_i \{ X_i, \text{ such that } X_i \vee ((A \ominus (n+1)B) \oplus B) = A \ominus n B$$

Define $SK_\infty(A, B)$ as follows

$$SK_\infty(A, B) = \bigwedge_k (A \circ kB)$$

The set of all skeleton components $(SK_n(A, B), n \geq 0$ we shall call the skeleton of A by the structuring element B.

These skeleton components allow to reconstruct A as follows

$$A = SK_0(A, B) \vee \left(\bigvee_{n > c} (SK_n(A, B) \oplus n B) \right) \vee SK_\infty(A, B) \qquad (2)$$

Let us prove that the equation (2) holds.

First we show that

$$SK_0(A, B) \vee (A \circ B) = A \qquad (3)$$

We have

$$SK_0(A, B) \vee (A \circ B) = (\bigwedge_i \{ X_i, \text{ such that } X_i \vee (A \circ B) = A \vee$$

$(A \circ B) = \bigwedge_i \{ X_i \vee (A \circ B)) = A$. We used here the infinite distributivity of the lattice L. So the infimum and the supremum are commutative operations in L.

Now we prove that

$$(SK_n(A, B) \oplus n B) \vee (A \circ (n+1) B) = A \circ n B \qquad (4)$$

We have

$$((\wedge_i \{X_i, \text{ such that } X_i \vee ((A \ominus (n+1)B) \oplus B) = A \ominus nB\}) \oplus nB) \vee$$
$$(A \ominus (n+1)B) = ((\wedge_i \{X_i | X_i \vee ((A \ominus (n+1)B) \oplus B) = A \ominus nB)) \oplus$$
$$nB) \vee (A \ominus (n+1)B \oplus B \oplus nB) = ((\wedge_i \{X_i\}) \vee (A \ominus (n+1)B \oplus B)) \oplus$$
$$nB = (\wedge_i (X_i \vee (A \ominus (n+1)B \oplus B)) \oplus nB = A \ominus nB \oplus nB = A \circ nB$$

Here we used the definition of dilation (i.e., distributivity of dilation with respect to the supremum) and infinite distributivity of the lattice L.

The opening of A by a structuring element nB is non-increasing under n i.e.,

$$A \circ nB \le A \circ (n+1)B \tag{5}$$

Using definition of opening we get
$$A \circ (n+1)B = A \ominus (n+1)B \oplus (n+1)B = A \ominus nB \ominus B \oplus B \oplus nB =$$
$$((A \ominus nB) \circ B) \oplus nB \le (A \ominus nB) \oplus nB = A \circ nB.$$ The inequality holds
while opening is an antiextensive operation.

It follows immediately from (4) and (5) that
$$SK_n(A,B) \oplus nB) \le A \circ nB \le A \tag{6}$$

Now we can show that the reconstruction formula (2) is true.

Substituting (4) for $n = 1$ into (3) we get
$$A = SK_0(A,B) \vee (A \circ B) = SK_0(A,B) \vee (SK_1(A,B) \oplus B) \vee (A \circ 2B).$$

Similarly, for every $k > 0$ we get the following formula
$$A = SK_0(A,B) \vee (\vee_{n \le k} (SK_n(A,B) \oplus nB)) \vee (A \circ (k+1)B) \tag{8}$$

Let us fix $k \in \mathbb{N}$ and consider the following expression
$$SK_0(A,B) \vee (\vee_{n=1}^{\infty} (SK_n(A,B) \oplus nB)) \vee (A \circ kB)$$
Then we have
$$SK_0(A,B) \vee (\vee_{n=1}^{\infty} (SK_n(A,B) \oplus nB)) \vee (A \circ kB) =$$
$$SK_0(A,B) \vee (\vee_{n < k} (SK_n(A,B) \oplus nB)) \vee (A \circ kB) \vee$$
$$(\vee_{n \ge k} (SK_n(A,B) \oplus nB) = A \tag{9}$$
Using (6) we get
$$\vee_{n \ge k} (SK_n(A,B) \oplus nB) \le A$$

Taking into account this inequality and (7) we get the last equality (9).

Thus $A = SK_0(A,B) \vee (\vee_{n=1}^{\infty} (SK_n(A,B) \oplus nB)) \vee (A \circ kB)$
Let us take the infimum on k in both sides of this formula
$$\wedge_k A = \wedge_k (SK_0(A,B) \vee (\vee_{n=1}^{\infty} (SK_n(A,B) \oplus nB)) \vee (A \circ kB)) =$$
$$SK_0(A,B) \vee (\vee_{n=1}^{\infty} (SK_n(A,B) \oplus nB)) \vee (\wedge_k (A \circ kB) =$$
$$SK_0(A,B) \vee (\vee_{n=1}^{\infty} (SK_n(A,B) \oplus nB)) \vee SK_{\infty}(A,B),$$
where $SK_{\infty}(A,B) = \wedge_k (A \circ kB)$

The second equality is true because in the lattice L the

116

property (1) is fulfilled. So we have

$$A = SK_0(A,B) \vee (\vee_{n=1}^{\infty}(SK_n(A,B) \oplus nB)) \vee SK_{\infty}(A,B)$$

Consider the question which symmetries of the original image $A \in L$ do preserve the skeleton transformation. Let $S(SK_n(A,B)$ be as before the set of all symmetries of $SK_n(A,B)$. It follows from the proposition 1 that for any automorphism $g \in S(A) \cap S(B)$ $g(SK_n(A,B)) =$

$g(\wedge_i \{ X_i, \text{ such that } X_i \vee ((A \ominus (n+1)B) \oplus B) = A \ominus nB \}) =$

$\wedge_i g(\{ X_i, \text{ such that } X_i \vee ((A \ominus (n+1)B) \oplus B) = A \ominus nB) =$

$\wedge_i \{ g(X_i), \text{ such that } X_i \vee ((A \ominus (n+1)B) \oplus B) = A \ominus nB \} =$

$\wedge_i \{ g(X_i), \text{ such that } g(X_i \vee ((A \ominus (n+1)B) \oplus B)) = g(A \ominus nB) =$

$\wedge_i \{ g(X_i), \text{ such that } g(X_i) \vee g((A \ominus (n+1)B) \oplus B) = g(A \ominus nB) =$

$\wedge_i \{ g(X_i), \text{ such that } g(X_i) \vee ((A \ominus (n+1)B) \oplus B) = A \ominus nB \} =$

$\wedge_i \{ X_i, \text{such that } X_i \vee ((A \ominus (n+1)B) \oplus B) = A \ominus nB \} =$

$SK_n(A,B)$, where $n = 1,2,\ldots$.

Here we used that

$$g((A \ominus (n+1)B) \oplus B) = (A \ominus (n+1)B) \oplus B \quad \text{and} \quad g(A \ominus nB) = A \ominus nB$$

for $g \in S(A) \cap S(B)$ (see Proposition 1).

Similarly it is possible to show that $SK_0(A,B)$ and $SK_{\infty}(A,B)$ are invariant with respect to any element $g \in S(A) \cap S(B)$. Then by Proposition 1 $g(SK(A,B) = SK(A,B)$ for every $g \in S(A) \cap S(B)$. Thus we proved the skeleton transformation preserves all the symmetries from the group $S(A)$ (B).

References

1. B.Birkhoff. Lattice theory, American Mathematical Society Colloquium Publications, vol.25, 1984.

2. R.M.Haralick, S.R.Sternberg, X.Zhuang, Image analysis using mathematical morphology, IEEE Trans. Pattern Anal. Machine Intell., 9, 1987, 532-550.

3. J.Serre. Image analysis and mathematical morphology, vol.21. Theoretical Advances, Academic Press, London, 1988.

4. H.J.I.M. Heijmans, C.Ronse. The algebraic basis of mathematical morphology. Part 1: Dilations and erosions, Computer Vision, Graphics, and Image Processing, 50, 1990, 245-295.

5. C.Ronse, H.J.I.M.Heijmans. The algebraic basis of mathematical morphology. Part 2: Opening and closing, Report AM-R8904, Centre for mathematics and computer sciences, 1989.

Nonlinear filtering of speckle noise in ultrasonic images

C. Kotropoulos*   I. Pitas *

1   Introduction

Speckle noise is a special kind of noise encountered in images formed by laser beams, in radar images as well as in envelope-detected ultrasound (US) B-mode images. It is an interference effect caused by the scattering of the US beam from microscopic tissue inhomogeneities. It has been found that the contrast/detail results for the envelope detection in diagnostic US are almost identical with the results for square law detection with the latter serving as upper limit for performance in lesion detection [6]. The detection of focal lesions from the point of view of communication systems has been considered in [7]. The suppression of speckle by an adaptive weighted median filter has been proposed in [3].

The main contribution of this paper is the design of optimal nonlinear filters for speckle removal in US B-mode images and the derivation of their properties. Speckle is modeled as multiplicative noise. At a first approach, the signal is assumed to be constant and the noise term to be Rayleigh random variable having unity expected value. The detection of the constant signal is expressed as a binary hypothesis-testing problem. The receiver operating characteristics for the optimal decision rule are derived by evaluating theoretically the probability of false alarm and the probability of detection. The problem of estimating the constant signal is also considered. It is proven that the maximum likelihood (ML) estimator of the signal is the L_2 mean filter multiplied by a constant scaling factor. The expected value and the variance of this estimator have been evaluated. The mean square error (MSE) in estimating the constant signal by using the ML-estimator has also been calculated. The use of an L-estimator of the constant signal is also proposed. L-estimators are defined as linear combinations of the order statistics, i.e., the observations arranged in ascending order of their magnitude inside the filter window [1]. The L-estimator which minimizes the mean square error between the L-estimator output and the signal is designed. At a second approach, the signal is assumed to be random variable. The structure of the optimal decision rule is again derived. The maximum a posteriori probability (MAP) estimator of the intensity (i.e., squared) signal has also been found.

2   Detection of a constant signal from speckle

Let z be the envelope-detected observed signal, m be the signal and n be a noise term statistically independent of m. It is assumed that the signal m is related to the observation z by:

$$z = mn \tag{1}$$

The probability density function (pdf) of the observed random variable (r.v.) z is considered to be Rayleigh [4]:

$$f_z(z) = \frac{z}{\sigma^2} \exp[-\frac{z^2}{2\sigma^2}], \quad z > 0 \tag{2}$$

---
*Department of Electrical Engineering, University of Thessaloniki, Thessaloniki 540 06, GREECE

It can be easily proven that if the signal m is constant and equals $\sigma\sqrt{\pi/2}$ and the noise term n is Rayleigh r.v. having unity expected value, then the pdf of the r.v. z is given by (2). In the following, the model (1) will be used.

Let us assume that we have a set of N observations $z_1, z_2, \ldots, z_N$ denoted by a vector $\mathbf{z} = (z_1, z_2, \ldots, z_N)^t$ in the observation space $\mathcal{R}^N$. Let $\mathbf{n} = (n_1, n_2, \ldots, n_N)^t$ be a vector of N independent identically distributed Rayleigh noise random variables. Let us assume the following two hypotheses:

$$H_k : \mathbf{z} = m_k \mathbf{n} \qquad k = 0, 1 \tag{3}$$

created by the probabilistic transition mechanisms:

$$f_{z_i|H_k}(Z_i|H_k) = \frac{Z_i}{\sigma_k^2} \exp[-\frac{Z_i^2}{2\sigma_k^2}] \qquad Z_i > 0, \quad i = 1, \ldots, N \quad k = 0, 1 \tag{4}$$

The Bayes criterion [8] leads to the likelihood ratio test (LRT) :

$$\Lambda(\mathbf{Z}) = \frac{f_{\mathbf{z}|H_1}(\mathbf{Z}|H_1)}{f_{\mathbf{z}|H_0}(\mathbf{Z}|H_0)} \overset{H_1}{\underset{}{\gtrless}} \theta \tag{5}$$

By substituting (4) to (5) the following optimal decision rule results:

$$\sum_{i=1}^{N} Z_i^2 \overset{H_1}{\underset{}{>}} \frac{2\sigma_0^2\sigma_1^2}{\sigma_1^2 - \sigma_0^2}(\ln\theta - 2N\ln\frac{\sigma_0}{\sigma_1}) = \gamma \quad \text{for } \sigma_1^2 > \sigma_0^2 \tag{6}$$

$$\sum_{i=1}^{N} Z_i^2 \overset{H_1}{\underset{}{<}} \frac{2\sigma_0^2\sigma_1^2}{\sigma_0^2 - \sigma_1^2}(2N\ln\frac{\sigma_0}{\sigma_1} - \ln\theta) = \gamma' \quad \text{for } \sigma_1^2 < \sigma_0^2 \tag{7}$$

where θ, γ and γ' are thresholds.

Let R_0 be the decision region under the hypothesis H_0 and R_1 the corresponding decision region under the alternative hypothesis. The probability of *false alarm* and the probability of *detection* for the decision rule (6) are given by:

$$P_F = \int_{R_1} f_{\mathbf{z}|H_0}(\mathbf{Z}|H_0)d\mathbf{Z} = Pr[\sum_{i=1}^{N} Z_i^2 \geq \gamma|H_0] \tag{8}$$

$$P_D = \int_{R_1} f_{\mathbf{z}|H_1}(\mathbf{Z}|H_1)d\mathbf{Z} = Pr[\sum_{i=1}^{N} Z_i^2 \geq \gamma|H_1] \tag{9}$$

The plot of P_D versus P_F for various γ as varying parameter is defined as the receiver operating characteristic. The threshold γ is expressed as follows:

$$\gamma = \frac{2d^2\sigma_0^2}{d^2 - 1}(\ln\theta + 2N\ln d) \tag{10}$$

where $d = \sigma_1/\sigma_0$. It can be proven [2] that the probability of false alarm is given by:

$$P_F = \int_{\frac{\gamma}{2\sigma_0^2}}^{\infty} \frac{\xi^{N-1}}{(N-1)!} \exp(-\xi)d\xi = 1 - \mathcal{I}_\Gamma(\frac{\gamma}{2\sigma_0^2\sqrt{N}}, N-1), \quad d \geq 1 \tag{11}$$

where $\mathcal{I}_\Gamma(u, M)$ is the incomplete Gamma function:

$$\mathcal{I}_\Gamma(u, M) \overset{\triangle}{=} \int_0^{u\sqrt{M+1}} \frac{x^M}{M!} \exp(-x)dx \tag{12}$$

The probability P_D is evaluated as follows:

$$P_D = 1 - \mathcal{I}_\Gamma(\frac{\gamma}{2d^2\sigma_0^2\sqrt{N}}, N-1), \quad d \geq 1 \tag{13}$$

From (11,13) and (10), it can be seen that the probabilities of false alarm and detection are independent of σ_0. A similar analysis holds for (7). The receiver operating characteristic becomes superior as d increases (decreases) when $d > 1$ (when $d < 1$) or with the increase of the length N when d is kept constant.

3 Estimation of a constant signal from speckle

In this section we estimate the parameter m in (1) if n is multiplicative noise independent of m which is distributed as follows:

$$f_n(\mathcal{N}) = \frac{\pi \mathcal{N}}{2} \exp[-\frac{\pi \mathcal{N}^2}{4}] \quad \mathcal{N} > 0 \tag{14}$$

Let us suppose that we have a set of N observations. Then:

$$f_{z|m}(\mathbf{Z}|M) = \frac{\pi^N}{2^N M^{2N}} \prod_{i=1}^{N} Z_i \exp[-\frac{\pi Z_i^2}{4M^2}] \tag{15}$$

The ML-estimate of M maximizes the log-likelihood function $\ln f_{z|m}(\mathbf{Z}|M)$. Therefore:

$$\frac{\partial}{\partial M} \ln f_{z|m}(\mathbf{Z}|M)|_{M=\hat{m}_{ML}(\mathbf{Z})} = 0 \tag{16}$$

or equivalently:

$$\hat{m}_{ML} = \frac{\sqrt{\pi}}{2} \sqrt{\frac{1}{N} \sum_{i=1}^{N} Z_i^2} \tag{17}$$

Thus, it has been proven that the ML-estimator of the constant signal is the L_2 mean scaled by the factor $\frac{\sqrt{\pi}}{2}$.

Let $\pi(N)$ be the following polynomial of N:

$$\pi(N) \triangleq \frac{\Gamma[N + \frac{1}{2}]}{\sqrt{N}(N-1)!} \tag{18}$$

then, the expected value of the ML-estimator, its variance and the mean square estimation error are given by [2]:

$$\mathrm{E}[\hat{m}] = \pi(N)M \qquad \mathrm{var}[\hat{m}] = (1 - \pi^2(N))M^2 \qquad \mathrm{E}[(\hat{m} - M)^2] = 2(1 - \pi(N))M^2 \tag{19}$$

Another class of estimators found extensive applications in digital signal and image processing are the L-estimators which are based on the order statistics. The output of the L-estimator of length N is given by:

$$y(k) = \mathbf{a}^t \mathbf{z}_r(k) \tag{20}$$

where $\mathbf{a} = (a_1, \ldots, a_N)^t$ is the L-estimator coefficient vector and $\mathbf{z}_r(k) = (z_{(1)}^k, z_{(2)}^k, \ldots, z_{(N)}^k)^t$ is the vector of the observations arranged in ascending order of magnitude (i.e., order statistics). We shall design the L-estimator which minimizes the mean square error (MSE) $\mathrm{E}[(y(k) - m)^2]$ under the constraint of unbiased estimation for the model (1). The unbiasedness condition implies that the L-estimator output will converge to the estimated constant signal in an ensemble-average sense and results in the following equation in vector notation:

$$\mathbf{a}^t \overline{\mu} = 1 \tag{21}$$

where $\overline{\mu} = (\mathrm{E}[n_{(1)}], \mathrm{E}[n_{(2)}], \ldots, \mathrm{E}[n_{(N)}])^t$ is the vector of the expected values of the order statistics. The superscript k is dropped out due to stationarity. Let $\mathbf{n}_r = (n_{(1)}, \ldots, n_{(N)})^t$

be the vector of the ordered noise samples and $\mathbf{R} = E[\mathbf{n}_r\mathbf{n}_r^t]$ be the correlation matrix of the ordered noise samples. The MSE is written as follows:

$$MSE = m^2(\mathbf{a}^t\mathbf{Ra} - 1) \tag{22}$$

The L-estimator coefficient vector $\mathbf{a}$ which minimizes (22) under (21) is given by [1]:

$$\mathbf{a} = \frac{\mathbf{R}^{-1}\overline{\mu}}{\overline{\mu}^t\mathbf{R}^{-1}\overline{\mu}} \tag{23}$$

In order to calculate $\mathbf{a}$ we need matrix $\mathbf{R}$ whose elements are moments of the order statistics for the Rayleigh distribution with parameter σ. In our case the parameter σ equals $\sqrt{2/\pi}$, as can be seen from (14). The evaluation of the elements of the correlation matrix $\mathbf{R}$ and the vector $\overline{\mu}$ in a computationally efficient manner is treated in [2]. It has been found that the higher order statistics are weighted by larger coefficients for various L-estimator lengths and that there exists an almost linear increase in magnitude of the L-estimator coefficients $\mathbf{a}$ with the order number i.

4   Generalization to a random lesion signal

In most practical cases it is unrealistic to consider a constant signal hypothesis. Without any loss of generality the following binary hypothesis problem will be assumed:

$$\begin{aligned} H_1 : z &= mn \\ H_0 : z &= n \end{aligned} \tag{24}$$

where m, n are random variables. Our aim is to perform detection and estimation based on this model. Since m is a r.v., the conditional density of the observations assuming H_1 is given by:

$$f_{z|H_1} = \int_{\chi_m} f_{z|m,H_1}(Z|M,H_1)\; f_{m|H_1}(M|H_1)dM \tag{25}$$

where χ_m is the domain of the r.v. m. If n is a Rayleigh r.v. distributed as (14) then the conditional density of the observations under the hypothesis H_1 and the condition that m is known is given by:

$$f_{z|m,H_1}(Z|M,H_1) = \frac{1}{M}f_n(\frac{Z}{M}) = \frac{\pi Z}{2M^2}\exp(-\frac{\pi Z^2}{4M^2})\; M > 0 \tag{26}$$

The conditional density of m assuming H_1 must be chosen in such a way that it represents a realistic model and it is mathematically tractable. A Maxwell density with parameter Λ fullfills both requirements. Thus:

$$f_{m|H_1}(M|H_1) = \frac{4\Lambda^{3/2}}{\sqrt{\pi}}\; M^2\;\exp(-\Lambda M^2) \tag{27}$$

By substituting (27) in (25) we obtain:

$$f_{z|H_1}(Z|H_1) = \pi\Lambda Z\exp(-Z\sqrt{\Lambda\pi}) \tag{28}$$

It can be seen that the resulted density is a Gamma density. Such a result is very reasonable, because it is known that speckle can be modeled by a Gamma density function [5, pp. 226]. Based on N observations the log-likelihood test leads to:

$$\sum_{i=1}^{N} Z_i^2 - 4\sqrt{\frac{\Lambda}{\pi}} \sum_{i=1}^{N} Z_i \overset{H_1}{\underset{>}{}} \frac{4}{\pi}(\theta - N\ln 2\Lambda) = \gamma'' \tag{29}$$

The problem of the estimation of the signal m will be treated next. The (MAP) estimate of the signal is defined by:

$$\frac{\partial}{\partial M} f_{m|\mathbf{z}}(M|\mathbf{Z})|_{M=\hat{m}_{MAP}(\mathbf{z})} = 0 \tag{30}$$

By applying the Bayes theorem we obtain:

$$(\frac{\pi}{4} \sum_{i=1}^{N} Z_i^2)\frac{1}{M^4} - (N-1)\frac{1}{M^2} - \Lambda = 0 \tag{31}$$

Therefore the MAP estimate of the squared signal $s = m^2$ is given by:

$$\hat{s}_{MAP}(\mathbf{z}) = \frac{\frac{\pi}{2}\sum_{i=1}^{N} Z_i^2}{(N-1) + \sqrt{(N-1)^2 + \pi\Lambda\sum_{i=1}^{N} Z_i^2}} \tag{32}$$

It can be seen that for $\Lambda = 0$ the MAP estimate of m reduces to the form of the ML-estimate of the constant signal.

5 Experimental results

In US community, simulated US B-mode images are used in order to evaluate the performance of various filters in speckle suppression and to select parameters (such as filter length and thresholds involved) in the image processing task. A simulation of an homogeneous piece of tissue (4×4 cm) with a circular lesion in the middle with diameter of 2cm has been used. The lesion differs from the background in reflection strength (+3dB). Background and lesion have an equal number density of scatterers ($5000/cm^3$). We have examined the success of the following strategies in lesion detectability: (1) thresholding the original image without any processing (2) filtering the original image by the 9×9 arithmetic mean filter and thresholding the filtered image (3) filtering the original image by the 9×9 ML-estimator of the constant signal and thresholding the filtered image (4) filtering the original image by the 9×9 L-estimator and thresholding the filtered image. We have compared the performance of the above-described strategies using as figures of merit the area under the ROC in each case and the probability of detection P_D for a threshold chosen so that the probability of false alarm P_F to be $\simeq 10\%$. Some experimental evaluations of

Table 1: FIGURES OF MERIT FOR LESION DETECTION ON SIMULATED US B-MODE IMAGE

Method	Area under ROC	$P_F(\%)$	$P_D(\%)$	Threshold
image thresholding	0.634570	10.8031	26.4860	25
ar. mean 9×9	0.738165	11.5512	37.8067	20
ML-estimator 9×9	0.743776	12.2488	40.8185	19
L-estimator 9×9	0.745246	11.5047	39.5872	19

these figures of merit are shown in Table 1. It can be seen that the proposed nonlinear filters are relatively better than the arithmetic mean with respect to the area under the ROC and the probability of detection for the same probability of false alarm.

Acknowledgements

This work has been supported by a grant from the National Scholarship Foundation of Greece and the Bodosaki Foundation.

References

[1] A.C. Bovik, T.S. Huang, D.C. Munson, "A generalization of median filtering using linear combinations of order statistics", *IEEE Trans. on ASSP*, vol. ASSP-31, no. 6, pp. 1342-1349, December 1983.

[2] C. Kotropoulos and I. Pitas, "Nonlinear filtering of speckle noise in ultasound B-mode images", *IEEE Trans. on Medical Imaging*, under review.

[3] T. Loupas, W.N. McDicken and P.L. Allan, "An adaptive weighted median filter for speckle suppression in medical ultrasonic images", *IEEE Trans. on Circuits and Systems*, vol. CAS-36, no. 1, January 1989, pp 129–135.

[4] A. Papoulis, *Probability, Random Variables and Stochastic Processes*, McGraw-Hill, 1984.

[5] I. Pitas and A. N. Venetsanopoulos, *Nonlinear digital filters: Principles and Applications*, Kluwer Academic, 1990.

[6] S.W. Smith, R.F. Wagner et al., "Low contrast detectability and contrast/detail analysis in medical ultrasound", *IEEE Trans. Son. Ultrason.*, vol. SU-30, pp. 156–163, 1983.

[7] J.M. Thijssen, "Focal lesions in medical images: A detection problem", *Proc. NATO-ASI Mathematics and Computer Science in Medical Imaging*, M.A. Viergever and A. Todd-Prakopek, eds., pp. 415-440, Springer, Berlin, 1988.

[8] H.L. Van Trees, *Detection, Estimation and Modulation Theory*, J. Wiley & Sons, 1968.

LOCAL CRITERIA, LOCALLY ADAPTIVE LINEAR AND RANK FILTERS

AND NEURAL-LIKE NETWORKS FOR PICTURE PROCESSING

Leonid P.Yaroslavsky[1]

The digital picture processing techniques that are taking shape now may be regarded from the viewpoint of computer implementation either as structured, or non-structured.The former methods make use of special-purpose software units handling sample vectors rather than of individual picture samples. The latter ones are those that can not be represented in the computer by standard units larger than the usual arithmetic and logic operations over the individual signal samples. Non-structured methods,as a rule,appear at the initial stage of approaching meaningful picture processing problems and as this process proceeds they grow into structured ones. Structured methods offer ways to higher computational efficiency and to design of special purpose hard- and software for picture processing computers.

The well established methods of linear filtration relying on fast algorithms for convolution and spectral analysis typify structured methods. The recently proposed locally adaptive linear filters are of further extension of this class.

The linear algorithms for filtration of discrete signal $a = \{a_k\}$, $k = 0,1,...N-1$ may be described as the following transformation

$$\mathbf{a} = \{ a_k \} = \{ \Lambda_k(a_k) \}$$

with $\Lambda(a_k)$ being a linear function of a_k :

$$\Lambda(a_k) = \lambda_0 a_k + a_k ,$$

and a_k being a weighed sum of the rest of signal samples.Those samples that are involved into the weighed sum with nonzero weights form the so called spatial neighborhood of a given sample.In adaptive linear filters the weight λ_0 as well as the weight coefficients involved into calculation of a_k depend on the signal samples themselves.

---

[1]Institute of Information Transmission Problems, Academy of Sciences of the USSR, 19 Yermolovoy str., 101447 Moscow, USSR

Currently, a new class of structured nonlinear algorithms is being formed. It can be described by the following transformation:

$$\hat{a} = \{ a_k \} = F(a) = \{ \Phi_k (a_k) \} ,$$

where $\Phi_k(a_k)$ is, generally saying, a nonlinear function whose form is defined by rank and/or order statistics of the set of signal samples within some neighborhood of a sample a_k , a neighborhood being a subset of the samples in the sequence of value ordered signal samples (a variational raw) formed from the samples spatially surrounding the given one.

The distinguishing feature of rank filters as well as of adaptive linear ones is their adaptivity enabling them to overcome the major drawback of the classical and most widely used in picture processing linear filtration, spatial inertiality that hinders its application to picture processing.

The present paper attempts at discussing the local adaptive linear filters and rank ones from a common standpoint and at demonstrating that they complement each other and can be used depending on a priori constraints that may be included into the filter design for each particular application, and on the signal parameters that may be used for filter design and adaptation.

Unified consideration of adaptive linear and rank filters is based on newly introduced class of the local criteria of processing quality which regards pictures as a combination of interpretation objects (details) carrying information for a specific user and a background, i.e. the component that in this specific application carries no information. The quality measure defining the class of local processing criteria is as follows:

$$\mathbf{AVLOSS}(k,l) = \mathbf{AV}_{imsys}\mathbf{AV}_{bg}\mathbf{AV}_{obj} \{ \sum \mathbf{LOC}(m,n;a_{k,l})\mathbf{LOSS}(\hat{a}_{m,n},a_{m,n}) .$$

where $\mathbf{AV}_{imsys}$, $\mathbf{AV}_{bg}$ and $\mathbf{AV}_{obj}$ denote statistical averaging, respectively over the intrinsic noise of the imaging system generating the picture, the background component of the picture and unknown parameters of objects under interpretation, and $\mathbf{b} = \{ b_{m,n} \}$ is a vector of processing picture samples, m,n are integer coordinates of the samples, $\hat{\mathbf{a}} = \{ \hat{a}_{m,n} \}$ is a vector of the resulting picture samples, $\mathbf{a} = \{a_{m,n}\}$ is a vector of "true" picture samples that are desired as the result of processing, $\mathbf{LOSS}(a_{m,n}, a_{m,n})$ is a function of losses due to the deviation of each (m,n)-sample of the processed picture from a true one, $\mathbf{LOC}(m,n; a_{k,l})$ is a locality function that is nonzero for those neighbors of the pixel $(a_{k,l})$ on a raster over which the loss function is to be averaged and zero for the rest of the pixels; the pixel $a_{k,l}$ is referred to as central element of the neighborhood determined by the locality function.

The following types of the neighborhood are introduced:

KSN-neighborhood, or the subset of K pixels that are Spatially Nearest to the given one.

EV- neighborhood, or subset of pixels in the predefined spatial window, whose values deviate from the value of the central pixel at most by a predefined quantities $(+\varepsilon_v; -\varepsilon_v)$.

KNV-neighborhood, or subset of K pixels in the predefined spatial window, which are Nearest in Value to the central pixel.

ER -neighborhood, or subset of pixels whose ordinal numbers in the variational raw(i.e.in the sequence $\{ v(r): v(r) \leq v(r+1) ; r = 1, \ldots, N \}$ of pixels ordered with respect to their increasing values ; N being a size of the spatial window) or ranks deviate from that of the central pixel at most by some pregiven quantities($+\varepsilon_r, -\varepsilon_r$).

CL- neighborhood,or subset of pixels whose values fall into the same Cluster or mode of the histogram over a predefined spatial window as that of the central pixel.

Optimal processing is aimed at an estimate $a_{k,l}(b_{m,n}; \mathbf{NBH})$ providing minimum of the averaged loss function $\mathbf{AVLOSS}(k,l)$. Consequently the corresponding algorithm will be optimal on the average. However,it is often desirable to determine an algorithm optimal for each particular picture which means that one must abandon averaging of the loss function over some random parameters of the picture under processing. Optimal algorithms, if realizable, will be adaptive in this case to those random factors which were omitted from averaging in the optimality criteria. Moreover since the criterion defines the averaged value of the loss function within a local neighborhood and for each picture element,these algorithms will be locally adaptive. This implies that picture must be processed by a sliding window, shape and size of which is determined by the initial **S**-neighborhood.

126

Design of linear locally adaptive filters is based on a quadratic loss function

$$\text{LOSS} \; (\; a_{m,n} \; ; \; \hat{a}_{m,n} \;) = | \; a_{m,n} - \hat{a}_{m,n} \; |^2$$

and the following locality function:

$$\text{LOC} \; (\; m,n \; ; \; a_{k,l} \;) = \left\{ \begin{array}{ll} d_{k-m,l-n} & , \quad |k-m| \leq N \; ; \; |l-n| \leq N \; , \\ 0 & , \quad \text{otherwise}, \end{array} \right.$$

defining the spatial neighborhood of $(2N+1)(2N+1)$ pixels size with weights $\{d_{m,n}\}$.

Optimal rank filters are generated if loss function is not quadratic and/or locality function define neighborhoods other then previous spatial one. They are described in terms of the following basic operations:

SIZE(NBH) - quantity of pixels which form the neighborhood;

MEAN(NBH) - arithmetic mean over the neighborhood;

MED(NBH) - median of the variational row over the neighborhood;

MIN(NBH) - minimum over the neighborhood;

MAX(NBH) - maximum over the neighborhood;

MODE(NBH) - a value which corresponds to the highest maximum of the histogram of signal distribution over the neighborhood;

RAND(NBH) - a random value whose distribution coincides with the histogram of signal distribution over the neighborhood.

RANK(NBH) - a rank of the given pixel in a variational row formed over the neighborhood.

In this way different linear and rank filters can be designed for noise suppression, image deblurring, local contrasts enhancement, detection and localization of objects, extraction of picture details and their boundaries.

The locally adaptive filters may be implemented by means of parallel recursive filtration, described elsewhere. It should, however, be noted that even with these effective algorithms, picture processing time for locally adaptive filtration could be rather high. Computer implementation of rank filters may be based on recursive algorithms of calculation of local histograms and their parameters

Recently the radical new ways for implementation of the rank filters as well as locally adaptive linear filters have appeared. They are connected with ideas of parallel computing and neural networks. The notion of neural networks is very popular now but has no exact definition, although their main idea is always an idea of of a computational network, composed of a set of processors working in parallel. The rank filters as well as locally adaptive linear ones can be very elegantly projected onto parallel computational network which possess the following features:

    i)It consists of a set of the simple processor units ("neurons").

    ii)The units may be of only two types:

        - Transforming units (T-units), which transform input signal in accordance with some look-up table. Each T-unit has one signal input, one output and may have several control inputs, which control parameters of the look-up table.

        - Summation units (S-units) which perform summation of the input signals. S-units may have several inputs and one output.

    iii)All units are arranged by the layers. The layers are streamlined.The units of the one layer work in parallel. Each subsequent layer begins its operation after completion of the previous layer operation.

    iiii)All input signals of the units may serve as signal ones for both T- and S- units, and as control ones for T-units.

    iiiii)The units of one layer may be connected only with the units of another layer. There may be feedback connections between the layers.

Due to shortage of space we illustrate these networks by a simplest one isolation the **EV**-neighborhood:

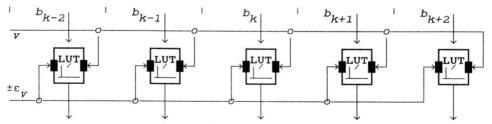

on-zero output for those of $\{b_k\}$ which belong to **EV**-neighborhood

    - Window look-up table:

$$a_{out} = a_{in1}, \text{ if } in2-in3 \le a_{in1} \le in2+in3;$$

$$a_{out} = 0 , \text{ otherwise.}$$

FROM MUSIC STAVES TO BRAIN FISSURE THROUGH A DISTANCE BASED ENERGY FUNCTION

NICOLAS MERLET *

Abstract

The detection of lines has lead to an abundant literature during the last ten years. It should be noticed however that most of the work on this topic has dealt solely with thresholded images (Hough) or with an edge-detector followed by a thresholding (Cox-Boie-Wallach), leaving aside the real problem of the perturbation of a thresholding by noise.

Rejecting the use of a thresholding, we propose here a method for detecting imperfect lines directly in the numerical original image, using an energy function based on the concept of distance. Those lines need only to have a privileged direction - they may even be sinuous - and may contain wide interruptions. The energy function is determined, relatively to the wished tolerances, by integrating a potential function of the direction and the grey-level values of two pixels.

We apply this function to the detection of staves in a music score and of the brain fissure in NMR images. Comparison with other methods prove the efficiency, simplicity, rapidity, robustness and wide range of applications of this energy function.

1 Introduction

The concept of energy is fundamental in image processing, in both segmentation and texture analysis. The modeling may be global (Gibbs distribution) or local (conditional probabilities) and it may correspond to a field of elastic deformations, to a distance, or a movement.

The usual approach consists of defining for a given pixel x a neighborhood V_x (a topology on a discrete lattice being pre-defined) and a function ϕ of the initial numerical image restricted to V_x, more precisely the relationship $\phi(V_x, f/V_x)$. The resulting models may be simple or complex, stationary or not in relation with the spatial dependency of the data.

We develop here an energy function based on the concept of distance for detecting imperfect lines, which may be even sinuous and interrupted, because of noise, digitization problems, and physical reality.

After having defined precisely this energy function we will present a theorem showing its close bound with the notion of distance, in section 2. We give then a theorem of characterization of the kernel of the energy function, which will lead us in section 3 to a fast algorithm of segmentation. We apply this new energy defined relatively to an attraction pole and privileging a direction to the segmentation of staves in a music score (numerical images obtained from a scanner) and of the brain fissure in NMR (section 4). Section 5 will be devoted to the discussion of the method and to the comparison with other methods.

---

*The Hebrew University of Jerusalem, Department of Computer Science, Givat Ram, 91904 Jerusalem, Israel

2 Distance based energy function

2.1 Reminder

Let us first recall some basic notions of the theory of Markov random fields which will be useful in the following. [BESAG][CHALMOND]

We denote by S the lattice of the image to study.

<u>Definition 1 :</u> We call neighbourhood system on S a family $\mathcal{N} = \{\mathcal{N}_s \subset S/s \in S\}$ such that :
- $s \notin \mathcal{N}_s$,
- $\forall (s_1, s_2) \in S^2, s_1 \in \mathcal{N}_{s_2} \Longleftrightarrow s_2 \in \mathcal{N}_{s_1}$.

The elements of $\mathcal{N}_s$ are the neighbours of s.

<u>Definition 2:</u> $c \subset S$ is a clique relatively to $\mathcal{N}$ iff :
- $card(c) = 1$,

or

- $card(c) \geq 2$ and any two different elements of c are neighbours.

$card(c)$ is the order of the clique.

In the hexagonal lattice,
- there are 6 cliques of order 2 corresponding to the 6 directions of the lattice,
- there are 6 cliques of order 3 corresponding to the 6 elementary triangles of the lattice,
- there are no cliques of order greater than 3.

In the following, for avoiding connectivity problems we will consider only the hexagonal lattice, and the usual neighbourhood relationship (6 neighbours for each point).

We will denote by :
- $\mathcal{C}_2$ the set of cliques of order 2 (or 1),
- $\mathcal{C}_3$ the set of cliques of order 3 (or 1),
- $P(x, y)$ the set of paths from x to y,
- $\mathcal{F}(S, \mathcal{R}^+)$ the set of functions from S into $\mathcal{R}^+$.

We can now define a potential and an energy on these cliques.

2.2 Energy function

For a given path between two points x and y we want first to define a cost.

<u>Definition 1:</u>

Let us define a potential $\phi : \mathcal{C}_n \mathrm{x} \mathcal{R}^{+^n} \longrightarrow \mathcal{R}^+$ ($n = 2$ or $n = 3$).

Let x and y be two points of S, and γ a path between them.

We denote $\gamma : x_0 = x,...,x_i \in \gamma,..., x_p = y$.

We call *attraction cost along* γ the functional μ :

$$\mu(\gamma) = \min_{(c_i) \in \mathcal{C}_n^p / \forall i \in 0, p<, x_i \in c_i, x_{i+1} \in c_i} \sum_{i=0}^{i=p-1} \phi(c_i, f/c_i).$$

We define an energy derived from this cost, and then a distance.

<u>Definition 2:</u>

We call *attraction energy* U between two points x and y of S the opposite of the minimum value of the attraction cost along any path between x and y :

$$U(x, y) = - \min_{\gamma \in P(x,y)} \mu(\gamma).$$

> **Theorem 1 :** We suppose that ϕ does not depend on the order of the grey-level values of the clique and that it verifies the following constraint :
>
> $$\forall c \in \mathcal{C}_n, \forall f \in \mathcal{F}(S, \mathcal{R}^+), \phi(c, f/c) = 0 \iff card(c) = 1.$$
>
> Then $\Delta(x, y) = -U(x, y)$ is a distance function on S.
> We call it the *directional numerical distance.*

The separability condition follows from the constraint, and the triangular inequality may be shown by combining two paths. For the sake of brevety, we do not develop the complete proofs here, they may be found in [Merlet].

Remarks : 1- These conditions on ϕ are necessary.

2- In general, Δ is not regular (there may be gaps in the values of Δ according to the values of ϕ).

We notice that elementary local properties furnished us a high-level global notion.
A second theorem will give us both an algorithm for computing Δ and a new method of segmentation.

> **Theorem 2 :**
> Let us consider a function $R : S \longrightarrow \mathcal{R}^+$ such that :
>
> $$\forall x \in S, R(x) \neq 0 \implies R(x) = \min_{c \in \mathcal{C}_n, x \in c, x_i \in c} \{R(x_i) + \phi(c, f/c)\}.$$
>
> We denote by S_0 the kernel of R : $S_0 = \{x \in S, R(x) = 0\}$.
> Then we have two important results :
> 1- $\forall x \in S, R(x) = \Delta(x, S_0)$,
> 2- S_0 is the set of the minima of R.

The first point may be proved by induction on the length of the shortest path (shortest *in the meaning of the distance* Δ) from S_0 to x.
The second point follows from the equation verified by R.([Merlet]).

3 Segmentation algorithm

We want now to show how Theorem 2 is useful both for computing Δ and for grey-level pattern recognition. We present algorithms for cliques of order 2, since this is the version we used in our applications. However, the following algorithms may be easily extended to n=3.

3.1 Computation of the directional numerical distance function

Algorithm 1 :
Initialization :
We consider the image Im defined in the following way :
$$Im(x) = \begin{cases} 0 & \text{iff } x \in S_0 \\ +\infty & \text{else.} \end{cases}$$

Iterations : We perform until convergence, alternatively forwards and backwards, the following operation :

$$Im(x) \longleftarrow \min_{x_i \in \mathcal{V}_x} \{Im(x), Im(x_i) + \phi(x, x_i, f(x), f(x_i))\}$$

Proofs of convergence and correctness follow directly from Theorem 2.([Merlet])

3.2   Algorithm of pattern recognition

We want now to use Δ for recognizing features in grey-level images. We suppose that a potential ϕ has been chosen that characterizes locally (see applications) a given type of features. More precisely, a feature passing through two given points (or sets of points) corresponds exactly to the shortest path between these sets *for the distance Δ associated to ϕ*.
We already know that $R(x) = \Delta(x, S_0)$, so S_0 must be one of these two sets of points. We call S_1 the second set. One should notice that S_0, S_1, and ϕ are all defined relatively to a particular application.

Algorithm 2 :
Initialization :
We consider the following 2 images : 1- Im1 : grey-level image R (got from algorithm 1).
2- Im2 : binary image defined by :
$$Im2(x) \begin{cases} > 0 & \text{iff } x \in S_1 \\ = 0 & \text{else.} \end{cases}$$

Iterations : We perform until convergence the following operations (propagation of the labels) :

$$\text{If} \begin{cases} Im2(x) = 0 \\ x_i \in \mathcal{N}(x) \\ Im2(x_i) > 0 \\ Im1(x_i) = Im1(x) + \phi(x, x_i, f(x), f(x_i)) \end{cases}, Im2(x) \longleftarrow Im2(x_i)$$

Due to the property verified by R, $Im2$ contains at convergence the shortest paths between S_0 and S_1. ([Merlet]).
Remark : One should notice the possibility of getting different features at the same time, if for example S_1 has several connected components. In this case, Im2 is defined as a labeling of S_1. The result is a labeling of the corresponding features, according to the connected components they originate from.

4   Applications

Let us stress first the following points : - R is determined uniquely by (S_0, ϕ) or (S_0, Δ),
- Δ is determined uniquely by ϕ.

Thus, for any application we must define S_0, S_1, and ϕ (solely). S_0 and S_1 are defined obviously as the extremities (in the meaning of Δ) of the features to be detected.
However, the determination of ϕ requires some search since the only constraint imposed on it so far is : $\phi(c, f/c) = 0 \Longleftrightarrow card(c) = 1$.

As a consequence, there is an almost infinite number of possible choices for ϕ.
For guiding our search, we impose for our both applications further constraints :
- ϕ depends uniquely from the orientation of the clique, not from its localization :
$$\phi(c, f/c) = \phi(\theta(x\vec{x}_i, \vec{i}), f(x), f(x_i))$$

132

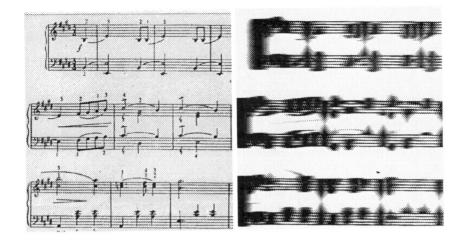

Figure 1: a- original image. b- numerical distance.

- ϕ depends only from one of the two values $f(x), f(x_i)$. (The problem of the asymmetry may be solved by using the maximum/minimum of the both values).
- ϕ is of the form : $\phi = k.h$
  where : - k is a variable which may take 6 different values according to the direction of the clique
          - h is a function of the grey-level of x.

More precisely, we separate the notions of direction and grey-level.

Let us now develop this search in our both applications.

4.1   Recognition of the staves of a music score

Our original image (Fig. 1a) is obtained by scanning a music score. We want to recognize the staves in it.

These staves may be defined as paths presenting the following characteristics :
        - they join the left vertical sticks to the right ones
        - they have low densities
        - they have a privileged direction, horizontally but with a slight slope
        - they may be interrupted by impression defaults.

Thus, we may first define the following elements :
- S_0 is the left vertical stick,
- S_1 is the right vertical stick, (these sticks were obtained by a vertical binary opening of a thresholded image, and are represented in Fig. 2a)
- k = 1 for the horizontal direction ; k > 1 for the other directions.

From a deeper study of the image, we could define the following properties for h :
- h is continuous (there is no significative sudden variation in the grey-level image)
- h is increasing (the staves have low-densities ; thus the higher the density, the greater the distance)
- the scale of values for h corresponds to the grey-level scale, for simplifying the storage,
- h is defined relatively to the histogram of the image (the histogram varies greatly from one music score to an other).

Hence, we defined two grey-level values from the histogram, t_1 and t_2 such that :
- between 0 and t_1, there is no physical meaning to variations of grey-level : $h(z) = 1$.
- between t_1 and t_2, there may be pixels on the staves having these higher values
  (transition region) : $h(z) = a_1.z + b_1$, with $a_1 > 0$.
- over t_2, we have values corresponding to the background or to interruptions of the staves.
  h must increase rapidly : $h(z) = a_2.z + b_2$, with $a_2 >> a_1$.
Finally, we determined precisely the values of the parameters :
- b_1 and b_2 are determined by continuity,
- for determining precisely k, a_1, and a_2, we used typical configurations such as :
    - interruptions of the staves and their maximum admitted width,
    - staves changing line and maximum slope admitted,
    - contrast of the features with the background.
These three values are defined relatively to the histogram.

Function h is drawn in Fig.2b. ϕ is not necessary unique, it is possible to use other constraints for guiding the search.
The corresponding distance function $\Delta(x, S_0)$ is shown in Fig. 1b, and the result of the propagation is presented in Fig. 2a.

Results :
The same function ϕ was used with 100 % success in 4 music scores having different slopes and histograms, each image containing more than 20 lines.
The computation of ϕ needed a dozen scannings, the propagation only 2. The five lines of the staves are recognized at the same time, for all the staves of the page.

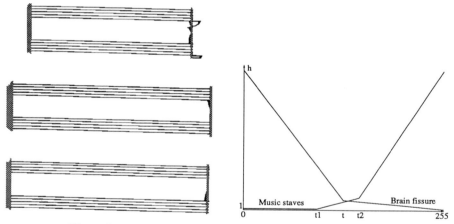

Figure 2: a- segmentation, S_0 and S_1. b- h functions.

4.2 Recognition of the brain s fissure in NMR images

Our aim was to recognize the brain fissure in images of nuclear magnetical resonance (NMR), obtained with a Gyrex computer of the ELSCINT society. The initial image is shown in Fig. 3a.

The brain fissure may be characterized by the following facts :
    - it joins the upper and lower border of the brain,
    - it has a high density,

134

- the privileged direction is vertical, possibly with a slight slope and even sinuosities,
- it may be interrupted.

Thus, following the same method :
- S_0 is the point of the lower border meeting the fissure (recognized by a binary horizontal morphological closing),
- S_1 is the corresponding point on the upper border. Unfortunately, it can not be recognized easily in all slices. Hence, we have found a new use for the information contained in Δ : this point corresponds to the minimum value of Δ on the upper border.
- $k = 1$ for the vertical direction ; $k > 1$ for the other directions.

And we defined h in the following way : (Fig. 2b)
- h is continuous,
- h is decreasing (the fissure corresponds to higher values),
- h has values in the grey-level scale,
- h is defined relatively to the histogram and to a value t determined from it :
    - over t : h has low values and decreases with a slight slope : $h(z) = a_2.z + b_2$, with $a_2 > 0$.
- between 0 and t : h has higher values, and decreases with a greater slope : $h(z) = a_1.z + b_1$, with $a_1 >> a_2$.
b_2 is determined by continuity, and b_1, a_1, a_2 from typical configurations.

The corresponding distance function $\Delta(x, S_0)$ is shown in Fig. 3b, and the result of the propagation is presented in Fig. 3c.

Results :

We recognized the fissure on 45 slices (3 patients), with a success of 100 %, using the same function ϕ for all.

For improving the computation time, we used a trick : we computed ϕ performing scannings only in one direction. The result was only an approximation of the distance function, but the number of scannings was reduced to two. The propagation was performed in two scannings, thus the fissure was recognized in 4 scannings. (We obtain in fact a double line, corresponding exactly to the double aspect of the fissure).

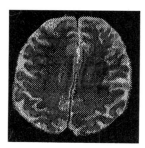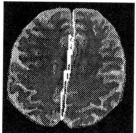

Figure 3: a- original image. b- numerical distance, S_0 and S_1. c- segmentation superposed on the original image.

5 Discussion

We remark that during the search for the values of the parameters, a major issue was to find a compromise between the importance given to grey-level irregularities and directional irregularities : more precisely, when the grey-level value becomes irrelevant to the feature, at which grey-level value should another direction produce a smaller distance function. Technically, this corresponds to defining the scale of k and h. For the music staves, which are narrow and relatively high contrasted features, and where direction changes are few (a dozen e.g. for all the width of the page), k must take much greater values than for the sinuous brain fissure (respectively, 2000 and 25).

Symmetrically, the grey-level scale for the energy is wider for the brain fissure since extremely low grey-level values do not occur on the fissure. In both cases, h looks like an approximation of an exponential. This is due to the chosen application, where the probability of a pixel belonging to the feature varies monotonously to its grey-level. This shape for h is not a general necessity.

We want to stress that most methods of line detection are based on a thresholding ; some are performed on a binary image obtained after a thresholding ([Hough]), others perform a final thresholding after an edge detection ([Cox]). Thus, for the general case there may be problems for fixing this threshold value, especially when there is much noise. Besides, the fine grey-level information may be completely neglected. The problems are even greater when the process is purely local (noise).
Some methods have dealt with the problem of exploiting grey-level information (following the ridges), using local neighborhood-based propagation.
Our method deals with these two problems of grey-level information and of global information by the use of a global grey-level energy function.
An other type of methods of line detection is based on the use of a filter ([Canny]), they are aimed more to edge detection than recognition of a particular pattern, so the purpose is different. However, we can stress the relative simplicity of our method, both on the theoretic and practical points of view. The number of operations is comparable, and better if the algorithm uses some "short-cuts", such as using scanning in one direction (brain fissure).
An other classical method of line-detection is the snakes method ([Kass]). The applications are quite different. The snakes in particular deal with the problem of movement of a contour through time, and with the detection of virtual contours, which is out of the field of applications of our attraction energy. On the other side, for a fixed pattern, all the grey-level information is synthesized before any propagation by the attraction energy, while snakes perform much computation during the propagation. Algorithm 1 has most of its computation performed in the interest zone automatically (zone where the energy values change the most). Besides, only one point is propagated, not a complete line. Thus, we spare computation time (only 4 iterations for detecting the brain-fissure and getting a continuous feature). Furthermore, we do not need any initial guess.
We may notice that the numerical directional distance generalizes usual distances. Effectively, the (pseudo-) euclidean distance corresponds to a n.d.d. where ϕ is uniformly equal to the constant 1, and the grey-weighted distance defined by [Rutowitz] to a n.d.d. where ϕ is equal to the grey-level value of a pixel. Our distance develops this notion by taking into account both a *function* of the grey-level and the local direction of the path.
Other methods have extracted the information of minimum-cost paths ([Martelli], [Hart]). By creating an energy function, we avoided the computational problems : the propagation simply follows decreasing values. Besides, we worked on the image, and not on a graph, and here too we used a function of the grey-level and directional information.

There are several ways of considering this distance based energy function. The general field of applications is the following : we have a feature (or a set of features) joining two extrem points (sets of points), and it may be characterized by some grey-level criterion and (eventually) by a direction preference. It may be interrupted and its direction may vary, even be sinuous. Then, we look for a distance function such that the shortest path between the extrem points for this distance is the feature. For this, we simply have to define the corresponding local potential.

We should stress that through these developments we have joined important notions, such as distance to energy and global information to local information. Besides, we illustrated the importance of non-stationary energies and potentials.

The algorithms are performed in less than a dozen scannings, sometimes in 4 scannings (brain fissure). This rapidity is due to the fact that they privilege the zone of the feature (where the energy values change) and that they are both recursive : the change of one pixel's value is taken into account during the same scanning. One should notice that the number of scannings is linear to the number of sinuosities of the feature.

Two major drawbacks could be mentioned. First, we need to know the extrem points of the feature to be detected. However, it is not a strict constraint since the five lines of the music staves are obtained with the same energy in the same propagation, and since the start of the propagation is determined automatically for the brain. This last example shows the importance of the distance function for representing global information, independently from pattern recognition, by synthesizing local information.

Second, there is a search process for determining ϕ, which is naturally not limited. We proposed to impose constraints for guiding the search and to define the parameters relatively to the worst admitted configurations. Since ϕ may take into account wished tolerances (such as allowed angle of deviation and maximal length admitted for the interruptions), and since it may be computed automatically from the histogram, we manage to combine robustness and wide range of applications.

6   Conclusion

As a conclusion, the efficiency, simplicity, rapidity, robustness, and wide range of applications of our method make it powerful for detecting imperfect lines in numerical images. Further developments may be envisioned. On the theoretic point of view, one could study the relevancy of this method and theorems to square lattices, and to cliques of higher orders (4 for example). Other applications could be tried too, including the use of cliques of order 3 for edge detection.

Acknowledgements

The author would like to express his gratitude for their efficient and kind medical and technical help to Aharon Peretz from the Elscint society (Haifa), and to Pr. Moshe Gomori, Haim Karger and Suzanne Yaffe from the Hadassah Hospital (Jerusalem).

7 References

BESAG J. [74]. "Spatial Interaction and the Statistical Analysis of Lattice Systems".
   J.R. Statist. Soc., vol. JRSS B-36, 1974, pp. 192-236.
CHALMOND B. [88]. "Image Restoration Using an Estimated Markov Model".
   Signal Processing 15 (1988), pp. 115-129.
COX I.J., Boie R.A., Wallach D.A. [90]. "Line Recognition". IEEE 1990, pp. 639-645.
DIJKSTRA E. [59]. "Note on Two Problems in Connection with Graphs".
   Numerische Mathematik, vol. 1, pp. 269-271.
HART P.E., Nilsson N.J., Raphael B.[68]."A Formal Basis for the Heuristic Determination
   of Minimum-Cost Paths". IEEE Trans.Sys.Man.Cyb. (1968), vol. SMC-4, pp. 100-107.
HOUGH P.V.C. [62]. "Methods and Means for Recognizing Complex Patterns". US Patent.
KASS M., Witkin A., Terzopoulos D. [87] "Snakes : active contour models".
   IEEE 1987, pp. 259-268.
MARTELLI A. [72]. "Edge Detection Using Heuristic Search Methods".
   Comp. Graphics Image Proc., vol. 1, pp. 169-182.
MERLET N. [91]. "Matching brains in spect and nmr imaging". Int. rep. Heb. Un. Jer.
RUTOWITZ D. [68]. "Data structures for operations on digital images". Pictorial pattern
   recognition (G.C. Cheng et al., eds.), pp. 105-133. Thompson, Washington DC, 1968.

UNSUPERVISED TEXTURED IMAGE SEGMENTATION USING MARKOV RANDOM FIELD AND CLUSTERING ALGORITHMS

A. Mosquera, D. Cabello, M.J. Carreira and M.G. Penedo[1]

ABSTRACT

A model-based approach to texture segmentation is presented in this paper, adopting Markov's random field as an image model. The algorithm includes three main components: optimal window size estimator, parameter estimator and clustering algorithm.

In order to estimate the optimal window size we define a codifference matrix, obtained as a generalization of the erosion operation from binary images to multiple gray level images. By parametrizing the structured element, the sum function of the codifference matrix provides information about the optimal window size. With that window size and for each position of the image, a maximum probability estimation of the parameters of the model is carried out. The segmentation problem is then transformed into a clustering problem on the multidimensional measurement space which we solve by searching for the centers of the classes on multidimensional histogram.

The results obtained on images generated artificially as a visualization of Markov's field model show the validity of the algorithm we propose.

INTRODUCTION.

An important task in image analysis systems is the segmentation process. It consists in the partition of an image into a set of elementary regions characterized by the fact that some property is constant. Although these coherent regions not always coincide with significant regions, they will constitute the elements for the interpretation of the scene; therefore, error in the segmentation process will lead to incorrect interpretations of the image.

In the literature there is a great variety of strategies for approaching the segmentation problem. They respond to two basic ideas: detection of local discontinuities or detection of local areas of the image with homogeneous properties (Haralick and Shapiro, 1985; Nevatia, 1986). Nevertheless, the presence of textures in the image induces unsatisfactory segmentations with both types of methods if they are applied using the grey level as the relevant feature. We must then consider the problem of separating regions with different textures in the image.

Most of the algorithms in the literature for the segmentation based on textures respond to the classical structure of a supervised classifier; that is, an 'a priori' knowledge of the number of classes (textures) and a design set are available, (Vickers and Modestino, 1982; Peleg et al., 1984; Hsiao and Sawchuk, 1989). The purpose of the algorithm we present in this work is to approach texture based image segmentation by means of an unsupervised algorithm which is able to detect borders between regions with different textures within a scene with no prior knowledge of the number and types of textures it may find.

The work we present here starts by considering a model for texture. In the literature we find a great number of established image models (Kashyap, 1986; Kashyap and Eom, 1989). Different types of applications require different image models; we are interested in the study of microtextures, and the best way of modeling them is by means of autoregressive models, among them Markov's random field.

---

[1]*Departamento de Electrónica. Facultad de Física. Universidad de Santiago de Compostela. 15706 Santiago de Compostela. SPAIN.*

The basic idea of the algorithm we propose consists in, once the model for the texture has been chosen, establishing an optimum window size over the image for the estimation of its parameters. By shifting this window over the image and characterizing the central pixel by means of the parameters estimated in its neighborhood, the problem of segmentation is transformed into a clustering problem on a multidimensional measuring space whose axis are the different features extracted. We have therefore developed a clustering algorithm which performs a search for class centers in multidimensional histograms based on the definition of local centroids and a displacement, within an iterative scheme, of the probability masses towards their centroids. The elementary regions arise when the information provided by this clustering algorithm is translated into the spatial domain of the image.

The results obtained on images generated artificially as a visualization of Markov's field model show the validity of the algorithm we propose.

MARKOV FIELDS AS IMAGE MODELS.

In a Markov field model, the intensity of the pixels of an image $y(s)$ is a linear combination of the intensities of the pixels located in a small area surrounding 's', plus an additive gaussian noise $e(s)$ with a null mean value. Thus, if we consider our finite network Ω and observations $\{y(s), s \in \Omega\}$ with a null mean value, the Markov field model can be formulated as follows:

$$y(s) = \sum_{r \in N} \phi_r \, y(s+r) + e(s) \ , \qquad s \in \Omega_i \tag{1.a}$$

$$y(s) = \sum_{r \in N} \phi_r \, y_1(s+r) + e(s) \ , \qquad s \in \Omega_b \tag{1.b}$$

where r and s are two dimensional vectors of integer components and N is the set of neighbors. Ω_i and Ω_b constitute mutually exclusive and totally included sets resulting from a partition of the network: Ω_i is the inside set and Ω_b the border set. They are defined, respectively, by the following expressions.

$$\Omega_b = \{ \ s \ / \ s \in \Omega \ \text{and} \ (s+r) \notin \Omega \ \text{for some} \ r \in N \ \} \tag{2.a}$$

$$\Omega_i = \Omega - \Omega_b \tag{2.b}$$

The term $y_1(s+r)$ of expression (1.b) is given by

$$y_1(s+(k,l)) = y[(k+i-1) \bmod M+1, (l+j-1) \bmod M+1] \tag{3}$$

for a network of size M*M; that is, we consider a toroidal representation of the network (Kashyap and Chellappa, 1983).

Once the image model has been established, we must attach this model to a given image; this implies an estimation of its parameters $\{\Phi, v\}$ in the image, where $v = E[e^2(s)]$. Hassner and Sklansky (1980) and Cross and Jain (1983) propose using the 'codings' method (Besag, 1974) for the case of binary and binomial variables, and perform an estimation of the maximum probability of the parameters within each coding. However, as pointed out by Kashyap and Chellapa (1983), this is not an efficient estimation method due to the partial utilization of the data. If we take a Gaussian Markov field model with $N = \{(0,1), (1,0), (0,-1), (-1,0), (-1,1), (1,1), (1,-1), (-1,-1)\}$, characterized by a parameter vector $\Phi = \text{col} \ (\phi_{0,1}, \ \phi_{1,0}, \ \phi_{0,-1}, \ \phi_{-1,0}, \ \phi_{-1,1}, \ \phi_{1,1}, \ \phi_{1,-1}, \ \phi_{-1,-1})$, the consistent estimation scheme proposed by Kashyap and Chellapa is given by the following expressions:

$$\Phi^* = [\ \sum_{\Omega'} q(s) \ q(s)^t \ ]^{-1} \ \sum_{\Omega'} q(s) \ y(s) \qquad (4.a)$$

and

$$v^* = (1/M^2) \ \sum_{\Omega'} \ (y(s) - \Phi^{*t} \ q(s))^2 \qquad (4.b)$$

where

$$q(s) = \text{col} \ [y(s+r); \ r \in N] \qquad (5)$$

Then, to approach the segmentation process, we must previously perform an estimation of the value of the parameters in the surroundings Ω' of each pixel of the image; we will then obtain new images in which the value of the pixels will reflect the value of the corresponding parameter in that position of the image. According to the image model and the parameter vector we are considering, the texture will finally be characterized by four features which globally characterize the 2 order Markov field in the four principal directions: horizontal, vertical and main and secondary diagonal, and which are obtained as the semi-addition of the corresponding parameters ϕ.

An important task prior to the estimation of the properties is the selection of the window size Ω' which is adequate for the process of estimating the parameters. This window must be large enough for the estimation of the parameters to be correct and small enough to be able to detect small regions in the image. This apparent contradiction has been the object of some studies in the literature (Khotanzad and Chen, 1989). To solve it we have developed a method for the automatic selection of the optimum window size based on a co-difference matrix which is obtained as the generalization of the operation of erosion in a binary image by an structured element into images with multiple grey levels.

An approximation to the concept of texture based on structural elements, in binary images, was proposed by Matheron (1967) and Serra and Vercherey (1973). Their basic idea is to define a structural element as a set of cells (pixels) which constitute a specific shape and generate a new binary image by displacing the structural element over the whole image, eroding with this element the figures made up of contiguous cells with a value of one.

Let's see the erosion operation. Following Haralick's (1979) nomenclature, we first define the displacement of a set. Let Z be the set of integers, $Z_1, Z_2 \in Z$ and $H \subseteq ZxZ$. For any pair $(i,j) \in ZxZ$, the displacement $H(i,j)$ of H in the subset Z_1xZ_2 is defined by:

$$H(i,j) = \{(m,n) \in Z_1xZ_2 \ / \ \text{for some } (k,l) \in H, \ m = k+i, \ n = l+j\} \qquad (6)$$

Let then Z_1xZ_2 be the spatial domain of a binary image I and let F be a subset of cells in Z_1xZ_2 of value one in image I. The erosion $F \ \theta \ H$ of F by H is given by

$$F \ \theta \ H = \{ \ (m,n) \in Z_1xZ_2 \ / \ H(m,n) \subset F \} \qquad (7)$$

The eroded image J obtained by the erosion of I using the structural element H is defined as:

$$J(i,j) = 1 \qquad \text{iff} \quad (i,j) \in F \, \theta \, H \qquad\qquad (8)$$

The number of elements in erosion $F \, \theta \, H$ is proportional to the area of points with value one in the image. Texture properties can be then obtained from the erosion processes by an adequate parametrization of the structural element and determining the number of elements of the erosion as a function of the value of the parameter. For example, a structural element made up of two pixels can be parametrized by means of the distance between them. The normalized erosion area as a function of the distance is, in this case, the autocorrelation function of the image. If we consider a texture as the repetition of a pattern on a background, the mean distance between consecutive maxima in the autocorrelation function will inform us about the mean distance between two consecutive patterns.

This approximation is only applicable to binary images. We are interested in images which are multivalued in their grey level. To solve this problem we propose the following generalization: Let H be the structural element (set of cells); we call co-difference matrix J of an image I obtained by means of the structural element H

$$J(i,j) = \sum_{\{(m,n)\}} |I(m,n) - I(i,j)| \qquad\qquad (9)$$

where $\{(m,n)\}$ is the set of cells resulting from the displacement $H(i,j)$ of structural element H. We can now measure texture properties in multivalued images by parametrizing the structural element. As an example, figure 1 shows the codifference matrices obtained from an image with 4 levels of gray by means of a structural element made up of two cells in the same line and parametrizing using the distance between them (from 0 to 8). Again, the sum of the elements of the codifference matrix as a function of the distance will produce information about the image. Thus, the mean separation between

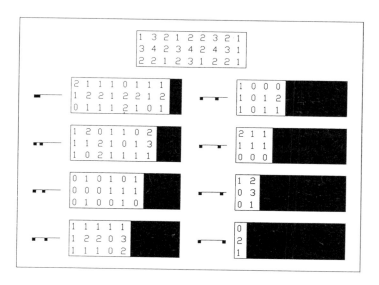

Figure 1. Example of codifference matrices for different structural elements (distance between cells from 0 to 8).

142

relative minima of the codifference sum function will indicate the mean distance between consecutive patterns. Figure 2 shows this codifference sum function for the example of figure 1; the relative minima appear approximately as multiples of 3 cells. This implies that in the horizontal direction there is a periodic repetition of the image approximately every 3 cells.

Consequently, for the selection of the size of the window adequate for the parameter estimation, we calculate the codifference matrix for two series of structural elements, one made up of two cells in the same line and another by two cells in the same column and both parametrized by means of the distance between them. This way, we obtain functions which are similar to the one shown in figure 2. By estimating the mean distance between minima we obtain the mean values of

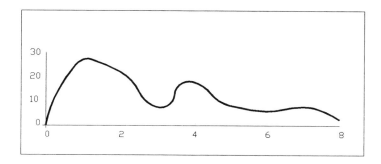

Figure 2. Codifference sum function.

periodic repetition in the horizontal and vertical directions. We will choose as window size the smallest integers which are larger than twice each mean value.

CLUSTERING IN THE MULTIDIMENSIONAL SPACE.

Once the directionality features in each coordinate of the image have been estimated, the segmentation problem is transformed into a clustering problem in multidimensional histograms. To solve it we have developed a clustering algorithm which performs a search of the class centers in multidimensional histogram based on the definition of local centroids and a displacement, within an iterative escheme, of the probability masses towards their centroids. This algorithm is a generalization of the one proposed by Spann and Wilson (1985,1988). According to them, to define the local centroids we consider the probability density $p(\mathbf{X})$, where $\mathbf{X} = (\mathbf{x}_1, \mathbf{x}_2, ..., \mathbf{x}_n)$ is the feature vector, which is n-dimensional in general. The local centroids defined for each point $(x_1, x_2, ..., x_n)$ of the n-dimensional class space will be given by:

$$\mu(x_1, ..., x_n) = (x_1, ..., x_n) +$$

$$+ \left(\frac{\int_{-w_1}^{w_1} x_1' \, p(x_1 + x_1') \, dx_1'}{\int_{-w_1}^{w_1} p(x_1 + x_1') \, dx_1'}, ..., \frac{\int_{-w_n}^{w_n} x_n' \, p(x_n + x_n') \, dx_n'}{\int_{-w_n}^{w_n} p(x_n + x_n') \, dx_n'} \right) \quad (10)$$

whenever the probability density $p(\mathbf{X})$ admits a decomposition of the type:

$$p(\mathbf{X}) = \sum_i p(\mathbf{x}_i) \tag{11}$$

Expression (10) shows that the local centroid for each point $(x_1, x_2, ..., x_n)$ is a n-dimensional vector whose components are the centers of mass of the different components of the probability density calculated in windows of size 2w and centered in that point, as can be seen in figure 3.

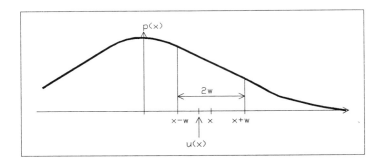

Figure 3. Calculation of a component of a local centroid

It is trivial to see that expression (10) can be extended to a discrete class space just by substituting the integrals by sums. In practical situations in the field of digital image processing, the components $p(\mathbf{x}_i)$ of the probability density will correspond to histograms of the different features used. Therefore, in this field, the restriction imposed by expression (11) is not important. Spann and Wilson (1988) demostrate that for this case the definition of the local centroids preserves the local classes.

The idea of the clustering algorithm is to shift the probability masses from each point $(x_1, x_2, ..., x_n)$ towards their local centroids, given by (10), obtaining them a new probability density as

$$p'(x_1, x_2, ..., x_n) = \sum_i (n_i(x_1, x_2, ..., x_n) *$$
$$\delta((x_1, x_2, ..., x_n)\text{-}\mu_i(x_1, x_2, ..., x_n))) \tag{12}$$

where $n_i(x_1, x_2, ..., x_n)$ are the areas of each probability density $p(\mathbf{x}_i)$ and $\delta((x_1, x_2, ..., x_n)\text{-}\mu_i(x_1, x_2, ..., x_n))$ is Dirac's delta function, and continue until there are no changes in the histogram observed. This is implemented by means of two nested iterative schemes. The external one enlarges the window w_i until the number of local centers does not change, and the internal one calculates the new probability density $p'(x_1, x_2, ..., x_n)$ until it does not vary.

The algorithm can be summarized in the following steps (in the discrete case): Let $h^0(x_1, x_2,...,x_n)$ be the initial value of the histogram for the point $(x_1, x_2,..., x_n)$, w the window size to be used in the calculation of the local centroids and NL_w the number of classes obtained for this window size; then:

step 1) $w := 1; NL_0 := 0; h(x_1, x_2, ..., x_n) = h^0(x_1, x_2, ..., x_n)$
step 2) $p(x_1, x_2, ..., x_n) = h(x_1, x_2, ..., x_n)$
step 3)   calculate, by expresion (10), the local centroids for each point $(x_1, x_2,...,x_n)$

144

step 4)   displace the probability masses towards their centroids and update the histograms using expresion (12)

step 5)   **If** $p'(x_1, x_2, ..., x_n) \neq p(x_1, x_2, ..., x_n)$ **Then**

        $p(x_1, x_2, ..., x_n) = p'(x_1, x_2, ..., x_n)$

        Goto step 3

    Else

        NL_w = number of points are non zero value on histogram

    End if

step 6)   **If** $NL_w \neq NL_{w-1}$ **then**

        $h(x_1, x_2, ..., x_n) = h^0(x_1, x_2, ..., x_n) + p'(x_1, x_2, ..., x_n)$

        $w = w + 1$

        Goto step 2

    End if

step 7)   Number of classes = NL_w

    Class centers = points are non zero value on histogram

Span and Wilson's algorithm (1988) only implies the aforementioned iterative scheme (stabilization of $p'(x_1, x_2, ..., x_n)$); consequently, the number of final classes depends on the size of the window and the 'peakiness' of the original histogram. With our algorithm we have managed, on one hand, to eliminate the dependence on the window size by introducing a second iterative scheme which calculates the optimum window, and, on the other, to reduce the dependence on the 'peakiness' of the original histogram by preserving, in each external iteration, the results produced for lower windows (step 6). With respect to the convergence properties, although they are difficult to determine (Wilson, 1984; Spann and Wilson, 1988), both iterative schemes converge in a small number of iterations.

For the final classification of the pixels in the spatial domain of the image, we assign each point to the nearest local clustering center using the city-block distance in the feature space.

RESULTS.

To try out the validity of the segmentation algorithm we propose, we have generated textures which are a visual representation of the Markov field model using 8 parameters and the algorithm proposed by Metrópolis et al. (1953), (Mosquera, 1989). We have then tried our segmentation

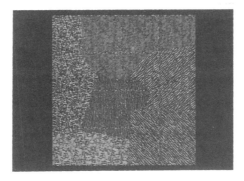

Figure 4. Artificially generated image that includes multiple textures which are a visual representation of Markov fields with different values for the parameters.

algorithm on different combinations of textures. Figure 4 shows a 256 * 256 pixel image which includes multiple textures.

The optimum window size for the estimation of parameters given by the codifference sum functions for the two series of structural elements we have indicated before was 6x6 pixels. Once the parameters of the model were estimated and the features which characterize the texture in the surroundings of each pixel were obtained, before the application of the clustering algorithm, we have performed a smoothing operation on the data to eliminate local noise and then we have normalized it. In the smoothing process we have considered a window which is identical to the one used for the estimation of the parameters.

As we have already pointed out, after the process of finding the class centers, the classification of the pixels in the spatial domain of the image is carried out in terms of the city-block distance to each clustering center in the feature space, assigning them to the nearest one. In order to take into account in the segmentation process both global information in the feature space and the spatial organization of this data in the image space, the resulting regions which present a size smaller than 100/(1.5*NL) % of the total pixels are eliminated. The classification of these pixels is carried out in a latter step by means of an algorithm which is typical for the growth of the regions nearby.

Figure 5 shows the final results of the segmentation process on the image we consider. In the figure we show both the contour image obtained (fig. 5.a) and the contours superimposed on the original image (fig. 5.b). We can observe the good concordance of these contours with those perceived on the original image. From this we can conclude that the algorithm we propose presents high segmentation quality on images which respond to the Markov field model.

ACKNOWLEDGEMENTS.

This work was supported by Xunta de Galicia, XUGA20602A90.

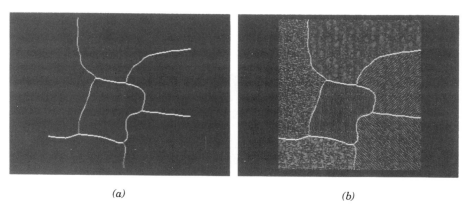

(a)   (b)

Figure 5. Results of the segmentation process. (a): contours obtained,
(b): contours on original image.

146

REFERENCES.

[1]. Besag, J.: Spatial Interaction and the Statistical Analysis of Lattice Systems. J. Royal Statist. Soc., series B, 36 (1974), 192-236.

[2]. Cross, G. R. and A.K. Jain: Markov Random Field Texture Models, IEEE Trans. Pattern Analis. Machine Intell., vol. PAMI-5 (1983) 1, 25-39.

[3]. Haralick, R. M.: Statistical and Structural Approaches to Texture, Proc. IEEE, 67 (1979) 5, 786-804.

[4]. Haralick, R.M. and L.G. Shapiro: Image segmentation techniques. Computer Vision, Graphics and Image Processing, 29 (1985), 100-132.

[5]. Hassner, M. and J. Sklansky: The Use of Markov Ramdon Fields as Models of Texture. Computer Graphics and Image Processing 12 (1980), 357-370.

[6]. Hsiao, J.Y. and A.A. Sawchuck: Supervised textured image segmentation using feature smothing and probalilistic relaxation techniques. IEEE Trans. Pattern Anal. Machine Intell., vol. PAMI-11 (1989) 12, 1279-1292.

[7]. Kashyap, R. L. and R. Chellappa: Estimation and Choice of Neighbors in Spatial-interaction Models of Images. IEEE Trans. Inform. Theory, vol. IT-29 (1983) 1, 60-72.

[8]. Kashyap, R.L.: Image models. In "Handbook of pattern recognition and image procesing" (T.Y. Young and K.S. Fu, eds.), Academic Press Inc., New York, 1986.

[9]. Kashyap, R.L. and K.B. Eom: Texture boundary detection based on the long correlation model. IEEE Trans. Pattern Anal. Machine Intell., vol. PAMI-11 (1989) 1, 58-67.

[10]. Khotanzad, A. and J.Y. Chen: Unsupervised Segmentation of Textured Images by Edge Detection in Multidimensional Features. IEEE Trans. Pattern Anal. Machine Intell., vol. PAMI-11 (1989) 4, 414-421.

[11]. Matheron, G.: Elements Pour Une Theorie des Milieux Poreux, Masson, Paris, 1967.

[12]. Metropolis, N.; A.W. Rosenbluth, M.N Rosenbluth, A.H. Teller and E. Teller: Equations of State Calculations by Fast Computing Machines. J. Chemin. Phys., 21 (1953), 1087-1091.

[13]. Mosquera, A.: Simulacion del Campo de Markov. Segmentacion de Imagenes basada en texturas". Graduation Thesis, Universidad de Santiago de Compostela, 1989. (In Spanish).

[14]. Nevatia, R.: Image segmentation. In "Handbook of Pattern Recognition and Image processing" (T.Y. Young and K.S. Fu, eds.) Academic Press Inc., New York, 1986.

[15]. Peleg, S.;J. Naor, R. Hartley and D. Avnir: Multiple resolution texture analysis and classification. IEEE Trans. Pattern Anal. Machine Intell. Vol. PAMI-8 (1986) 4, 518-523.

[16]. Serra, J. and G. Verchery: Mathematical Morphology Applied to Fibre Composite Materials. Film. Sci. Tech., 6 (1973), 141-158.

[17]. Spann, M. and R. Wilson: A Quad-tree Approach to Image Segmentation Which Combines Statistical and Spatial Information. Pattern Recognition, 18 (1985) 3/4, 257-269.

[18]. Spann, M. and R. Wilson: Image Segmentation and Uncertainty. Research Studies Press Ltd.,London, 1988.

[19]. Vickers A.L. and J.W. Modestino: A maximun likelihood approach to texture classification. IEEE Trans. Pattern Anal. Machine Intell. vol. PAMI-4 (1982) 1, 61-68.

[20]. Wilson, R.: A Class of Local Centroid Algoritms for Classification and Quantisation. Proc. IEEE Conf. Comput. Sys. Sig. Proc., Bangalore, India,1984.

SEGMENTATION OF MULTISIGNAL IMAGES WITH KOHONENS SELFLEARNING TOPOLOGICAL MAP

Ansgar Springub[1], Dinu Scheppelmann[1], Hans-Peter Meinzer[1]

1. Introduction

For the 3D-Visualisation of a set of medical tomographical images (i.e. MR-images) it is necessary to make a segmentation at first. In the German Cancer Research Center in Heidelberg we use an improved Kohonen Map algorithm for the segmentation of medical images. In this paper we present the algorithm and the difference of our implemented method to the original Kohonen Map algorithm.

For the input of the Kohonen-Map we use three different signals of the same image. For the segmentation of an MR-image for example it is possible to use three (or more) images of one slice with different paramenters (T1, T2, proton density). Therefore we get for each pixel a three dimensional vector instead of a skalar. Figure 1 shows the feature space of a MR-image with three parameters.

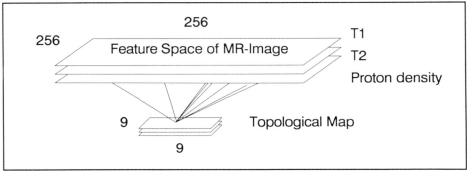

Fig 1: The three dimensional feature space of a multimodal MR-image (T1, T2, proton density). Each feature vector corresponds to a map vector.

The algorithm generates a two-dimensional Topological Map with a three dimensional vector in each map unit. Every point in the feature space corresponds to an image point in the Map. The order of points in the signal space and in the output plane are topologically similar.

The objective of the algorithm is to classify the feature-vectors. Vectors with similar feartures should gather in the same group and vectors with different features in different groups. The result of the method is similar to a conventional cluster analysis algorithms, but the partitions are often more optimal. Unfortunately the algorithm is very time consuming.

In the first part the original Kohonen algorthm will be described and then the differents of the original algorithm to our method will be presented.

2. The Kohonen Map

In [3] and [4] Teuvo Kohonen describes a algorithm to generate a topological map. The input

---

[1]   German Cancer Research Center, Dep. Medical and Biological Informatics. Im Neuenheimer Feld 280, D-6900 Heidelberg, Germany.

signals are any n-dimensional feature vectors.

The algorithm generates a map. A map is a plane with m x m units. Every unit contains a n-dimensional vector. Figure 1 shows a map with 81 units.

At first all map vectors will be initialized with random numbers. Then all vectors of the feature space (x_i) are scanning sequentially all units of the map and searching for the unit with the most similar vector. A widly applied similarity criterion is the Euclidean distance. If we define the best match to be due as the unit with index c, the c can be determined by the condition:

Similarity Matching:

$$\|x(t_k)-m_c(t_k)\|=\min_i\{\|x(t_k)-m_i(t_k)\|\} \tag{1}$$

t_k stands for a discrete time index.

Around the determined unit c, a topological neighborhood N_c is defined such that all units that lie inside a certain radius from unit c are included in N_c. After the searching of the most similar unit, this vector and all vectors inside the neighborhood N_c will be adapted with the following rule.

Updating:

$$m_i(t_{k+1})=m_i(t_k)+\alpha(t_k)[x(t_k)-m_i(t_k)] \quad for \ i\in N_c, \tag{2}$$

$$m_i(t_{k+1})=m_i(t_k) \qquad otherwise.$$

The gain factor α should be a decreasing function of time in order to guarantee convergence to a unique limit. $\{ \alpha(t_k); t_k = 0,1,...; 0 < \alpha(t_k) < 1 \}$.
Kohonen propose to define the topological neighburhood N_c in the beginning faily wide and then it is let to shrink with time. (see Fig. 2)

Kohonen remarks that it is a problem to find the optimal gain sequence. The sequence $\alpha(t_k)$ can be choosen as a linearly decreasing function of t_k whereby the process then automatically stops when $\alpha(t_k)=0$.

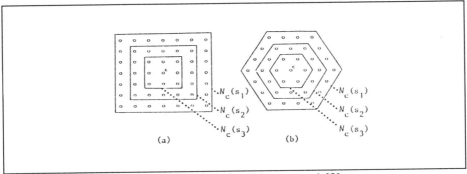

Fig 2: An Example of topological neighbourhood ($s_1 < s_2 < s_3$) [3].

The two phases of the process 1) *Localisation of the best matching unit* and 2) *Increasing the matching at this unit and its topological neighborhoods* have to processed for all vectors of the feature space sequentially. The whole learning process must be repeated until $\alpha=0$ is reached.

3. The Kohonen Map for Image Segmentation

After generating a map it is possible to use this map for the image classification. Each vector of the feature space which correspondents to a pixel of the image, matches by using the Similarity Matching condition (1) with one unit of the generated map. If all feature vectors which matches in the same unit will be gathered, then the image can be classified in as much classes as units the map have. Moreover, since similar map vectors lies in the same neighborhood on the map, it is possible to join similar map units to groups, to reduce the number of classes. The advantage of this method is, that the number of classes don't have to be fixed at the beginning of the process.

4. The Difference of our method to the original method of Kohonen

In Heidelberg we made some changes in the algorithm [1,2,5]. After some tests we found out that we get the best results with the following changes of the original algorithm.

4.1 Learning Mask

Kohonen uses for the adaptation a neighbourhood with equal weights for the adaptation of all neighbourhood units. In our approach we use a *Gauss-weighted learning mask* with adaptation weight factors, depending on the distance to the central map unit. The greater the distance to the central unit is, the lower is the adaptation factor.
The size of the learning mask decreases from one adaptation process to another until only the central unit will be left.

4.2 The adaptation weight factor

The main difference of our method to the one of Kohonen is the individual weight factor α for each map unit depending on the frequency of adaptation. Kohonen uses a constant weight factor for each map vector which is monoton decreasing from one adaptation process to another. The Kohonen process ends, when the weight factor reaches a determined value $(\alpha=0)$.

In our case we implemented an individual weight factor for each map vector depending on the frequency of the adaptations of each vector. The result is that feature vectors with a low frequency will be represented in the feature map as well as feature vectors with high frequency.
For the determation of the individual weight factor we count the feature vectors which matches to each map unit. For each map position we determine the weight factor with

$$w_t = \frac{\textit{number of actual matching vectors}}{(\textit{amount of all matching vectors before}) + (\textit{number of actual matching vectors})}$$

150

4.3 The Adaptation

For the input of the map we don't use the single feature vector. Instead of the single feature vector we gather all vectors which matches to a single map unit and determine the mean value of all matching vectors. This mean feature vectors are used as input vectors for the adaptation of the map.

Therefore we need the values from the last determined map to calculate the weight factors and the mean vectors. Using this three parameters we can calculate the new map.

4.4 The stop learning condition

Since we don't use the monoton decreasing sequence $\alpha(t_k)$, we need a new stop condition for the algorithm. A good stop condition is the rate determined of the vectors matching on the old map to the vectors matching on the same units in the new map. If 97% of the feature vectors matches to the same map units the adaptation process ends.

After adaptation of the actual map it is sometimes useful to enlarge the size of the map using an interpolation, and then start the adaptation again. A bigger map results more map vectors and more image classes. But the advantage of the map is that the similar map vectors are in the same neighbourhood and very often large regions of the map have similar map vectors. This vectors can be gathered to one class.

5. Example

The example demonstrates the segmentation of a multimodal MR-Images using a 3x3 Map. The Figure shows the original images (T1, T2, proton density) and the segmentation result. All the feature vectors of the white areas are corresponding to the same map unit (only three classes are presented).

Beside the use of this algorithm for MR-images it is also possible to use it for single modal images and to fill the other planes of the feature space with preprocessed results of the image (filter operations, morphological operations,...).

6. Conclusion

The segmentation of MR-images is very difficult. Therefore it is necessary to use all available information. With the described method it is possible to make an image segmentation using three different images of the same slice.

The algorithm generates a topological correct feature map. The feature vectors corresponding to the same map units belonging to the same image class. Similar map vectors lies in the same neighbourhood and they can be gathered. All corresponding feature vectors are therefore united too and the number of classes is decreasing.

Therefore it is not necessary to fix the expected number of image classes before starting the algorithm in opposite to the conventional cluster analysis.

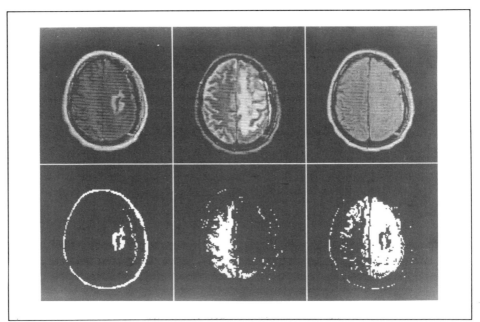

Fig 3: Results of an image segmentation of an MR-image using a 3x3 map

REFERENCES

[1] Bertsch, H; Dengler, J; Klassifizierung und Segmentierung medizinischer Bilder mit Hilfe der selbstlernenden topologischen Karte. In Paulus E (Ed), 9.DAGM-Symposium Mustererkennung (1987) pp 166-170, Springer Informatik Fachberichte 149, Berlin, Heidelberg.

[2] Bertsch, H.: Die selbstlernende topologische Merkmalskarte zur Bildsegmentierung und Klassifikation. Dissertation. Universität Heidelberg, Fakultät für theoretische Medizin, 1990.

[3] Kohonen, T.: Clustering, Taxonomy and Topological Maps of Patterns. Proc 6th Int Conf on Pattern Recognition (1982), Munich pp 114-128

[4] Kohonen, T.: Self-Organization and Associative Memory. Springer Series in Information Sciences 8, Heidelberg 1984

[5] Saurbier, F.: Automatische Segmentierung aus CT- und MR- Bildern mit Hilfe der Topologischen Karte. Diplomarbeit. Universität Heidelberg, Fakultät für theoretische Medizin, 1989.

Development and implementation of methods for the segmentation of bond-wedges

W.Eckstein, W.Glock,
Technische Universität München
Institut für Informatik / Lehrstuhl Professor Radig
Orleansstraße 34, 8000 München 80

Abstract

The aim of this project was to develop a prototype-system which can recognize defects caused by wedge-bonding during microchip production automatically and knowledge based. In order to extract the relevant parts of the image and make a decision about the state of a wedge-bond, proper methods of image processing were developed and tested. Based on the data of the segmented image, additional geometric information was computed and a final result was resumed.

Aiming at a high flexibility in use for different chip types, special attention was paid to developing a training-function for knowledge acquisition. This module guarantees the ability to configure the system for a new chip-type by using some test-images, parameterize the image processing techniques and have a tool for supervised learning.

Introduction

Automatic, optical controlling techniques for printed circuit boards have been in use for a rather long time, but the examination of chip structures like the bonds on microchips is often done by visual controlling.

The presented prototype system has been conceived for the controlling of wedge-bonds. Wedge-bonding is the oldest and mostly used method of linking the contact on the chip with the corresponding one on the chip case. The contact is build by a thin gold or aluminium wire with a diameter of 10 to 50 micrometer. This wire is pressed on the pad by supersonic and heat.

The area of examination was limited to the surrounding of the pad on the chip and the parts of the wire nearby. Typical sorts of defects for this complex are the missing of the bondwire, insufficient conducting caused by pollution of the pad surface or multi-bonding. The functionality and suitability of an automatic supervision system and the chosen processing techniques are shown in the following chapters.

Preconditions for the system

The main documents for the functional design were the rules for quality-ensurance for the visual controlling of bonding by DEC [DEC 88]. The presented prototype system supports the controlling of the geometric data of the bond wire, the location of wire and pad, and the total number of defects detected by the system.

The programming environment consists of a workstation (VAX-station 3200), the operating system VMS and a transputer system with an interface to a microscope for taking the images from the examined chip-areas.

The rule-based programming language for the prototype was VAX-OPS5 V.2.2 [BRO 85, RAD 87]. The image processing operations were available by using the image interpretation system HORUS through a C interface.

Besides these preconditions the following characteristics of the problem had to be dealt with:

- visible, 3-dimensional structures on the surface of a microchip are to be analysed,
- location variable (e.g. bond wire) and invariable (e.g. circuits) components are parts of the scene,
- there are many different textures in the image caused by the high integration of the chip structures,
- focussing and depth of focus of the microscope objective have considerable influence in the analysis and the used techniques,
- the interval of time for examination must be less or equal to the time used for taking one image,
- the methods for the segmentation of the scene must fit into different types of chips, besides being robust and adaptable.

The list of criteria described in the previous chapter lead to the following system.

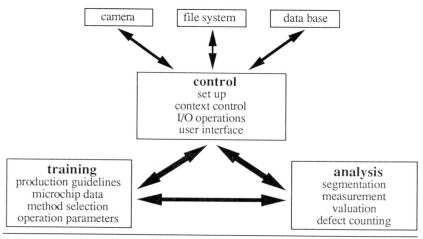

Image 1. Components of the prototype and their functionality.

There are three main parts:

- controlling of the program and the interactions with the user interface,
- a function-module for the training of new chiptypes, data acquisition and configuration of the processing methods,
- analysing of images taken from chipbonds and preparation of the data for evaluation and the final generation of the conclusion.

The development and implementation of the system under OPS5 was mainly influenced by the model oriented methods for knowledge-based systems. Due to this modular concept, it is easy to add other techniques for segmentation or additional functions.

The flow of the program is controlled by a mechanism using context-elements for synchronisation.

Segmentation Methods for the Bond Scenery

The segmentation of the images of the bond and the extraction of the relevant parts are the main tasks of automatic control.

For a classification of a bond-complex the following objects are necessary to make a decision whether the current bond is correct or not:

• bond wire and

• pad splitted into correct and polluted or damaged parts of the surface.

Two special techniques have been selected out of the amount of known methods using thresholding and clustering. These support the criteria: processing speed, robustness and flexibility and are provided by the HORUS-system.

Both methods use one original image of the expected bond (image A) and a transformed image (image B). The size of the filter operation is 3x3 or 5x5. Best results were gained with texture transformations (5x5) and mean filtering (3x3 and 5x5).

The size of the filter is influenced by the size of the demanded texture elements in the image. These values are selected because we search small structures (crystalline silicium surface) with a diameter of 3 to 5 pixels dependant on the magnification of the microscope.

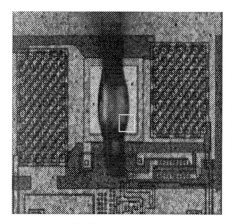 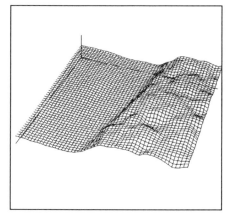

Images 2 and 3. Pads are more textured than wires.

(a) Clustering

This method is using the frequency of characteristic combinations of grey-values of corresponding points in the two processed images. For each coordinate (x,y) in the scene belonging to the bond wire we compute a special clustering function $(g(A,x,y), g(B,x.y))$ using a training sample. The resulting pairs generate cluster in a two-dimensional feature space, which correspond to the training samples. The areas for pads are treated the same way.

Using the frequency of these pairs in a cluster and a threshold with which all values are compared, with only the higher ones being marked in the resulting cluster, we get a good criterion for reclassification of equivalent scenes. As an alternative a closing-technique or the approximation with ellipses can be used to exclude disturbing. Using the original image together with a lowpass image or a texture transformed image, the cluster algorithm is ready for the detection of the pads.

Image 2 shows a pad with a wire. The marked square is displayed in image 3 as a plot. The left part of image 3 is defocussed due to the thickness of the wire and thus generates a texture completely different from the pad. These textures can easily be separated using the cluster algorithm.

Out of the clustering method a second segmentation technique was developed, which is especially simple and robust.

(b) Dynamic Thresholding

This method is using the lowpass effect caused by defocussation of the chip structures outside the focus of the objective.

The fundamental principle is to compute the difference in grey values between the corresponding pixels of the two input images. Afterwards, these values are compared with a threshold.

The following formula is constructed including the lowpass filter and the thresholding and represents the criterion for marking a pixel in the resulting image.

$$\left(g(A,x,y) - \frac{1}{(2m+1)^2} \sum_{i=x-m}^{x+m} \sum_{j=y-m}^{y+m} g(B,i,j) \right) > t, \quad x = 1,\ldots,512; \ y = 1,\ldots,512; \ m = 1 \ \text{bzw.} \ 2$$

Especially the focussed parts of the scene on level of the chip substrate are marked, because these areas have an distinct local texture and are rather different from the grey value of the surrounding structures. The defocussed, homogenous bond wire hardly diverge from the corresponding parts in the lowpassed image. Consequently these image areas are not marked in the segmentation result. After a closing-step and the computing of the complement, we get the wire segment.

The marked square in image 3 is displayed in image 4. A horizontal cut through the original image (broken line) and the mean filtered image (5x5) (white line) shows the differences in regions which belong to the die.

In bad conditions for the CCD-camera in the microscope a second processing-step can be included to improve the result. An image taken from the bond is now focussed to the bond-wedge and then processed like the first image without complementation. The two results are joined together.

After processing one of the segmentation methods ((a) or (b)) the marked areas are processed with a binary median-filter to get bigger, connected regions. The contour is roughly smoothed by using an opening operation with a circle-mask and disturbing is excluded by a size classification.

Both methods (a) and (b) are used for the segmentation of the bond wire. In this case the dynamic threshold has a higher robustness related to bad illumination.

For the segmentation of the pad, clustering is used. The high grey value of the

156

undamaged, metal surface of the contact supports the generation of significant clustering. Trouble is caused by damaged or polluted pad-areas, which are very different in their appearance and are hard to classify. The possibility of making a classification with different damage-types is supported by splitting the examination into two parts. The first part generates results before the bonding-process, the second one afterwards. This recommendation is given for the realisation of a bond inspection system and will help to come up with better results.

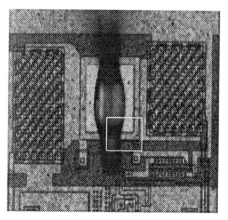 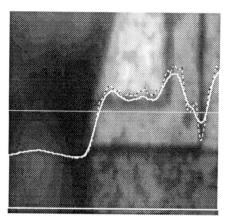

Images 4 and 5. Texture segmentation to seperate die and wire.

Extraction of Data for Evaluation

In order to evaluate the quality of a bond, the following criteria were tested:

• geometry and location of the bond wire and

• the condition of the pad-surface

To get the necessary geometric data of the bond wire segment, a rather ragged contour has to be made smoother before measurement. To improve the correctness of the values and minimize errors, the contour is smoothed by using a weighted cubic spline operator. Then the characteristic attributes, like thickness of the wire, length and width of the bond wedge and length of the wire are computed and compared with the conditions for visual inspection.

Training of the Operation Parameters for Analysis

For adapting the discussed methods to fit into the different chip types and to improve the flexibility, the system contains a module for the training of new chip types. This function allows us to control the behaviour of the system and configure the parameters of the single operation steps according to the examined chips. In an interactive training session the user can select different combinations of parameters and test the selected configuration with test images taken under real conditions. Selectable parameters are he value for threshold, size of operators, or attribute classes for the clustering operation (among others). Besides the ability to set fixed values to the different parameters, intervals can be selected, too. The training component then simulates a segmentation step for each value in the interval and presents all results. The trainer can now choose the best combination. In later versions of the system, controlled learning or automatic configuration will be added.

Image Processing System

For the realization of the image processing operations the IP-system HORUS [ECK87] is used. HORUS offers a language interface which was adapted to OPS5. It contains a wide range of procedures for the preprocessing, segmentation and interpretation of images. Moreover, it introduces the abstract data type image object.

Definition: An image object $O = (R, I_1, .. , I_n)$ consists of a region R and image functions I_i with the following characteristics:

Let X,Y be the ranges of the row and column indices of an image. Then each region R satisfies:

$$X \times Y \supseteq R$$

Let **R** be the set of all regions. An image function I_i is defined by:

$$I_i: \mathbf{R} \rightarrow G$$
$$(x,y) \rightarrow I_i(x,y)$$

where G = Byte + Integer + Float.

An image function assigns a grey value $I_i(x,y)$ to each pixel (x,y) of a region. An image object can contain any number of image functions. The definition of an image object leads to the following characteristics:

Object focus: The image object is the basis of the image processing. It is used for the iconic as well as the symbolic processing (the basic informations for the latter, e.g. features, are gained by image objects, too). Image processing operations can be characterized by their impact on image objects. Consider the following examples:

• Filter operation f (with one input and one output image)

$$(R, I_1, .., I_i, .. , I_n) \rightarrow (R, I_1, .., I_i, .. , I_n, f(I_i))$$

All components of the input object are transferred to the output object without any changes. The result of the filter operation is added to the image object as an additional component (image function).

• Morphological operation m

$$(R, I_1, .. , I_n) \rightarrow (m(R), I_1, .. , I_n)$$

The image functions I_n remain unchanged. The region of the output object is gained as the result of the operation m applied to R.

• Segmentation s: Let **O** be the power set of all image objects and $o = (R, I_1, .. , I_n)$; s is an equivalent relation of R, thus:

$$\forall r \varepsilon R \quad \exists \text{ one and only one } o' \varepsilon \mathbf{O} \text{ with } o' = ([r]_s, I_1, .. , I_n).$$

The input object is splitted into a set of new image objects, each of them containing

158

one subregion.

The general definition of an image processing operator F in HORUS is given by:

$$F: P(\mathbf{O}) \rightarrow P(\mathbf{O})$$

Thus each time the operator is engaged any number of image objects (typically 100 up to 10,000) is processed.

Overlapping invariance: Each image object is stored in its own data structure. Therefore, the typical problems arising in connection with binary image implementations (e.g. ´fusion´ as a result of a dilation) do not occur.

Region dependent processing: Operators are restricted to the region of an object (especially when dealing with filtering or segmentation). This leads to a significant reduction of the computational load in many applications.

Example for the Implementation in VAX-OPS5 and HORUS

The previous chapters were basically concerned with the theoretical aspects and the acting of the selected techniques. The following simple OPS5-rule is an example for the implementation of a small task and demonstrates the interaction with the HORUS-system. The target of this rule is to get the bond wire segment using the threshold-technique and to start the binary median operator on the result.

```
(P Bond_Wire_Segmentation
  ( Control    ^ActContext bond_wire_segmentation_dyn_threshold
  ( ImageObj   ^IState loaded ^IType <focus> ^Image1 <image> )
  ( BondPara   ^BPState loaded ^BondType <focus> ^WireFilterSize <fsize>
               ^WireDyn_Thresh <dyn_thr_offset>
               ^WireCountSize <csize> ^WireCountThresh <cthresh> )
-->
  ( BIND <Z1> (f_lowpas <image> <fsize> <fsize> 1 2 ) )
  ( BIND <Z2> (f_dyn_threshold <Z1> <dyn_thr_offset> 1 2 ) )
  ( BIND <Z3> (f_count <Z2> |full| <csize> <csize> <cthresh> ) )
  ( MAKE ImageObj
         ^Image1 <Z3>   ^IType <focus>   ^BondNo <BNo>   ^IState ltc_ready)
)
```

The condition part (left side) of this rule tests the working memory of the OPS5-system as to whether a context element is stored for program controlling and assigns the images and parameter sets to variables. These are processed by the initiated operations in the acting part of the rule (right side) and the results are stored in the working memory.

Integration of the System in an Industrial Environment

As a part of the quality control for chip production, the presented chip-bonding examination system must be placed between the chip-mounting and chip-sealing. Image 6 shows the structure of this system.

The search of oxidation defects on the pad surface and the examination of the bonding results must be handled in two different processing steps. This has the advantage of simpler subtasks and more efficient controlling.

Besides the configuration of the controlling-system by the training function, data from other parts of the production-process like construction data in chip development can be automatically recorded.

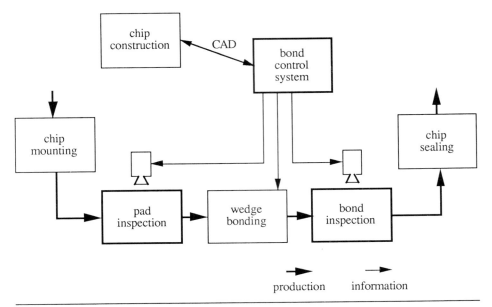

Image 6. System architecture in an industrial environment.

The permanent storing of controlling data allows the permanent supervision of production quality. Faults can be reported very fast to other parts of the production and actions to abolish the causes can be initiated.

Conclusions

In this report we have presented a prototype system for the automatic, optical examination of bonds on microchips. The developed thresholding method combined with a contour smoothing technique using a cubic spline operation was qualified for the segmentation of the bond wire and extraction of the geometric data.
The segmentation of the pad was fitted by the clustering. For enhancing the spectrum and robustness of the clustering, more test sequences and tests with different image attributes and combination had to be done. There would be better results using color- or IR-images because of more favourable classification possibilities.

Literature

[BRO 85] Brownston L., Farrell R., Kant E., Martin N.: "*Programming Expert Systems in OPS5*", Addison-Wesley, 1985;

[CAN 86] Cantoni V., Carrioli L., Cozzi L., Ferretti M, Ziliani R.: "*Automatic Pads Recognition for I.C. Bonding*", ICPR 1986

[DAR 88] Darwish A.M., Jain A.K.: "*A Rule Based Approach for Visual Pattern Inspection*", IEEE Transactions on Pattern Analysis and Machine Intelligence, Vol. 10, No 1, January 1988

[DEC 88] "*Ceramic Pre-Seal Inspection Criteria*", document# AYA20046F, DEC, February 1988

[ECK 88] Eckstein W.: "*Das ganzheitliche Bildverarbeitungssystem HORUS*", 10. DAGM - Mustererkennung 1988, Proceedings, Zürich 1988

[HAY 88] Hara Y., Doi H., Karasaki K., Iida T.: "*A System for PCB Automated Inspection Using Fluorescent Light*", IEEE Transactions on Pattern Analysis and Machine Intelligence, Vol. 10, No. 1, January 1988

[KUR 89] Kurbel K., Pietsch W.: "*Expertensystemprojekte:Entwicklung, Organisation,und Management*", Springer-Verlag, Informatik-Spektrum 12/89, S.133-146

160

[RAD 87] Radig B., Krickhahn R.: *"Die Wissensrepräsentationssprache OPS5"*, Vieweg, 1987;

[SPÄ 83] Späth H.: *"Spline-Algorithmen zur Konstruktion glatter Kurven und Flächen"*, Oldenbourg-Verlag, 1983;

[YOD 88] Yoda H., Ohuchi Y., Taniguchi Y., Ejiri M.: *"An Automatic Wafer Inspection System Using Pipelined Image Processing Techniques"*, IEEE Transactions on Pattern Analysis and Machine Intelligence, Vol. 10, No. 1, January 1988

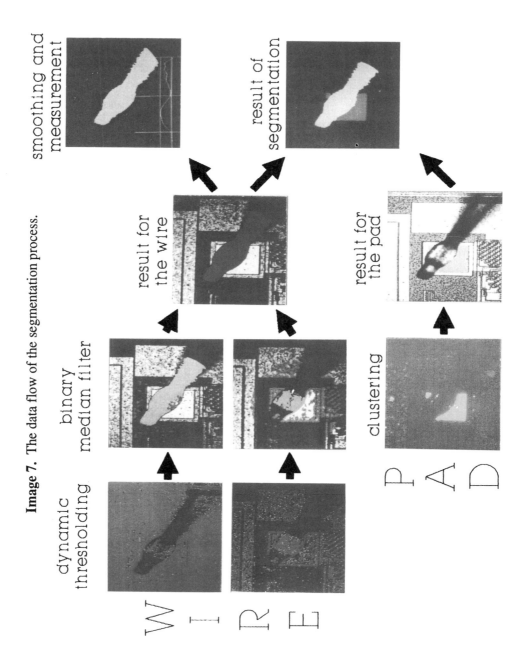

Image 7. The data flow of the segmentation process.

AN ADAPTIVE ALGORITHM FOR IMAGE BINARY
QUANTIZATION AND EDGE DETECTION

V. V. Gritsyk and R. M. Palenichka [*]

Abstract

A new adaptive algorithm for signal or image binary quantization is described. The proposed algorithm is recursive and based on thresholding scheme with variable threshold. It is mainly designed for segmentation of a video signal received during the raster format scanning of the bilevel image.

1. Introduction

The binary quantization consists in dividing an image or signal into a set of two-class segments which may correspond to an object (foreground) or a background. It is the basic preprocessing technique in many applications of signal and image recognition and visual data compression . A large number of image quantization algorithms has been reported and among them are some adaptive algorithms for image thresholding to obtain a binary image [1-4]. The developed techniques are time -consuming and sensitive to noise in low-contrast video signal. The algorithm to be presented is based on a detection of abrupt transitions in pixel values for two neighbouring pixels using the given image model. The main part of the algorithm can be used for robust adge detection.

2. Image Video Signal Model

The underlying mathematical model of a video signal (obtained as a result of the image line scanning) can be presented as

$$g(i) = r(i) + n(i), \tag{1}$$

where $r(i)$ is the piecewise constant function with alternating high and low level of pixel values; $g(i)$ is the signal value at

---

[*]   Institute of Physics and Mechanics of the Ukrainian SSR
       Academy of Sciences,   5 Naukova st., 290601 Lvov, USSR

162

point i; n(i) is the white normal (Gaussian) noise with zero
mean and covariance function d*Ó(i), where Ó(i) is the discrete
delta function, d is the noise variance. Also known is the
length M of the possibly shortest segment of constant values.

For two-dimensional image modelling we have used the
notions and operations of mathematical morphology and image
algebra. In this case the set of specified structural elements
was used instead of the linear segments [5].

3. Technique for Binary Quantization

The process of binary quantization consists in assigning a
zero to low grey-level and a unity to high grey-level for every
image pixel. The basic approach to solve the problem is the
following adaptive thresholding of the video signal:

$$f(i)= \begin{cases} 1 & \text{if} \quad g(i) >= x(i) \\ 0 & \text{if} \quad g(i) < x(i) \quad , \end{cases} \qquad (2)$$

where f(i) is the binary value of the segmented ouput. To
achieve high performances of the quantization algorithm the
threshold value x(i) should be calculated at each point using
the pixel values in a neighbourhood, i.e. letting the threshold
to be a local function. To meet many practical conditions the
locally adaptive thresholding must be implemented in real time,
i.e. in a raster format scanning of the entire image.

Considering the binary quantization as a procedure of
two-class classification in accordance with (2), the optimal
threshold may be derived by minimization of the probability of
misclassification. Let us have at point i an abrupt transition
of brightness from a to b(fig. 1). Then in the context of image

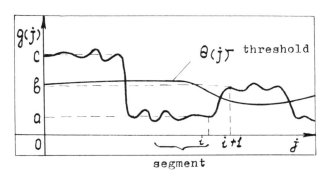

Fig.I

segment

local model the approximate value of the optimal threshold $x(i)$ at point i, minimizing the probability of misclassification, can be presented in the following recurrent form

$$x(i) = w(i)*x(i-1) + (1-w(i))(a+b)/2 \quad , \qquad (3)$$

where $w(i)$ depends on the probability $q(i)$ of abrupt transition (edge) at point i and also on the value of a, b ; $x(i-1)$ is the threshold value at the previous point. The probability q can be calculated at point i using the Bayes' rule on the basis of the following random variable (statistic):

$$u(i) = \frac{\tilde{g}(i) - \tilde{g}(i+1)}{\sqrt{(m-1)S(i)+(n-1)S(i+1)}} \sqrt{mn(m+n-2)/(m+n)} \quad , \qquad (4)$$

where $\tilde{g}(i)$ and $\tilde{g}(i+1)$ are the local mean values for two non-overlapping segments relating to point i and $(i+1)$; $S(i)$ and $S(i+1)$ are the local variances; m and n are the segments lenght, where $\max(m;n)=M$. For evaluation of the mean $\tilde{g}(i)$ and the variance $S(i)$ the most homogencous neighbourhood (signal segment of length M) is selected using the maximum likelyhood principle. For the specified video signal model the segment number $K(i)$ can be obtained as follows:

$$K(i) = \arg \min_{k} \{S_k(i)\} \quad , \qquad (5)$$
$$k = i-(M-1)/2 , \quad i+(M-1)/2 .$$

In context of the image local model the proposed statistic $u(i)$ has t distribution with $(m+n-2)$ degrees of freedom. In order to reduce the computation time the probability $q(i)$ may take only three values:

$$q(i) = \begin{cases} 0 & \text{if} \quad |u(i)| < T1 \\ 1/2 & \text{if} \quad T1 < |u(i)| < T2 \\ 1 & \text{if} \quad |u(i)| > T2 \end{cases} \qquad (6)$$

where T1 and T2 are two critical points of t distribution with (m+n-2) degrees of freeedom, assuming the value of the given significance level. For this end in (3) the levels of brightness a and b are substituted for their local estimates $\tilde{g}(i)$ and $\tilde{g}(i+1)$, respectively. Thus, the value of q(i) is evaluated using the statistical hipothesis testing.

The main disadvantage of the algorithm is its dependence on length M of the minimal line segment, which might equals unity. To eliminate this disadvantage it is suggested to obtain not the one-dimensional but the two-dimensional estimates of g (i) and S (i) in the local regions, the examples of which are shown in Fig. 2. These regions and their parameters are determined proceeding from the local two-dimensional image model [5]. In order to reduce the computation time and to implement adaptive thresholding in real time for this case a fast algorithm was developed[5]. In this algorithm the main idea consists in substitution of the regions in fig. 2 with the regions, which have equal size and the same form.

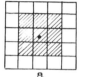

a   b   c

Fig.2

Another method to improve the quantization quality at low additional expenses of time consists in realization of the one-dimensional quantization but simultaneously row- and column-wise in the image matrix. This enables to increase the power of the criterion of type (6) at the specified significance level. Also the better results of the quantization can be obtained using Wald's sequential analysis technique. For this case we should consider not only one following point (i+1) but several neigbouring points to given point i.

4. Conclusion

The developed algorithm was tested for video signals with different edge heights and different noise levels and showed good results. The quantization errors arise only on those sections where the standard noise deviation is close to half

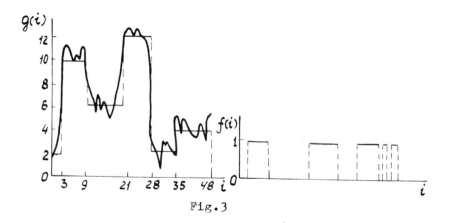

Fig.3

the value of the edge height or exceeds it (fig. 3). The suggested algorithm allows to segment the image invariantly to the value of the edge heights and tolerantly to the action of additive noise with the zero mean. Insignificant algorithm modification allows to use it in case of the video signal model with smoothly varying edge, as well as for the signals consisting of long segments with smoothly varying brightness.

References

1. Wezka I. S. A survey of threshold selection techniques //Computer Graphics and Image Processing. - 1978. - vol. 7, p. 259-265.

2. Sahoo P. K., Soltani S. and Wong A. K. A survey of thresholding techniques //Computer Vision, Graphics and Image Processing. -1988. -vol. 41, p. 233-260.

3. Pérez A. and Gonzalez R. C. An iterative thresholding algorithm for image segmentation// IEEE Trans. on Pattern Analysis and Machine Intelligence. - 1987. - vol. 9, p. 742-751.

4. Lee S. U. and Chung S. Y. A comparative performance study of several global thresholding techniques for segmentation // Computer Vision, Graphics and Image Processing. -1990. - vol. 52, p. 171-190.

5. Gritsyk V. V., Palenichka R. M. Adaptive signal smoothing based on a polynomial approximation //Avtomatica. -1989. - N2, p. 43-50 (in russian).

A CONTRIBUTION TOWARD MODEL DRIVEN SEGMENTATION AND SEGMENTATION FEEDBACK

Hans-Haiko Seifert, Dominik Giewald 1)

1. The aim of segmentation and modelling

Suppose, that an "object" is a structure which is determined by man according to it's semantical content. A "segment" is a set of pixels with the same label resulting from the segmentation process, first of all not necessarily reflecting a semantical content.

But there is a gap between finding segments as connected subsets of pixels with e.g. similar features and our general aim in practice: finding segments with a semantical content as demanded in a specific application. In general we are interested in a "Object-Segment-Idendity" (OSI) pointed out as beeing successful by a semantical analysis (matching the segmentation result with a semantical object model (SOM)) .

To find a way out of this dilemma we favourized first of all one approach:

If we would able to identify a photometrical model of the objects representing the intensity function without any perturbations we could compare it with the well known requirements of segmentation algorithms. If the model identification is good enough the OSI is optimal.

The general image model consists of the following submodels:

a) Photometrical object model (POM)

not necessarily decribing the intensity function as beeing constant inside an object but also variable. The model parameters are for example:

- average grey level of an object
- deviation of grey levels inside an object
- contrast between averages
- minimal contrast at object borders etc.

b) Geometrical object model (GOM)   having coarse information about

- compactness of objects
- extendedness of objects
- neighbourhood relations between objects

c) Perturbation model (PM)   describing the influence of

- Shading
- Unsharpness of edges
- Noise

during the scanning process.

Fictively, we would like to have a segmentation algorithm which gives

- in an efficient way
- for images with different complexity (POM)

---

1) TU Dresden
   Fakultät Informatik
   Institut für Datenbanken und künstliche Intelligenz
   Mommsenstraße 13
   O-8027 Dresden

- and different degrees of perturbations (PM)

- good results (OSI)

But a real aim is to choose an algorithm/combination of algorithms with appropriate uniformity predicates and parameters which works well in an efficient way for a given application. This decision is based upon a certain set of model parameters we get from reference images (see fig. 1).

By the way, we have got a general theory of perturbations as first of all not beeing perturbations but "phenomenons". For example: an "unsharpness-like" phenomenon may be caused either by the PM (unsharpness) or by a adequate POM, i.e. the phenomenon may be a segment itself. Obviously, the elimination of a part of the POM would provide to mis-segmentations. The decision about the real reason of a phenomenon is made with semantic apriori knowledge in the module "subsequent processing".

Nevertheless we have to overcome the following problems:

1) Possibly, the POM or PM were not representative in general, even for the reference image.

2) We don't want to segment reference images but images of a certain application. We cannot exclude a changing lighting (PM/POM) or changing object characteristics (POM) or a changing scenery (POM/GOM) at all.

3) Possibly, the resolution is not good enough.

These problems are providing to mis-segmentations:

- undersegmentation if at least one segment is missed or the segment doesn't represent the complete object, or

- oversegmentation if there is a set of segments instead of one object

These kinds of missegmentation are pointed out by a matching of the segmentation result with a SOM. In any way, there is a need of correcting the segmentation result. But note, that an wrong/incomplete SOM wrongly can provide to oversegmentation.

2. Segmentation feedback and data structures

Starting from the often discussed feedback of segmentation and structural analysis we realized the possibility of correcting segmentation results at two levels:

a) Sometimes perturbations which were not represented in PM, or not corrected during the pre-processing are producing rather innocent defects. These defects are quite easily repairable without any semantical apriori knowledge as used in a higher level analysis module and corrected in a low level analysis module.

b) The high level analysis based upon the SOM evaluates the segmentation and the low level result. This module provides to

- further correction (if the matching of the model and a union of some segments without own semantics is successful)

- feedback with a new segmentation using new parameters, new predicates or a new algorithm, respectively.

Three image representations are to be discussed:

- The grid point image (segmented image)

168

The <u>cell list</u> [KOVALEVSKY] is an efficient mean used for image description and consists of variously dimensional elements: 0-cells (branching points), 1-cells (border lines), 2-cells (segments). These elements are containing topological and metrical information <u>Quadtree structures</u> are often used for a structural analysis. If quadtree-structures just exist as a result of the split-and-merge-segmentation they may be preferred in the lower level analysis module to cell lists.

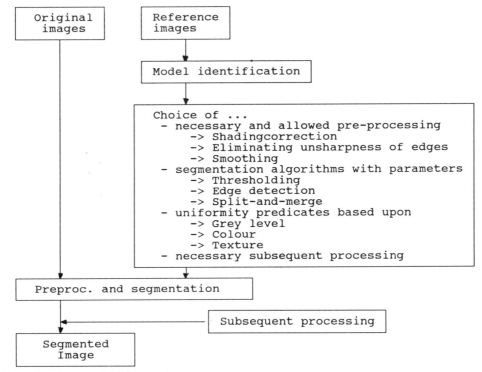

Fig. 1   Segmentation scheme

The cell list structure meets in a better way the analysis requirements and the quadtree structure the requirements of segmentation.

In general we obtain cell lists and quadtrees one from the other via the appropriate grid point image (see fig. 2 modules 3 and 4). Indeed, these conversions are considerably time consuming. Therefore we decided to design an algorithm converting structures directly from cell lists to quadtrees and vice versa.

The advantage of a direct conversion in module 3) in fig. 2 is evident. But we have to discuss the second conversion (module 4 from cell list to quadtree).

3. An Example

Let the initial segmentation be of edge detection type, i.e. after the analysis step there are available the segmented image and the cell list.

Suppose, a matching procedure in the high level analysis module failes, e.g. "undersegmentation" is detected. Thus there are well segmented parts in the image but there is at least one object inside of at least one of the well segmented parts which does not correspond to an appropriate segment according to a given semantical object model (see fig. 3).

We suppose that there is needed another uniformity predicate as a next step (e.g. colour).

Then we decide to convert the actual (well segmented) part of the cell list into a quadtree for a further segmentation with other parameters.

We designed a conversion algorithm (from cell list to quadtree) working in two passes [GIEWALD] (see fig. 3).

1)   Finding all vertical parts of segment boundaries in the cell list . By this the quadtree sizes
      at the boundaries and the labels are just determined (linear part of the algorithm)

2)   Merging all quads in the interior of the segments as great as possible (Expensive part of
      the algorithm).

After the conversion we obtain a quadtree representing only that part segmented up to now (the exterior segment). The segment inside is not represented yet (see fig. 3). Note that for getting this structure we didn't test any uniformity predicate. Till now we have to build up the more detailed quadtree from the top to the down (i.e. down from the actual leaves of the quadtree) by testing the new uniformity predicate (e.g. for the red, green, and blue component). To get an impression of the advantage of the direct conversion , imagine that for building up the quadtree containing only the exterior segment we have to test the uniformity predicate from the top (i.e. the whole region of interest) to the down. Tillnow the further subdivision is the same as after the direct conversion.

4. Conclusion

In order to perform a local re-segmentation we are preferring the direct conversion from the cell list to quadtree if

      there is no quadtree available yet

      we can determine a region of interest containing the object we are looking for (i.e.

      according to the semantical object model there is expected at least one segment inside

      of another one which was just segmented well.

Otherwise, there is a need of complete re-segmentation (excluding those segments having been segmented well).

5. References

[KOVALEVSKY]   Kovalevsky, V.A. "Finite Topology as applied to Image Analysis".
                Computer Vision, Graphics, and Image Processing. 30.2(1989):141-161

[GIEWALD]   Giewald, D. "Entwicklung eines Algorithmus zur Konvertierung von
                Zellenlisten in quadtree-Daten". Dipl. Dresden,1991.

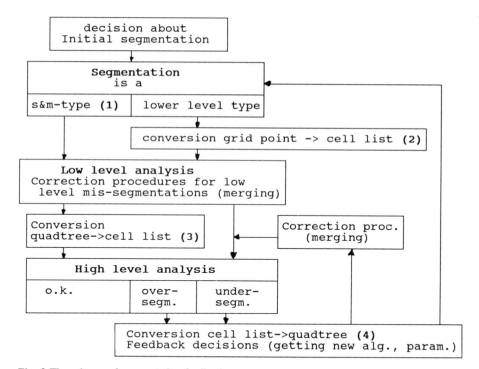

Fig. 2 The scheme of segmentation feedback

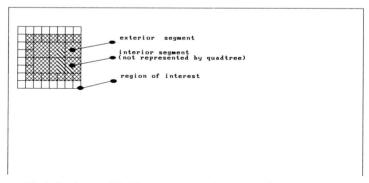

Fig.3 Quadtree subdivision not representing an interior segment

IMAGE INTERPTETATION BY ALGEBRAIC TOPOLOGY

Wolfgang Wilhelmi

University of Passau
Faculty of Mathematics and Computer Science
Innstraße 33, D-8390 Passau

1. Introduction

A lot of practical problems, where methods of image processing and computer graphics have to cooperate are not well supported by the corresponding conceptual models and data representations. This is particulary true for the avoidance of unreasonable geometric configurations generated automatically from visual observations or in another nonconstructive way. If one utilizes principles which avoid inconsistencies a priori (e.g. the Winged Edge Structure - WES), most of automatic aquired image data would be excluded due to temporary but necessary inconsistencies. Another drawback of recent models is the difficulty of computing elementary topological characteristics as the number of components, of holes etc.. Another problem not solved yet adequately is the well known sensitivity of topological features against rounding errors.

Therefore a modelling approach is developed which supposes an arbitrary decomposition of the geometric object, the identification of its cells, and a not necessary complete or error free observation of the incidences between these cells.

It will be shown, that this information together with certain expectations on topological characteristics of a permissible configuration (esp. the orientability) can help to solve the following tasks by computing invariants and filtering out unexpected configurations.

- Checking the correctness of mesh generation and triangulation schemes.
- Fast omputation of topological features.
- Decision making on topological similarity (homology) of objects.
- Resolving of unknown (hidden) incidences.
- Adding incidence data for higher dimensional cells, e.g. for fleshing out wire frames.

Probably the first paper on topological methods for image processing was published by Rosenfeld /1/. However, they have not been applied to the before mentioned tasks and were restricted to certain paradoxa and deciability problems due to the discretization of the embedding space, cf. /2,3,4,5/. Kovalevski /6/ has introduced the notion of the cellular comlex as a conceptual model for raster images. Connolly /7/ gives a convincing example for the use of algebraic topology concepts for computer models of molecules. A data base with explicitely stored topological information /8/ was used by Kovalevski and the author for processing of technical drawings.

The classical work by Markovsky and Wesley /9/ on fleshing out wire frames does not clearly distinguish between topological and metric information; this is expressed by the central notion "illegal intersection". The simplification and generalization of the presented procedures seem to be difficult without the theory of complexes. Many authors represent topological relations by graphs /10/, i.e. by twodimensional complexes. This results in the restriction either to 2D-embeddable configurations /11/ or to the proposition of a prohibitory element like the before mentioned WES /12/.

The problems of rounding has lead to the conclusion that explicit topological information should be avoided at all /13/; nevertheless it must be extracted and checked by expensive computation /14/. It seems better to ensure a rounding error resistive technique by observing topological features. The recent development in Computational Geometry has emphasized the general data structure problem /15/; unfortunately this work is oriented toward the efficient implementation of classical algorithms, not to the consistency problem.

2. Applied Algebraic Topology
2.1. Fundamentals

The complex is a generalization of geometric objects (especially Euclidean polyhedra) and was introduced 1862 by Listing. It consists of elements called q-cells, where q is the dimension of the cell ($q \geq 0$, q integer). The geometric interpretation of q-cells is easy: A 0-cell corresponds to a vertex, a 1-cell to an edge, a 2-cell to a surface patch etc.. A relation may exist between two cells of different dimensions may: The q-cell y is a face of the r-cell z ($q < r$) which is noted as $y < z$. The cell y is called also a q-face of z. The geometric interpretation is again obvious: If two elements of different dimension contact each other, the relation "$<$" is satisfied. Later on we will use the notion of incidence: y and z are incident if $y < z$ or $z < y$ or $y = z$. One can constitute a theory of complexes in axiomatic manner as shown in topological textbooks /16/. We only need some additional postulates.

(I) The complex K is finite, i.e. it has a finite number of cells. As a corollary follow that the dimension of K

$$k = \dim(K) = \max(\ \dim(z),\ z \in K) \tag{1}$$

is finite and every q-cell ($q > 0$) is adjoined by a finite number of cells (K is local finite).

(II) The complex is pure. $x < z$ and $\dim(x) < \dim(z)+1$ implies the existence of a cell y with $x < y < z$. If $\dim(z) > 0$, then exists at least one cell y with $y < z$.

Let us use the following symbols:

a_q ($q=0,\ldots,k$) – the number of q-cells
$z^q{}_i$ ($i=1,\ldots,a_q$) – the i-th q-cell

Finite pure complexes may be represented by a sequence of k-1 incidence matrices

$$J^q = ||\ j(z^{q-1}{}_i,\ z^q{}_i)\ ||\quad (q=1,\ldots,k) \tag{2}$$

with the incidence function

$$j\ (x,\ y)\ =\ \begin{cases} 1 \text{ if } x < y \\ \\ 0 \text{ else} \end{cases} \tag{3}$$

Our current research is based on a preliminary system of observation matrices B^q ($q=1,\ldots,k$) which corresponds to the incidence system with the exception that there are a few elements where the corresponding incidence is uncertain (designated by a value of -1). Such uncertainity may be introduced by hidden or fuzzy incidences and rounding errors. From the observation matrices a set of incidence systems can be generated in a purely combinatorial way. If the observation system has n positions with -1 then 2^n incidence systems are generated. The following procedures allow to select those instantiations which ensure that the complex models a consistent geometry.

One will soon realize that relevant applications of incidence information must be completed by a concept related to the orientation of cells. We propose a formal approach according to Tucker /16/ by introducing an orientation function $e(x,y)$ of two cells with the following properties.

(I) $e(x,y)$ has integer values only.
(II) $e(x,y) = 0$ implies $x < y$ and $\dim(y) = \dim(x) + 1$.
(III) For any 2 cells x, y with $\dim(y) = \dim(x) + 2$ the following condition holds true:

$$\sum_{z \in K} e(x,z)\ e(z,y) = 0 \qquad\qquad (4)$$

A complex together with such a function $e(.,.)$ is called a oriented one. The function $e(x,y)$ may be interpreted as the relative orientation between incident cells x,y with dimensions different by 1. There are 2 approaches for defining this function.

- The complex 'represents an Euclidean polyhedron. Any cell is given an arbitrary orientation. The orientation function takes the value 1, if the incident arguments have compatible orientations, and the value -1 otherwise.
- The complex is given by an incidence system. An unknown is assigned for every 1-valued element. The nontrivial expressions (4) constitutes then a bilinear system. A particular solution of it gives a possible instantiation of the orientation function. The corresponding algorithm is outlined in section 3.

In any case we can represent the oriented finite complex by a sequence of matrices similar to the incidence system; we call it the boundary system. Non zero elements are allowed only when the corresponding incidence elements have the value 1.

$$E^q = ||\ e(z^{q-1}{}_i,\ z^q{}_i)\ || \qquad (q=1,\ldots,k) \qquad\qquad (5)$$

Now the concept of a q-chain will be introduced. It corresponds to an integer vector $\underline{v}^q$ with a_q components arranged in the enumeration order of the q-cells. The non zero elements of $\underline{v}^q$ define the carrier set of the chain. The integer components $v^q{}_i$ are called chain coefficients and may be interpreted as multiples of occurences of the corresponding cell. The boundary of a q-chain is a (q-1)-chain given by

$$\underline{v}^{q-1} = E^q\ \underline{v}^q \qquad (q=1,\ldots,k) \qquad\qquad (6)$$

If the left side of (6) vanishes, then the particular q-chain is called a q-cycle. The postulate (4) in a rewritten formula

$$E^{q-1}\ E^q = 0 \qquad (q=2,\ldots,k) \qquad\qquad (7)$$

means that the boundary of any boundary is a cycle. The complex is called a chain complex
Now we consider all (k-1)-cells which are faces of exactly 1 k-cell and those q-cells $(q=0,\ldots,k-2)$ which are incident to them. This subcomplex K^* is called the boundary complex of K and is closed, because by definition $x \in K^*$ and $y < x$ implies $y \in K^*$. K^* may not exist for certain complexes. The cells of K^* are used to label corresponding rows and columns of the boundary system (5) with the goal to exclude them from further processing. The system of matrices generated by discarding the labeled columns and rows describe the relative (in respect to its boundary) topology of the complex. We call it the relative boundary system

$$R^q = A^q\ E^q\ B^q \qquad (q=1,\ldots,k), \qquad\qquad (8)$$

where A^q and B^q are simple matrices accomplishing the before mentioned deletion of columns and rows. It is easy to show that the postulate (4) holds true because K˙ is closed.

$$R^{q-1} \ R^q = 0 \qquad (q=2,\ldots,k) \tag{9}$$

Fig.1 illustrates the general flow of information from data acquisition to the establishment of several relative boundary systems.

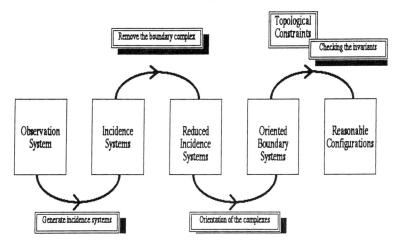

Fig.1 Processing stages of topological analysis

It should be noted that the reduction K-K˙ is done before orientation in the incidence system. For the following investigations a_q is the number of q-cells in K-K˙.

2.2. Topological Invariants

Let us apply a finite number of the following elementary operations to the matrix R^q.

(Ia) Exchange of two rows.
(Ib) Exchange of two columns.
(IIa) Superposition of an integer multiple of one row onto another.
(IIb) Superposition of an integer multiple of one column onto another.

Then we can achieve a unique representation.

$$P^q \ R^q \ Q^q = S^q \tag{10}$$

with the block matrix

$$S^q \ = \ \begin{Vmatrix} I^q & 0 & 0 \\ 0 & T^q & 0 \\ 0 & 0 & 0 \end{Vmatrix} \tag{11}$$

$n_q \times n_q$ – identity matrix I^q
$s_q \times s_q$ – diagonal matrix T^q of q-dimensional torsion numbers t^q_i.

$$T^q = \left|\left| \begin{array}{cccc} t^q_1 & 0 & \ldots & 0 \\ & & & \\ .. & .. & .. & .. \\ & & & \\ 0 & \ldots & 0 & t^q_{s_q} \end{array} \right|\right| \qquad t^q_i > 1 \; ; \; t^q_{i+1} \equiv 0 \bmod t^q_i$$

$a_{q-1} \times a_{q-1}$ - unimodular matrix P^q
$a_q \times a_q$ - unimodular matrix Q^q

S^q is called Smith's normal form of R^q. The rank r_q of S^q ($r_q = n_q + s_q$) and the number of q-cells a_q allow the computation of the q-th Betti number p_q. By definition let $r_0 = r_{k+1} = 0$.

$$p_q = a_q - r_q - r_{q+1} > 0 \qquad (q=0,\ldots,k) \tag{12}$$

Algebraic topology shows that the Betti numbers and the torsion numbers characterize the interior structure of a complex. Further it can be shown that Betti numbers are invariant against different decompositions of the geometric object. In the case of 3-dimensional polyhedra the Betti numbers may be interpreted as follows:

p_0 - number of components,
p_1 - number of holes,
p_2 - number of caverns,
p_3 - $p_3=1$ means that the modelled object is orientable.

The well known Euler characteristic of the k-dimensional complex K may be formulated also in an invariant form.

$$\begin{aligned} u(K) &= a_0 - a_1 + \ldots + (-1)^k \, a_k \\ &= p_0 - p_1 + \ldots + (-1)^k \, p_k \end{aligned} \tag{13}$$

The Euler characteristic gives the type of embedding manifold of the modelled geometric object.
The interpretation of the torsion number is supported by another notation of (10).

$$(P^q)^{-1} \, S^q = R^q \, Q^q \tag{14}$$

The columns of Q^q ($q=1,\ldots,k$) constitute the topological base of the complex. The last ones corresponding to the zero columns of S^q are the basic cycles. If the complex is not torsion free one can represent a particular boundary only by multiples $t > 1$ of another chain

$$t \, \underline{v}^{q-1} = R^q \, \underline{v}^q \tag{15}$$

A smaller multiplier than t does not exist. Well known examples of manifolds with torsion are the Möbius ribbon and the Klein bottle. In any case a complex with torsion is suspected of inconsistency and should be excluded from further consideration.

The examples of a cube, an open box, a regular ribbon, and a Möbius ribbon illustrate the meaning of the topological invariants (fig. 2, fig. 3). Because the boundary systems contain 1, -1, and 0 only, these are symbolically denoted by +, -, 0. The columns and rows of the boundary complex are labeled by circumflexes below and underlines.

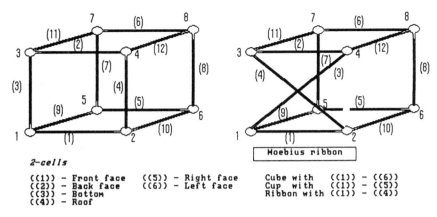

2-cells

((1)) – Front face   ((5)) – Right face   Cube with   ((1)) – ((6))
((2)) – Back face   ((6)) – Left face   Cup with   ((1)) – ((5))
((3)) – Bottom   Ribbon with ((1)) – ((4))
((4)) – Roof

Fig.2 Simple example: Cell arrangement

3.   Preliminary Algorithms
3.1. Deletion of $K^\bullet$

In the first fully formal step the boundary complex has to be removed. The algorithm is easy to understand and to implement. All incidence matrices J^q are processed starting from $q = k$ down to $q = 1$. Certain columns of the current incidence matrix are labeled as belonging to $K^\bullet$. For $q = k$ this property is given, if the column contains exactly one 1. For other q this label is assigned to columns index of them is the same as the index of labelled rows of the before prosessed J^{q+1}. A row will be labelled if it contains at least one 1 belonging to a before labelled column. Finally all labelled columns and rows, if any, are discarded. Additionally a table is updated, where the indices of the new matrices are mapped onto the news. This allow a better identification of the cells in the reduced complex.

3.2. Orientation of $K-K^\bullet$

Let the reduced incidence system be H^q $(q=1,\ldots,k)$. The algorithm starts at $q = k-1$ with the initial orientation

$$R^k = H^k \tag{16}$$

We assume that in all pairs (7) the right matrix R^{q+1} has been already defined. The left matrix R^q is only partially defined; it must contain zeros at the same positions as the corresponding matrix H^q. It is easy to see that we can consider the row vectors $\underline{r}^q_i$ $(i=1,\ldots,a_{q-1})$ indepedently. Let $\underline{c}^q_i$ $(i=1,\ldots,n^q_i)$ the vector of unknown elements of the row r^q_i. Then the following equation applies.

$$\underline{r}^q_i = G^q_i \, \underline{c}^q_i \tag{17}$$

$$G^q_i = || \, g^q_i(m,n) \, || \tag{18}$$

with

$$g^q_i(m,n) = \begin{cases} 1 \text{ if } c^q_{in} \text{ is the m-th component of } \underline{r}^q_i \\ \\ 0 \text{ else} \end{cases}$$

```
Cube
1 :  - 0 + 0 0 0 0 0 - 0 0 0
2 :  + 0 0 - 0 0 0 0 0 + 0 0
3 :  0 + - 0 0 0 0 0 0 + 0
4 :  0 - 0 + 0 0 0 0 0 0 -
5 :  0 0 0 0 - 0 + 0 + 0 0 0
6 :  0 0 0 0 + 0 0 - 0 - 0 0
7 :  0 0 0 0 0 + - 0 0 0 - 0
8 :  0 0 0 0 0 - 0 + 0 0 0 +

1 :  + 0 + 0 0 0
2 :  + 0 0 + 0 0
3 :  + 0 0 0 + 0
4 :  + 0 0 0 0 +
5 :  0 + - 0 0 0
6 :  0 + 0 - 0 0
7 :  0 + 0 0 - 0
8 :  0 + 0 0 0 -
9 :  0 0 - 0 + 0
10:  0 0 - 0 0 +
11:  0 0 0 - + 0
12:  0 0 0 - 0 +

--- 1-dim. boundary operator ---
            rank:    7
--- 2-dim. boundary operator ---
            rank:    5
   0. Betti number:   1
   1. Betti number:   0
   2. Betti number:   1
   Euler charact. :   2  (sphere)
```

```
Cup
1 :  - 0 + 0 0 0 0 0 - 0 0 0
2 :  + 0 0 - 0 0 0 0 0 + 0 0
3 :  0 + - 0 0 0 0 0 0 + 0
4 :  0 - 0 + 0 0 0 0 0 0 -
5 :  0 0 0 0 - 0 + 0 + 0 0 0
6 :  0 0 0 0 + 0 0 - 0 - 0 0
7 :  0 0 0 0 0 + - 0 0 0 - 0
8 :  0 0 0 0 0 - 0 + 0 0 0 +
                ^         ^   ^   ^

1 :  + 0 + 0 0
2 :  + 0 0 + 0
3 :  + 0 0 0 +
4 :  + 0 0 0 0
5 :  0 + - 0 0
6 :  0 + 0 - 0
7 :  0 + 0 0 -
8 :  0 + 0 0 0
9 :  0 0 - 0 +
10:  0 0 - 0 0
11:  0 0 0 - +
12:  0 0 0 - 0

--- 1-dim. boundary operator ---
            rank:    4
--- 2-dim. boundary operator ---
            rank:    4
   0. Betti number:   0
   1. Betti number:   0
   2. Betti number:   1
   Euler charact. :   1  (plane)
```

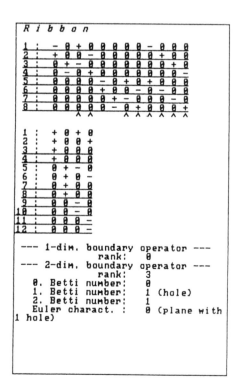

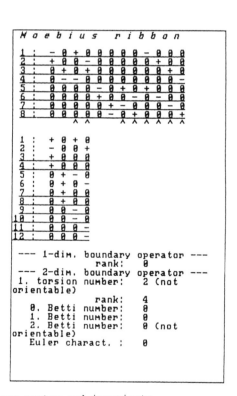

Fig. 3 Simple example: Boundary system and invariants
```
--- 1-dim. boundary operator ---
            rank:    0
--- 2-dim. boundary operator ---
            rank:    3
   0. Betti number:   0
   1. Betti number:   1  (hole)
   2. Betti number:   1
   Euler charact. :   0  (plane with
1 hole)
```

```
--- 1-dim. boundary operator ---
            rank:    0
--- 2-dim. boundary operator ---
   1. torsion number:   2 (not
orientable)
            rank:    4
   0. Betti number:   0
   1. Betti number:   0
   2. Betti number:   0 (not
orientable)
   Euler charact. :   0
```

By transposition one get the following homogenuous linear equation system

$$(R^{q+1})^T \; G^q_i \; \underline{c}^q_i = F^q_i \; \underline{c}^q_i = 0 \tag{19}$$

A particular integer solution of (19) with a maximal number of nonzero elements is required. If the rank of F^q_i is n^q_i only a trivial solution exists and it makes no sense to continue. However, this occurs infrequently and usually due to unknown incidences giving $n^q_i = 1$.
Equation (19) is solved by a division free version of the Gauss elimination procedure /17/. To get nonzero diagonal elements, exchanges of rows and columns have to be carried through. In the case of a column exchange the corresponding components of $\underline{c}^q_i$ changes their places. Finally we have the following system.

$$\begin{Vmatrix} P^q_i & Q^q_i \\ & \\ 0 & 0 \end{Vmatrix} \underline{c}^q_i = 0 \tag{20}$$

$P_q i$ is a upper triagonal matrix and the vector of unknowns $\underline{c}^q_i$ is a permutation of the original one. The unbound components of $\underline{c}^q_i$, i.e. those corresponding to the lower zero blocks in (20) are set to the product of all diagonal elements of P^q_i. Therefore the successive resolution of (20) gives integer values. It has been observed that in almost all examples the elimination procedure degenerates to simple exchanges of rows and columns and that the diagonal elements of P^q_i have the absolute value 1. Finally all components of the solution will be checked for a common divisor and divided by it if any.
The described procedure is very inexpensive because the order of (19) corresponds to the usually limited number of (q-1)-faces of the i-th q-cell. E.g., a 3-cell of a simplicial complex has only four 2-sides. On the other hand, for a given q the solution can be done in parallel with a maximum degree af parallelism of a_{q-1}. This expresses the locality of the orientation of a complex.

4.   Algorithms for Smith's Normal Form
4.1. The Fröberg-Sundström Procedure

Only a few publications exist about techniques for achieving the normal form of a matrix. Beyond verbal descriptions in mathematical text books /17/ an ALGOL program has been published by Fröberg and Sundström in 1967 /18/ where the elements are taken from the ring of polynomials rather than from integers. We will give an informal description of a slightly modified version, based on the following elementary functions:

(I) Find_Next_Pivot(matrix, divisor) returns the location and the value of a matrix element that has minimal remainder after division by *divisor*. Non zero elements are considered only. *divisor* = 0 means that no division take place.
(II) Reduce_Row(matrix, row, column) subtracts integer multiples of column *column* from all other columns in such a way that all elements of row *row* except that at *column* will be zero. It returns FALSE if that is not possible.
(III) Reduce_Col(matrix, column, row) subtracts integer multiples of row *row* from all other rows in such way that all elements of column *column* except that at *row* will be zero. It returns FALSE if that is not possible.
(IV) Discard(matrix, row, column) generates a new matrix from the old one by discarding the indicated row and column and returns the absolute value of the matrix element located at *row, column*.

```
for q = 1,...,k do
    {
    matrix = R^q; divisor = 0;
    do forever
        {
        matrix[row,column] =
        Find_Next_Pivot(matrix,divisor);
        divisor = matrix[row,column];
        if Reduce_Row(matrix,row,column)
                AND Reduce_Col(matrix,row,column) then
                {
                ; The next non zero diagonal element of
                ; Smith' normal  form in nondecreasing
                ; order of magnitude.
                factor = Discard(matrix,row,column);
                Output(factor);
                ; if factor equal 0 then leave;
                }
        }
    }
```

4.2. The New Algorithm

The proposed parallel algorithm relies on a new sequential one which is not as
efficient as the Fröberg-Sundström procedure. However, if the matrices are
sparse, it will be easy to parallelize. The main idea is to proceed along the
columns as long as possible and then to switch to the next appropriate
selected column. It should be noted that one can proceed also along rows. For
this we define the procedure Clear_Col(column) as follows. The internal
variables *vector* and *line* have been introduced to limit the pivot search to the
current entities.

```
Clear_Col(matrix,column)
{
divisor = 0;
do forever
    {
    vector = matrix[ ,column];
    matrix[row,column] = Find_Next_Pivot(vector,divisor);
    divisor = vector[row];
    if Reduce_Col(matrix,row,column) then
        {
        if Reduce_Row(matrix,row,column) then
            {
            Output(Discard(matrix,row,column));
            ; Diagonal element found, return 0.
            return( 0 );
            }
        else
            {
            ; Reduction impossible, search for a new pivot
            ; in the current row, return its column index.
            line = matrix[row, ];
            matrix[row,column]  =  Find_Next_Pivot(line,divisor);
            return( column );
            }
        }
    }
}
```

180

4.4. Parallel Algorithm

One can observe that the boundary system is usually sparse. If the new algorithm Clear_Col() is applied to a certain column then only a few others are affected. We can distinguish two types of dependency:

(I) The procedure Reduce_Row() changes only those columns where the current row contains a non zero element. We call a column dependent on another one if it has at least one non zero element in the rows where the latter does not vanish. This relation is symmetric and organizes a primary dependency graph G^*. Columns are mapped on vertices of this graph.

(II) One column usually depends not only on a single one. If a certain column has been selected any manipulation of other columns from which all dependent columns depend are not allowed. The dependency graph has to be extended by edges connecting all pairs of vertices having the initial distance 2. This is the final dependency graph G. Fig. 5 illustrates the 2 dependency types.

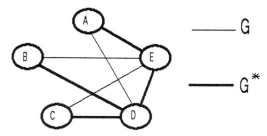

Fig.5 Data dependency types

Obviously we may process in parallel different sets of columns taking as pivot columns members of an independent set of the dependency graph G. All vertices adjacent in G^* to one member of the independency set constitute the processing set. The additional vertices adjacent in G are not processed but are not allowed to be pivots. The maximum degree of parallelism is given by the independency number $\alpha_0(G)$. However, the application of any algorithm for finding a maximal set of independent vertices is not feasible, because this task is NP-complete. Further it has to be carried through several times at run time, because the dependency graph changes by the transformation of the corresponding boundary matrix. One can observe that the "connectedness" of G will decrease until all vertices corresponds to orthogonal columns and so will have degree 0. A very simple heuristic for finding an usually not maximal independent set has been proved as adequate /19/. Take an arbitrary vertex as the next independent one together with all vertices adjacent to it and remove them from G. The removed set has no more than 1+D element where D is the maximum degree of G. The procedure is repeated until G is exhausted. The number of independent vertices is therefore

$$\alpha_M \geq |G|/(1+D) \ . \tag{21}$$

This simple approach yields an promising lower bound for parallelism. If simplicial complexes are used, the maximum degree is restricted due to the fact that a q-dimensional cell has exactly q+1 (q-1)-dimensional faces resulting in

$$D < (q+1)^2 \ . \tag{22}$$

E.g., the algorithm for unstructured mesh construction presented in /20/ generates simplicial cells (lines, triangles, tetrahedra). A complex fighter configuration is composed of 641,872 tetrahedra. The achievable $\alpha_M > 641,872/16 = 40,117$ is typical for massively parallel systems.

Fig. 4 outlines the differences between the 2 algorithms in respect to the finding of diagonal elements neglecting the outer iteration loops on q.

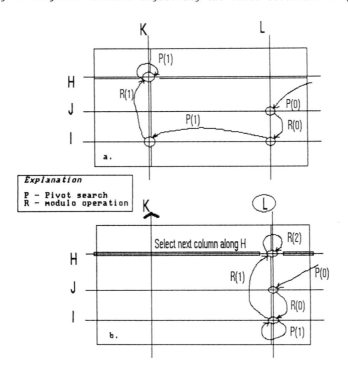

Fig.4 Two methods for finding Smith's normal form
a. Fröberg-Sundström procedure
b. New algorithm

So the final algorithm has the following form.

```
for q = 1,...,k do
    {
    matrix = Rq;
    column = Select_Col(matrix);
    while matrix is not empty do
        {
        column = Clear_Col(matrix,column);
        if column equal 0 then
            column = Select_Col(matrix);
        }
    }
```

The 2 algorithms are not functionally equivalent. The first one puts out the diagonal elements in monotonically increasing order and stops if the next one found is zero, i.e. all invariant factors have been found. The other works until the matrix is exhausted. It also depends on the selection of the start column and the next column if a diagonal element was found. This is expressed by the arbitrary function Select_Col().

5. Implementation

The current experimental implementation consists in the following independent programs.
TOPINP supports the manual generation of incidence systems, especially for test purposes. TINGEN generates all incidence matrices satisfying a set of observations on incidences. The number of cells in every dimension is assumed to be known before. TSTRIP detects the boundary of the complex, given by the incidence system, and transforms it to an open complex. TUCKER transforms an incidence system in a set of boundary matrices. TBETTI computes the topological invariants of a oriented complex given by a boundary system and allows the user to decide whether the complex meets his requirements or not.
Most of them are filters and can be chained to processing sequences by the pipe construction. Until now no direct connection to an image recognition system is established. Internally the data are organized as a set of twodimensional arrays. The input/output streams begin with global data (dimension, number of cells) and continue with tripels each of them containing the indices and the value of an element. A reserved tripel terminates the set for the current dimension. Obviously the practical application of the developed methods depends on the data base access. Either interfaces to existing image or graphic data bases have to be implemented or a new database that fairly supports the topological analysis must be defined.

References

1. Rosenfeld, A.: Connectivity in Digital Pictures. J.ACM 17 (1970) Nr.1, pp.146-160.
2. Tourlakis, G.; Mylopoulos, J.: Some Results in Computational Topology. J.ACM 20 (1973) Nr.3, pp.439-466.
3. Lee, C.-N.; Rosenfeld, A.: Holes and Genus of 3D Digital Images. Technical Report CAR-TR-170. University of Maryland - Computer Vision Laboratory, December 1985.
4. Lee, C.-N.; Rosenfeld, A.: Computing the Euler Number of a 3D Image. Technical Report CAR-TR-205. University of Maryland - Computer Vision Laboratory, May 1986.
5. Lee, C.-N.; Rosenfeld, A.: Simple Connectivity is not Locally Computable for Connected 3D Images. Technical Report CAR-TR-207. University of Maryland - Computer Vision Laboratory, June 1986.
6. Kovalevski, V.A.: Finite Topology as Applied to Image Analysis. Computer Vision, Graphics, and Image Processing 46 (1989), pp.141-161.
7. Connolly, M.L.: An Application of Algebraic Topology to Solid Modeling in Molecular Biology. The Visual Computer (1987), pp.72-81.
8. Kovalevski, V.A; Wilhelmi, W.: Automatic Processing of Technical Drawings. Proceedings of the 7. Int. Conf. on Pattern Recognition - Paris , 27-31. October 1986, pp.1297-1300.
9. Markowsky, G.; Wesley, M.A.: Fleshing Out Wire Frames. IBM J. RES. DEVELOP. 24 (1980), Nr. 5, pp.582-597.
10. Ansaldi, S.; De Floriani, L.; Falcidieno, B.: Geometric Modeling of Solid Objects by Using a Face Adjacency Graph Representation. SIGGRAPH 85, Vol.19 Nr.3, pp.131-139
11. Suk, M.; Oh, S.-J.: Region Adjacency and its Application to Object Detection. Pattern Recognition 10 (1986) Nr.2, pp.161-167.
12. Ken-ichi-Kobori; Futagami, N.; Nishioka, I.: Automated Generation of Simply Connected Solid Objects from Wire-Frame Data Using Operations on Graphs. The Visual Computer (1986) Nr.2, pp.335-341.
13. Takala, T.: Geometric Boundary Modelling without Topological Data Structures. Proc. EUROGRAPHICS 86, pp.116-128.
14. Milenkovic, V.J.: Verifiable Implementations of Geometric Algorithms Using Finite Precision Arithmetic. Artificial Intelligence 37 (1988), pp.377-401.
15. Günther, O.: Efficient Structures for Geometric Data Management. Lecture Notes in Computer Science 337. Springer-Verlag 1988.
16. Rinow, W.: Lehrbuch der Topologie. Deutscher Verlag der Wissenschaften, Berlin 1975.
1j7. Zurmühl, R.: Matrizen - Eine Darstellung für Ingenieure. Springer-Verlag, Berlin 1958.
18. Fröberg, C.-E.; Sundström, A.: Smith`s normal form (ALGOL-Programming) BIT 7 (1967), pp.163-169.
19. Griggs, J.R.: Lower Bounds on the Independence Number in Terms of the Degree. J. of Combinatorial Theory, Series B, 34 (1983), pp.22-39.
20. Gumbert, C.; Löhner, R.; Parikh, P.; Pirzadeh, S.: A Package for Unstructured Grid Generation and Finite Element Flow Solvers. Collection Techn. Papers AIAA 7th Appl. Aerodyn. Conf., Seattle (WA), July 31th - August 2nd 1989. pp.99-108.

MORPHOLOGICAL VORONOI TESSELLATION AND DELAUNAY TRIANGULATION

I.Pitas[1],   A.Maglara[1],   C.Kotropoulos[1]

ABSTRACT

A new method is introduced for implementing the Voronoi tessellation and the Delaunay triangulation. in the Z^2 plane. This method uses metrics on a discrete grid and discrete approximations of the euclidean metric. Mathematical morphology is used to implement Voronoi tessellation based on these metrics.

1. INTRODUCTION

Voronoi tessellation is a very important tool in computational geometry [4], object recognition [1] and image analysis [2]. Several important problems can be solved by employing Voronoi tessellation, for example Delaunay triangulation, convex hull, object decomposition into simple components (triangles).

Let $X=\{x_1,x_2,\ldots,x_N\}$ be a set of N points on a subset W. The **Voronoi Tessellation** is given by:

$$V(i)=\{x\in W: d(x,x_i)<d(x,x_j), j\neq i\} \tag{1}$$

$$Vor(X)=\cup V(i)$$

where : $W\subseteq R^n$ or $W\subseteq Z^n$ and d() is a distance function. V(i) is the Voronoi region of x_i and $Vor(\overset{\bullet}{X})$ is called the Voronoi diagram of X.

In this paper a novel algorithm for the computation of Voronoi tessellation is proposed. It is based on mathematical morphology. It construct Voronoi diagrams on the Euclidean grid Z^2 for any distance measure, e.g. Euclidean, Hausdorff, cityblock, chess-board, octagonal. Its computational complexity is of order $O(1/N)$.

Each Voronoi region V(i) contains all points of W that are closer to x_i than to any other x_j, $j\neq i$. This means that it can be obtained by "growing" all points $x_i, i=1,\ldots,N$ simultaneously until they occupy the entire W. When two Voronoi region collide, a boundary is formed and no further growth is allowed along this boundary. The growth mechanism is the **dilation** operator:

$$Y\oplus B^S= \underset{b\in B}{U} Y_{-b} =\left\{ x\in Z^2: B_x\cap Y \neq \varnothing \right\} = \left\{ x: B_x\uparrow Y \right\} \tag{2}$$

In the following section a presentation of distance functions is

---
1) Department of Electrical Engineering
University of Thessaloniki, Thessaloniki 54006, GREECE.

made. In section 3 a method for implementing the Voronoi tessellation by using various distance functions is given. Simulation examples are shown and conclusions are drawn in section 4.

2. DISTANCE FUNCTIONS

The notion of the distance between two points is fundamental in a number of geometrical problems. In the case of the Voronoi diagram, the Euclidean metric is used to find the points lying on the perpendicular bisector of two given points in R^2.

The best known distance measure between two points in R^2 is the Euclidean distance. A coordinate independent distance that can be used to calculated the Euclidean distance is the Hausdorff distance function, that is defined by using mathematical morphology

$$d_h(x,y)=\inf \left\{ \rho \; : \; x \oplus B(\rho) \uparrow y \right\} \tag{3}$$

where $B(\rho)$ is a disk of radius $\rho \in R^2$.

In order to define a distance measure in Z^2, grids with different connectivity are used. Such are the city block for a 4-connected and the chessboard distance for an eight-connected grid. When trying to approximate in Z^2 the connectivity of the R^2 grid, then the octagonal distance function has to be used. The best approximation of the Euclidean measure in Z^2 is given by:

$$d_z(x,y)=\left\{ n \in \mathbb{N} : \; n-0.5 \leqslant d_e(x,y) < n+0.5 \right\} \tag{4}$$

where d_e is the Euclidean distance of x,y in Z^2. An equivalent definition for (3) in Z^2 is:

$$d_h(x,y)=\inf \left\{ n \; : \; x \oplus B(n) \uparrow y \right\} \quad x,y \in Z^2, \; n=0,1,2,\dots \tag{5}$$

where $B(n)$ defines a structuring element of size n. There are several ways to construct a structuring element $B(n)$ of size n. In the following we present two distance functions based on (5) but using a different definition for $B(n)$.

The uniform-step distance (USD) is denoted by $d_{usd}(x,y)$ and defined by using (5), as follows [5]:

$$B(n)=\begin{cases} B \oplus B \oplus \dots \oplus B & (n \text{ times}), \quad n=1,2,\dots \\ 0, & n=0 \end{cases} \tag{6}$$

where B is the structuring function of unit size. B is a symmetric compact set in Z^2 containing the origin. When using a RHOMBUS (SQUARE) structuring element [3] then the city block (chessboard) distance function results. Eqs. (5)-(6) provide an easy iterative way for computing different measures by using dilation.

Another distance function is the periodically-uniform-step distance (PUSD). If $B_1, B_2, \ldots, B_m$ are all symmetric compact sets in Z^2 containing the origin, $B(m)$ of size m ($m \geq 1$) is given by [5]:

$$B(m) = B_1 \oplus B_2 \oplus \ldots \oplus B_m, \qquad (m \geq 1), \qquad B_1 \subset B_2 \subset \ldots \subset B_m \qquad (7)$$

For $n \geq m$ $B(n)$ is defined by:

$$B(n) = \begin{cases} pB(m) \oplus B(q), & n = pm+q > 0, \quad q < m. \\ 0, & n = 0 \end{cases} \qquad (8)$$

where $pB(m) = B(m) \oplus B(m) \ldots \oplus B(m)$, (p-times). If B_1, B_2 (m=2) are the RHOMBUS and the SQUARE structuring elements [3], then the octagonal distance function is evaluated. Eqs. (5),(7) and (8) can approximate the Euclidean distance in the grid Z^2 if the sets $B_1, \ldots, B_m$ are chosen carefully. A better approximation of the Euclidean distance in Z^2 can be found by using another class of distance functions based on a slightly different definition:

$$d_a(x,y) = \inf \left\{ k : X_k \uparrow y \right\}, \qquad k \in N$$

$$X_k = (X_{k-1} \oplus B_k) \cup S_k^+ \qquad k > 0, \qquad X_0 = x \qquad (9)$$

where B_k, $k=1,2,\ldots$ are symmetric structuring elements which contain the origin and S_k^+ is a set of points to be defined. When each structuring element B_k is chosen to be a RHOMBUS and denoted by B the set S_k^+ is given by:

$$S_k^+ = \left\{ z \in Z^2 : z \in \{ (X_{k-1} \oplus 2B) - (X_{k-1} \oplus B) \} \text{ and } d_z(z,x) = k \right\} \qquad (10)$$

where $2B = B \oplus B$ and $d_z()$ is given by (4). If S_k^+ is chosen as in (10), then X_k in (9) implements a recursive way for growing a disk in Z^2, centered on the point x. At each step k, the disk X_{k-1} is dilated by B and the points of S_k^+ given by (10) are appended. The sets S_k^+, $k=1,2,\ldots$ can be precomputed and stored.

In the following section the above metrics will be applied to the Voronoi tessellation.

3. VORONOI TESSELLATION

A new method for constructing the Voronoi diagram of a given set of distinct points in $X \subset W \subseteq Z^2$ will be presented. This method finds the Voronoi regions of a given set $X \subset W$ rather than the Voronoi edges and vertices. It uses successive region growing of the n-Voronoi region of each point, denoted as $N_n(i)$. The $N_n(i)$ region of a point x_i is the set of points already appended to x_i during the n previous growing steps. When two or more n-Voronoi

186

regions collide, the collision points form subsets of the Voronoi polygons and the growing stops in this direction. This procedure is repeated until no further growth is possible in $W \subseteq Z^2$. The overall algorithm is described as follows:

$$n_n(i) = \left\{ x \in \{W-X\} : x \in [n_{n-1}(i) \oplus B_n], \ x \notin e_n(i), \ x \notin N_{n-1}(i) \right\}, \quad n \geq 1$$
$$x_j \in \{X-x_i\}$$
$$n_0(i) = x_i \tag{11}$$

$$N_n(i) = N_{n-1}(i) \cup n_n(i), \qquad N_0(i) = \{ \ \}$$

where B_n is the n-th in order structuring element of $B(n)$. The set e_n contains the collision points of x_i at the growing step n:

$$e_n(i) = \left\{ x \in \{W-X\} : x \in \bigcup_{x_j} \left[D_n(i) \cap D_n(j) \right] \right\} \tag{12}$$
$$x_j \in \{X-x_i\}$$

$$D_n(i) = \{ x \in W : x \in X_n - X_{n-1} \} \tag{13}$$

$$X_n = x_i \oplus B(n)$$

The points in the set $e_n(i)$ have the same distance n from a point x_i and at least from another point x_j of X ($i \neq j$) by using (5). The set $N_n(i)$ contains all the points of $\{W-X\}$ that have been appended to x_i and are at a distance $k \leq n$. If $k_{max}(i)$ denotes the step in which the point x_i cannot grow any more, the Voronoi region V(i) of a point $x_i \in X$ is defined by using (11) as:

$$V(i) = N_{k_{max}}(i) \triangleq N_{k_{max}(i)}(i) \tag{14}$$

Thus the union of all $k_{max}(i)$-Voronoi regions of the points in X is equal to the Voronoi diagram of the set X. (11) is useful in practice because it allows the construction of the Voronoi neighborhoods recursively. A n-Voronoi neighborhood $n_n(i)$ contains the new points to be appended to the corresponding $(n-1)$-Voronoi region $N_{n-1}(i)$. Thus the $N_{n-1}(i)$ region grows to the $N_n(i)$ region. The set which contains the **boundary points** of V(i) is denoted by F(i) and is given by:

$$F(i) = \left\{ x \in \{W-X\} : x \in \{ N_{k_{max}}(i) - N_{[k_{max}-1]}(i) \} \right\} \tag{15}$$

where $(-)$ denotes set subtraction.

Let $X = \{x_1, x_2, \ldots, x_N\}$ be a set of N points. The basic idea of the algorithm is to grow each given point of X by growing the set $N_n(i)$. More precisely, at each step the points of $n_n(i), \forall \ x_i \in X$ are appended to $N_{n-1}(i), \forall \ x_i \in X$, thus resulting in the $N_n(i)$ regions, $\forall \ x_i \in X$. The set $n_n(i)$ is found by dilating $n_{n-1}(i)$ by B_n and then checking whether all points $x \in [n_{n-1}(i) \oplus B_n]$ have been appended to x_i

exclusively (and not to another point x_j, $j\neq i$ at the same time). We also check if the point x already belongs to a $(n-1)$-Voronoi region of a point x_j, $j\neq i$ of X. The iterative dilations stop when all points of W−X have been appended to one of the Voronoi regions.

The previously described method can be modified to construct the Euclidean Voronoi diagram in Z^2. In this case the distance function used to derive the definitions is given by (9). The only change to the above formulas is the set X_k, now defined:

$$\text{for } n=1: X_1 = (x_i \oplus B) \cup S_1^+ \tag{16}$$
$$\text{for } n>1: X_n = (X_{n-1} \oplus B) \cup S_k^+$$

where S_k^+ is given by (10) and B is the RHOMBUS structuring element.

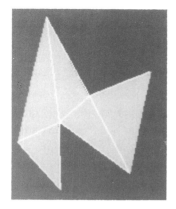

Figure 1: (a) Voronoi tessellation (b) Delaunay triangulation of binary object.

4. SIMULATIONS EXAMPLES AND CONCLUSIONS

The previously described method has been implemented in C programming language. The Morphological Voronoi tessellation using this method has been tested and found to be very successful, Figure 1a. This tessellation has also been used to obtain the Delaunay triangulation [4]. The Delaunay triangulation of a polygonal object X obtained by using this method is shown in Figure 1b. The set X_c of the corners of this object have been obtained by morphological operations:

188

$$X_c = X_E \cup X_{E'}$$
$$X_E = X - X_B \qquad (17)$$
$$X_{E'} = X^c - (X^c)_B$$

where X^c denotes the complement of X with respect to W and X_B denotes set opening [3]. The corner set X_c is used to obtain the Voronoi tessellation of X and, subsequently, its Delaunay triangulation.

In this paper a new method for performing Voronoi tessellation on a set of points in Z^2 has been presented. A general definition of a distance function has been used that is implemented by using the morphological operator of dilation as a growing mechanism. The proposed method is independent of the coordinate system. It allows the implementation of different tessellations based on different distance functions. e.g. the Euclidean, the Hausdorff, the octagonal, the chessboard and the city block. It has low computational complexity of order $O(1/N)$ and allows parallel implementation.

REFERENCES

[1] Levine,M.D. Vision in man and Machine, Mc Graw-Hill, 1985.
[2] Pitas,I., Kotropoulos,C., "Texture analysis and segmentation of seismic images", Proceedings IEEE International Conference on Acoustics Speech and signal Processing, Glasgow, 1989.
[3] Pitas,I., Venetsanopoulos,A.N., Nonlinear digital filters: principles and applications, Kluwer Academic, 1990.
[4] Preparata, F.P., Shamos, M.I., Computational Geometry, Springer-Verlag, 1985.
[5] Zhou,Z., Venetsanopoulos,A.N., "Pseudo-Euclidean morphological skeleton transform for machine vision", Proc. IEEE ICASSP, Glasgow, 1989.

A CONCEPT FOR RECOGNITION AND DESCRIPTION OF LINE OBJECTS

Reiner Göldner [1]

Abstract

A characterization of line objects is used to derive a method for a structural description of them. Relations between boundary structure and sceleton structure of the line object are deduced. They are used to find connections between segments of middle axis to get the whole sceleton.

Introduction

There are many problems in the field of pattern recognition connected with "lines" or "line objects". The recognition of bar codes, handwritten words or technical drawings are some of them as well as the detection of streets or rivers at air photos. Many algorithms in this field use methods of line thinning, gradient matching or the Hough-Transformation. This paper gives a structural approach to recognize and describe line objects using their boundary.

Characterization of line objects

To characterize line objects it is useful to distinguish between "stroke" and "line object". A stroke is something which was drawn, e.g. with a pencil or a brush. If we consider strokes such as handwritten characters or a scetch of a drawing we can find a characterization of a stroke. This characterization is closely connected with the process of generating this stroke. Most of the information we can receive from a drawn line we get from the way the pencil was moved. The color of the pencil and it's thickness are less interesting.

From that we can derive a definition of a *stroke* :

Definition:

Let $\mathbf{R}$ be the Euclidean plane with the vector addition $+$. Let $F \subset \mathbf{R}$ be a small and compact geometrical figure with the origin $\underline{o}$ as the central point and let $C \subset \mathbf{R}$ be a curve. Then the stroke S is the Minkowski-Sum of F and C :

$$S = \{ \underline{x} + \underline{y} \;\; : \;\; \underline{x} \in F \;, \; \underline{y} \in C \}$$

Figure 1 shows a curve C, a circle as figure F and the resulting stroke S. You can see that this definition corresponds to the process of drawing a line. Some additional restrictions about the

[1]   TU Dresden
Fakultät Informatik
Institut für Datenbanken und künstliche Intelligenz
Mommsenstraße 13
O-8027 Dresden

largeness of figure F and the shape of curve C can be made, but they are not essentiell. They are necessary to exclude the case that the stroke fills a large region (just like painting a wall).

This definition is fairly strong and not very suitable for use in structural recognition. We want to weak it by the following statements:

- the diameter of the figure F may be different at different positions (along C),
- the shape of the stroke may be rugged,
- the curve C may be replaced by a set of connected curves (sceleton SC).

Now we can characterize a *line object* :

A line object is a long, narrow geometrical figure that essentially can be described by a set of connected curves (sceleton) and some data about the width of several parts of the line object.

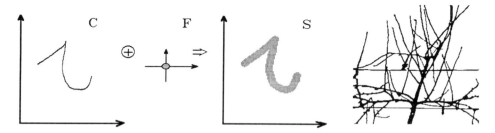

Fig. 1 Generation of a stroke   Fig. 2 Appletree

This characterization guarantees that we can consider a river or a tree in an image as a line object too (figure 2). There is a great difficulty to find general limits for length, thickness and roughness of line objects. These parameters are very important to prevent trouble while detecting lines. They have to be fixed using a-priori-information as good as possible.

Structural features

Line objects (LO) can be described by the sceleton lines (position and structure) and a width belonging to every point (or segment) of the sceleton. We already found this context between LO and sceleton. But there is another context between the LO and the boundary B of the LO. Considering a LO (figure 3) we can find parts of the LO, sections of the sceleton and sections of the boundary belonging together. E.g. section c' of the sceleton and sections c_1'' and c_2'' of the boundary belong to part c of the LO. This can be explained using the stroke definition. A section of the sceleton approximately creates (by drawing along it) the part of the LO and the section(s) of the boundary belonging to it.

Resulting from the stroke definition we attribute the structure of the LO to the structure of the sceleton. A sceleton consists of lines (middle axis) and branching points (connections of the lines). The arrangement of these elements determines the structure of the LO.

Consider now the boundary of the LO. The boundary of the LO is structured too and there is a context with the structure of the sceleton. If two segments of the boundary are neighbours (e.g.

c_1'' and d'' in figure 3) then the sections of sceleton (c' and d') respectively the parts of LO (c and d) belonging to the mentioned segments of boundary are neighbours too. This is important for detecting LO's via the boundary.

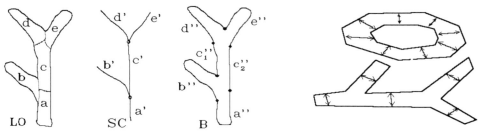

Fig. 3 Line object (LO), sceleton (SC) **Fig. 4** Opposite boundary
and boundary (B)   segments

To find candidates for parts of the sceleton it is necessary to use some geometrical information. It is important that two opposite segments of the (smoothed) boundary are nearly parallel and their distance is limited. This can be detected easily if a polygonal approximation of the boundary is used (figure 4).

Segments of middle axis

The following statements are all based on a polygonal approximation like it is used in cell lists to represent segmented digital images [KOVALEVSKY]. A slightly modified algorithm from [SCHIRMER] tests pairs of *straight sections of boundary (SSB)*. This algorithm detects a part of a LO if the two straight sections are opposite and parallel situated and if they have a limited distance. In this case the algorithm returns the beginning and the end point of that *section of* the *middle axis (SMA)* that lies between the two SSB (figure 5). SSB which are successfully used to build a SMA are called *assigned*. All such SMA are the basic elements to create the sceleton. They only have to be correctly connected.

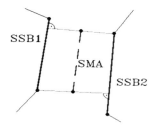

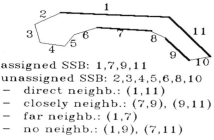

assigned SSB: 1,7,9,11
unassigned SSB: 2,3,4,5,6,8,10
 − direct neighb.: (1,11)
 − closely neighb.: (7,9), (9,11)
 − far neighb.: (1,7)
 − no neighb.: (1,9), (7,11)

Fig. 5 Boundary and SMA   Fig. 6 Neighbourhood of SSB

192

All we have to do now is to connect the SMA using the neighbourhood relations of the assigned SSB. Because there may exist some not assigned SSB disturbing direct neighbourhood of SSB we declare :   *2 assigned SSB are*

1)   *direct neighbours*   if they have one common end point,
2)   *closely neighbouring* if there is a short* path of unassigned SSB connecting them,
3)   *far neighbours* if there is a far* path of unassigned SSB connecting them,
4)   *no neighbours* if there is no path of SSB between them or if all paths between them
      contend at least one other assigned SSB,

(a measure for short* and far* has to be defined, e.g. the distance or the length of the path).

An example is shown in figure 6.

In an analogous way we declare the neighbourhood of SMA (remember, the SMA must be connected to built up the sceleton) :   *2 SMA are*

1)   *direct neighbours*   if they have one common end point,
2)   *closely neighbouring* if there is a short* way inside the LO from an end point of the first
      SMA to an end point of the second SMA,
3)   *far neighbours* if there is a far* way inside the LO from an end poind of the first SMA to an
      end point of the second SMA,
3a)   *indirect neighbours*   if they have the same (direct or indirect) neighbour at a branching
      point,
4)   *no neighbours* else,

(a measure for short* and far* has to be defined).

Strictly speaking we have to determine the neighbourhood for each end of each SMA.

In this sense we can distinguish 14 several combinations of pairs of assigned SSB to build a connection between two SMA. We can look at them and declare the neighbourhood of the SMA in each case. The result is indicated in table 1 and some examples are given in figure 7.

SSB	0	1	2	3	4
0		1	2	3	3*
1		_2	2	3	3*
2			_2	3	3*
3		SMA		_3	3*
4					\ 3a*/4

The numbers represent the neighbourhood of the SSB and SMA respectively with the meaning:
```
0  - the same (SSB only)
1  - direct neighbours
2  - closely neighbouring
3  - far neighbouring
3a- indirect neighbours (SMA)
4  - no neighbours
*  - indicates the occurence
     of a branching point
```

Table 1 Neighbourhood of SMA

Problems

There are some special cases that have to be excluded before using the above mentioned contexts. We want to have a look at some examples without discussion about it (figure 8).

In some other cases it is impossible to find out the correct neighbour of a SMA via neighbouring SSB (figure 9).

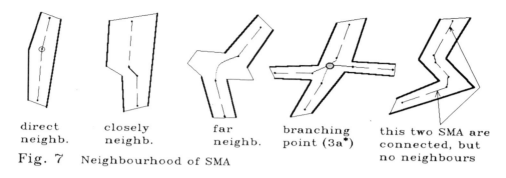

| direct neighb. | closely neighb. | far neighb. | branching point (3a*) | this two SMA are connected, but no neighbours |

Fig. 7   Neighbourhood of SMA

To solve these problems you have to use some other information (e.g. position and direction of the SMA) if you really want to get the whole sceleton. The easier way is to say: "That's not a line object!" . If you know that from a-priori-information that is right but I must reply that such structures may occure at cell lists of real images indeed. There is no way to avoid additional computations in this case.

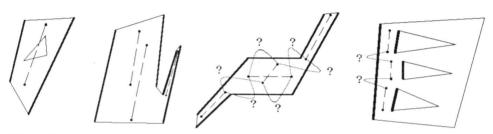

Fig. 8 Incorrect SMA   Fig. 9 Obscure neighbourhood of SMA

Concluding remarks

This concept is not suitable to supersede line thinning methods in grid point images because the computational complexity of the algorithms (including generation of boundary description) is rather high. But it may be profitable in connection with other boundary based methods of structural recognition.

References

[KOVALEVSKY]   Kovalevsky, V.A.
"Finite Topologie as Applied to Image Analysis". *Computer Vision, Graphics and Image Processing* . 30.2 (1989): 141-161.

[SCHIRMER]   Schirmer, H.
"An Algorithm for the Recognition of Line Objects". *Computer Analysis of Images and Patterns.* Mathematical Research 55. Berlin: Akademie-Verlag, 1989. 157-162.

CALCULATION OF THE CURVATURE OF THE EDGE OF
A ROAD WITH THE HELP OF REGULARITIES

Nikolai Metodiev Sirakov[1] Ivan Trebaticky[2]

Abstract

A method for the calculation of the curvature of the edges of
a road in our paper is proposed. It is based on the terms of regularities and consistency of regularities, and on the principles of
the independent observer.

Introduction

There are some important problems in the field of navigation
of a vehicle. The first problem is to separate the ground from the
road and determine the road's edges. The appearance of the road
edges in an image can greatly depend upon such things as:

1. daily weather conditions such as sunshine, shadows and poor
contrast, rain and reflection;

2. seasonal effects such as snow, ice and blow dust;

3. road design, edge and condition, painted line markers,
kerb-stones, grass or dust verges.

The solution of these problems greatly depends on the utilization of sensor and hardware or software filters [2]. We shall not
concentrate on that here.

The second problem is the problem of the calculation of the
curvature of the edge of a road. This is connected with the first
problem, and furthermore it is the second step in the navigation of
a vehicle and it follows the first step mentioned above.

In this paper we assume that the first problem is solved with
the help of some of the approaches which are suggested in the papers [3], [2]. After this we shall concentrate our attention on the
solution of the second problem. An approach for solving it is proposed in [2]. This method and all similar methods are elegant, but
they are slow and need a lot of computer power.

1) Institute of Mechanics and Biomechanics, Bulgarian Academy of
   Sciences, G. Bontchev str. Bl. 4, 1113 Sofia, Bulgaria
2) Institute of Technical Cybernetics, Slovak Academy of Sciences
   Dubravska cesta 9, 84237 BRATISLAVA, CSFR

Regularities which curves satisfied on the plane

Very excellent and elegant theoretical concepts in field of Regularities Structures in the book of prof. Grenander [1] are presented. But they are not efficient enough for application in real task. Definitions which have a good application in systems working in real time in the paper [4] are proposed.

Let $D = \{D_1,\ldots,D_k\}$ is a certain set of actions, and $S = \{S_1,\ldots,S_\ell\}$ is a set of conditions. Assuming N is a set of points in the plane.

Definition 1) We shall say, that N is regular with respect to (S_i, D_j), if every time when D_j is fulfilled, the points of N satisfy the condition S_i.

Let us assume that the set of action $D = \{D_1\}$, where D_1 is a next action: the moving of the line $x = \ell$ over the plane Oxz. Seven regularities in paper [6] are defined.

Now all curves in the plane, whose regularities satisfy can be defined (Figure 1).

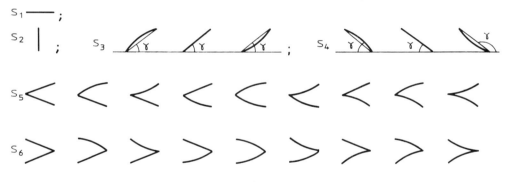

Figure 1

Definition 2) The regularity (S_i, D_j) is said to have changed at a point x, if (S_i, D_j) is satisfied until the point x-dx and at the point x, $(S_k, D_j) \neq (S_i, D_j)$.

Let us assume that we have a rectangular frame of the plane of the road. With the help of the following mapping:

$$\varphi : (x,y) \to (i,j), \text{ where}$$

$\left\lfloor \dfrac{x}{c} \right\rfloor = i$ $\left\lfloor \dfrac{y}{c} \right\rfloor = j$, and c is a step of the frame we can represent each curve from the plane over the vertices of the frame. For example, the curves which satisfy the regularity S_3 are mapped on the following configurations over the frame:

196

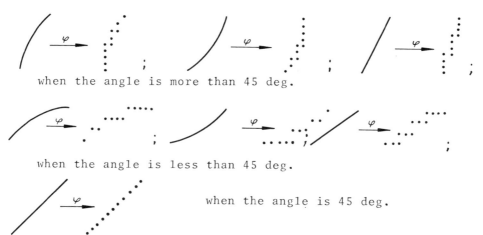

when the angle is more than 45 deg.

when the angle is less than 45 deg.

when the angle is 45 deg.

Figure 2

Independent Observer (IO)

Let us assume that there is an independent observer, who is tracking the movement of the curves point from the plane over the line x = ℓ, when this line is moving on the plane. In the beginning we shell formulate the criterions with the help of which the observer stop the moving line:

1. One or more nonzero regularities are changed [6].

2. d pillars which are zero, when the line moving over the plane.

3. The end of searching plane is found.

The conditions for which the independent observer must look are the following:

1. Direction of the movement of the point over the line

2. The shape of the segments with the help of which the movement over the line is realized: vertically $\vdots$, horizontally $\ldots\ldots$

3. The change of length of the segments with the help of which the movement over the line is realized:

decrement $\vdots$;   increment $\vdots$;   not change $\vdots$

Figure 3

With the help of the stop criterions and the conditions the indpendent observer can determine:

1. The type of regularities - from direction of movement of the point over the line - ↑ for S_3, ↓ for S_4, ↓↑ for S_5, ↑↓ for S_6, ≅ for S_1, O for S_2;

2. Angle γ - from the information of the shape of segments, and type of regularities.

3. The shape of the arc - convex, concave or straight line. The IO can make this conclusion from information of the type of regularities, angle γ, and change of length.

Let us define the next sequence:

$$e_1, e_2, \ldots, e_n, \ldots \qquad (1)$$

where the general element is $e_n = \{\mu_n,\ \nu_n,\ \ell_n\}$, where

μ_n is element from the set $\{\uparrow,\ \downarrow,\ \downarrow\uparrow,\ \uparrow\downarrow,\ \cong,\ O\}$;

ν_n is element from the set $\{V,\ H,\ VV,\ HH,\ VH,\ HV\}$, V - vertical, H - horizontal;

ℓ_n is element from the set $\{\ell_\uparrow,\ \ell_\downarrow,\ \ell_{\uparrow\uparrow},\ \ell_{\uparrow\downarrow},\ \ell_{\downarrow\uparrow},\ \ell_{\downarrow\downarrow}\}$. Here we assign with ℓ the length of the segment.

Each of the elements of the sequence corresponding to all points satisfying one and only one regularity.

$\uparrow, V, \ell_\downarrow$ - / ; $\uparrow, V, \ell_\uparrow$ - ╱ ;

$\uparrow, H, \ell_\downarrow$ - ╱ ; $\uparrow, H, \ell_\uparrow$ - ╱ ;

$\uparrow, V, \cong$ - / ; $\uparrow, H, \cong$ - ╱ ;

After all concepts expressed, we can conclude, that the edge of a road can be presented with the help of the sequence (1). And we are ready to formulate the following statements.

Statement 1. The point which connecting two neighborhood elements from sequence (1) is inflex point, when

$$\mu_i \equiv \mu_{i+1}, \qquad \ell_i \neq \ell_{i+1} \quad \text{and} \quad \ell_i, \ell_{i+1} \neq 0,\ \cong.$$

Statement 2. The curve which satisfy the regularities S_5 or S_6 is smooth if

$$\mu_i \equiv \downarrow\uparrow \quad \text{and} \quad \ell_i \equiv \ell_{\downarrow\downarrow} \quad \text{for}\quad S_5$$

$$\mu_i \equiv \uparrow\downarrow \quad \text{and} \quad \ell_i \equiv \ell_{\uparrow\uparrow} \quad \text{for}\quad S_6.$$

Calculation of the curvature

From all the formulated concepts and the statements it follows, that an independent observer can divide the edge of the road on straight lines and arcs which are presented on a figure 4.

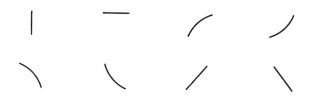

Figure 4

Now we can formulate the next statement.

Statement 3. Every arc which satisfies regularity S_3 or S_4 is arc from a circle.

For the calculation of the curvature of each arc we have to determine the circle redius. We can make this with the help of the theory of moments, and then

$$r^2 = \frac{\mu_{20} + \mu_{02}}{n} \tag{2}$$

where

$$\mu_{pq} = \int\limits_{+\infty}^{-\infty}\int (x - \frac{m_{10}}{m_{00}})^p \cdot (z - \frac{m_{01}}{m_{00}})^q \cdot g(x,z)\,dx.dz \tag{3}$$

and

$$m_{pq} = \int\limits_{+\infty}^{-\infty}\int x^p \cdot z^q \cdot g(x,z)\,dx.dz \tag{4}$$

n - is the number of the points.

With the help of the formulated concepts and FORTH language one version of program for calculation of the curvature of the edge of the road is created. The program using principles which are describe in [5]. The experiments with this program show the following results:

- recognition of regularitics and calculation of the sign of the curvature for 3-4 ms;
- calculation of radius of the circle for 8-10 ms;

working on the IBM personal computer, which have processor 80286. The time does not include perception of the date and determining of the road's edges.

Conclusion

In conclusion we can say that this method is not so exact as others, but it is faster than the others and allows working in real-time even with an IBM PC compatible personal computer.

This research is conducted for the guidance of vehicles in real time. For continuation of the research we need from sponsors.

R E F E R E N C E:

[1] Grenander U., "Regular Structures - Lectures in Pattern theory Volume III". Springer Verlag, New York, Heidelberg, Berlin, 1981.

[2] Kehtarnavaz N., Mohan S., "A Framework for the Estimation of Motion Parameters from Range Images", Computer Vision, Graphics and Image Processing, Vol. 45, 1989, pp. 88-105.

[3] Millios E., "Shape Matching Using Curvature Processes", Comp. Vision, Graphics and Image Processing Vol. 47, 1989, pp. 203-226.

[4] Sirakov N., Nedev N., "Approximation Analysis of Spatial Scenes with 3D Coordinates Data Obtained by Stereo Television Projection in Real Time", Computer Analysis of Images and Patterns, Mathematical Research, Vol. 55, Academie Verlag, Berlin, 1989, pp. 123-128, (Proc. of the III-rd Int. Conf. CAIP-89, Leipzig Germany, Sept. 8-10, 1989).

[5] Sirakov N., Dimitrov A., "Software application for recognition of 3D objects, represented as finite series of plane figures", Proc. of 6-th Cong. on Theor. and Appl. Mech., Varna, Bulgaria, 25-30.10.1989, Vol. 1, pp. 428-432.

[6] Sirakov N., "Application of regularities in pattern classification", Proc. on Int. Conf. "Mech. Appl. in Field of Robotics and new Materials", Sunny Beacg, 22-26.09.1988, pp. 309-315.

Multiresolution shape matching

Dmitry Chetverikov and Attila Lerch

Computer and Automation Institute,
Hungarian Academy of Sciences
Budapest P.O.Box 63
H-1518 HUNGARY

Abstract: Real-time recognition of planar shapes is usually based on either invariant shape features or contour matching. Contour matching is a precise but time-consuming operation. In this paper we present a simple but efficient multiresolution technique that considerably speeds up the process by using shape pyramids as an aid to matching. The proposed algorithm is tested with a large set of test shapes. Finally, the algorithm is compared to a composite shape recognition technique that combines a feature based pre-selector and a conventional contour matching algorithm.

1. Introduction.

This paper deals with rotation- and translation-invariant matching of planar shapes for recognition of flat objects represented by their complete contours. Matching is a precise but relatively time-consuming operation. Usually, it is used in applied two-dimensional object recognition systems when it is necessary to discriminate between similar planar shapes that cannot be reliably distinguished by their features such as area, invariant moments and the like.

Conventional approaches to contour matching are based on a comparison of two shape vectors for a range of orientations. Numerous shape vectors were proposed for flat object recognition. (See Pavlidis (1978) for a survey on shape representation.) In industrial applications, a shape is often represented by the distance between the centroid and the contour given as a function of angle. Yachida and Tsuji (1978) applied this method in an early machine vision system. The radial representation proved to be quite useful despite the fact that it can only be used when the radial function is single-valued.

The shape vectors are normally compared for the entire range of possible orientations. In some cases, the range can be reduced by using characteristic contour points or the orientation of the major axis of inertia, but generally the entire range is to be considered for rotation-invariant recognition. The number of operations required grows as N^2, where N is the number of contour points. If the shape set is large, or a high resolution is used, one might be interested in techniques that speed up the process of matching while preserving the classification accuracy. In particular, this applies to real-time industrial object recognition.

A variety of approaches to contour matching are described in literature. Many authors use structural matching based on specific structural features such as corners. Ballard and Brown (1982) discuss some of the structural matching methods. Neveu et.al (1986) apply a structural feature based multiresolution technique. The structural approaches are especially useful for recognition of incomplete or overlapping shapes. However, they are usually quite time-consuming. Another drawback is that most of them rely on contour features that are not easy to extract.

An alternative but somewhat similar approach is to use an approximation of the contour. Often, a polygon approximation is applied for this purpose (e.g. Cox et.al, 1989). A sophisticated method based on arcs and line segments was proposed by Mérő (1981). Such techniques are efficient if approximation conforms with typical contour features, otherwise they may be less robust than direct contour matching.

Mokhtarian and Mackworth (1986) applied the concept of scale-space introduced by Witkin (1983) to planar curves and two-dimensional shapes. In the scale-space, matching proceeds at varying levels of detail. Although theoretically attractive, this approach does not seem to be suitable for reliable real-time matching of a large set of shapes.

Yachida and Tsuji (1978) suggested using a shape feature based pre-selector prior to contour matching. In this pragmatic composite approach, a few shape features are used for preliminary classification thus significantly reducing the number of shapes involved in matching.

The goal of the present study is to apply a multiresolution approach in order to considerably speed up rotation-invariant matching of two-dimensional shapes without any noticeable loss in shape classification accuracy. The proposed matching technique can be efficiently used for real-time recognition of a large set of relatively simple, rigid shapes. This is supported by a test with more than fifty test shapes and an experimental comparison with the composite method by Yachida and Tsuji (1978).

2. The shape pyramid

The basic idea of the proposed algorithm is to apply a coarse-to-fine approach to a matching algorithm based on the radial representation of the contour. The concept of coarse-fine matching appeared in a study by Rosenfeld and Vanderbrug (1977) in a different context. Unlike Neveu et al (1986), we use direct, rather than structural, contour matching. The presented algorithm can be extended to other types of shape vectors as well. We select the straightforward radial representation because in this study the emphasis is laid on the concept of multiresolution matching rather than a particular shape description. For the sake of simplicity, the contours considered are assumed to have single-valued radial functions.

The radial representation of a planar shape contour is used to build a shape pyramid. A shape pyramid, which is a stack of contours of decreasing angular resolution, is obtained by a Gaussian filter followed by decimation, i.e. discarding every second contour point. This fast and effective procedure is analogous to the one proposed by Burt (1988) for image pyramids.

More specifically, let $R_0(i)$, $i=0,1,...,M-1$, be the original, full-resolution radial function of a closed contour. $R_0(i)$ is computed for M contour points defined by a sequence of rays cast from the centroid. The orientation of the i-th ray is $2\pi i/M$. $R_0(i)$ is the distance between the centroid and the intersection of the i-th ray and the contour. This function is processed by an approximation of the Gaussian filter applied by Burt (1988):

$$G = [1,4,6,4,1]/16 \tag{1}$$

The border points of the radial function are processed using a periodic extension of the function. Denote the resulting function by $G*R_0(i)$. After the Gaussian filtering, every second element of $G*R_0(i)$ is discarded to obtain a reduced-resolution contour $R_1(i)$, $i=0,1,...,M/2-1$.

The same two-step procedure is then applied to $R_1(i)$, etc. Finally, we obtain a shape pyramid which is a sequence of radial functions of decreasing angular resolution $R_k(i)$, $i=0,1,...,M/2^k-1$, where $k=0,1,...,K-1$ is the index of a pyramid level and K is the number of levels. The reduction factor of the shape pyramid is 2, hence the contour of the k-th level has $M/2^k$ points. A periodic extension of the functions is used for $i<0$ and $i>M/2^k-1$. Fig.1 shows examples of shape pyramids. Note that due to the Gaussian smoothing, all shapes tend to circles as k grows.

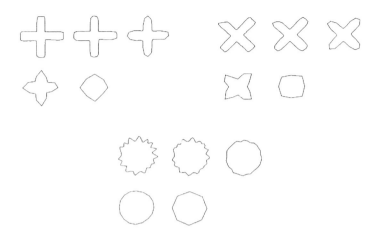

Fig.1. Examples of shape pyramids.

3. The matching algorithm

The sketch of the proposed matching algorithm is as follows. The algorithm matches a test shape against S reference shapes and finds the best matching reference shape. The shapes are represented by their shape pyramids. A measure of dissimilarity of two shape contours is introduced. The matching algorithm starts at the top level of the shape pyramid. At each level, the test shape is matched against reference shapes, and some of them are discarded. As matching proceeds top down, the decreasing number of the candidate reference shapes is controlled via a candidate reduction parameter. Only a few candidates remain at the base level of the pyramid where the final decision is always made. Because of the Gaussian smoothing, the difference between shapes decreases at low resolutions, therefore precautions are taken in order not to discard the true match. A tolerance parameter is introduced and certain candidate shapes are kept despite the reduction prescribed by the candidate reduction parameter.

More precisely, introduce a measure of dissimilarity of two contours A and B as

$$D(A,B) = \min_{m} \{ \sum_{i} (R^A(i)-R^B(i+m))^2 \}, \tag{2}$$

where $R^A(i)$ and $R^B(i)$ are the radial functions of A and B, respectively. At each level, the dissimilarity is computed between the test shape and all the remaining candidates. The values of D(A,B) are sorted. Applying the k-NN rule, a certain number of candidates with the least values of dissimilarity is selected for matching at a higher resolution. The rest of the candidates are discarded. Note that dissimilarity values computed at different levels are never compared.

A parameter FINCAND specifies the number of candidate reference shapes for the final decision at the base of the pyramid. This parameter determines the candidate reduction factor CANDREDUCT that defines the minimum number of candidate shapes for matching at each level of the pyramid. The relation between the two parameters is

$$S \geq FINCAND \cdot CANDREDUCT^{K-1} \tag{3}$$

If S is large enough, the minimum number of candidates at the k-th level is $S_k = S/FINCAND^{K-k-1}$. Otherwise, the algorithm may skip some of the levels unless the tolerance mechanism is activated.

The tolerance parameter TOLERANCE (%) defines the range of those shapes that are kept along with the S_k selected candidates. This is done if the dissimilarity of these shapes is within a tolerance limit from the level's lowest value D_{min}. In other words, a candidate shape passes a level if

$$D < D_{min}(1+TOLERANCE/100), \tag{4}$$

where D is the dissimilarity of the shape. The tolerance rule (4) is applied even if $S_k=0$, thus superseding the candidate reduction rule.

The final best match is selected from the candidates that arrive at the base level of the pyramid, as the shape with the minimum value of dissimilarity.

The matching algorithm has three variable parameters: the number of pyramid levels K, the minimum final decision set size FINCAND and the dissimilarity tolerance parameter TOLERANCE. K is limited by the basic contour resolution. Using large K means faster operation. However, discrimination of shapes becomes unreliable at high levels when many relevant features disappear because of the Gaussian filtering. Larger FINCAND and TOLERANCE improve classification accuracy at the cost of more computation.

4. Experimental results

Obviously, there is a tradeoff between the classification accuracy and the computational efficiency. The tradeoff depends on the values of the algorithm parameters. This section is devoted to classification experiments with two different sets of test shapes. The goal of the first experiment is to investigate how the classification accuracy and the execution time of the proposed matching algorithm depend on its parameters. We will demonstrate that by tuning the parameters it is possible to significantly reduce the execution time while preserving the classification accuracy.

Matching at the higher levels of a shape pyramid may be viewed as a pre-selection for the final decision-making at the base of the pyramid. The first test also compares the proposed multiresolution method to a conventional uniresolution matching algorithm preceded by a feature based pre-selector (Yachida and Tsuji, 1978). The second experiment shows that for certain tasks the proposed method may be preferable to the composite one. The programs were written in C and run on an IBM PC AT 286/12. Neither of the programs was optimized.

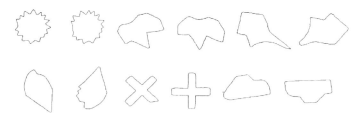

Fig.2. Some of the test shapes used in the first test.

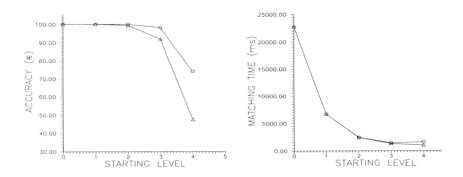

Fig.3. FINCAND=2; TOLERANCE: ▲=0, ▢=80.   Fig.4. See Fig.3.

First test

This extensive classification experiment used a set of 54 test shapes. (See Fig.2.) In this set, 26 shapes were included together with their slightly modified versions in order to test the discriminating power of the algorithms. The shapes were presented to the recognition system using a CCD camera and a frame grabber. The shape images were digitized to 256x256 size matrices and their contours extracted. The radial functions were computed and normalized so as to have a uniform mean value. This was done to exclude shape discrimination based on size. The shape pyramids were built with the base resolution of 128 points, which corresponds to the angular resolution of about 2.8°. Each of the 54 shapes was presented in 4 different positions and orientations. One of the 4 images was used as a reference, the other 3 were used as test samples. Totally, there were 54 reference shapes and 162 test shapes.

The main results of the first test are demonstrated in Figs.3-10. Figs.3 and 4 refer to the proposed multiresolution method only, while the other six compare the new algorithm to the composite one. In the latter case, the curves related to the composite method are shown dashed.

Fig.3 illustrates the dependence of the classification accuracy of the proposed algorithm on the number of pyramid levels K. In practice, the shape pyramids had the same number of levels (five),

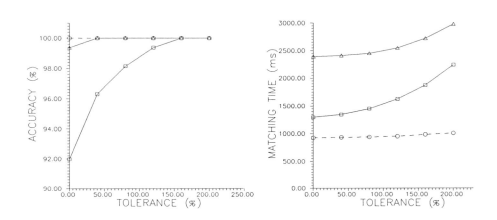

Fig.5. FINCAND=2;   Fig.6. See Fig.5.
      starting level:▲=2, ▢=3, O=composite

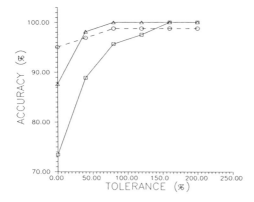
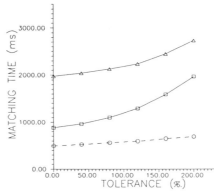

Fig.7. FINCAND=1. See Fig.5.   Fig.8. FINCAND=1. See Fig.5.

but the process of matching was initiated at a varying level called a starting level. Zero starting level corresponds to conventional uniresolution matching that yields 100% accuracy. The accuracy falls when the starting level exceeds 3. This is a limiting value for the given spatial and angular resolution. Note that there is a considerable difference between the zero and the nonzero tolerance curve.

Fig.4 shows a plot of matching time as a function of the starting level. Matching time is the mean processor time per classified shape. This does not include the time needed to compute the radial function and the pyramid (or the features in the composite method) because this time is negligible compared to the matching time. The plot shows a drastic decrease of execution time when the multi-resolution approach is used.

The remaining plots compare the proposed algorithm to the composite one. In the composite approach, the features used for pre-selection were the shape factor (perimeter^2/area) and two invariant moments (e.g. Pavlidis, 1978). These features are often applied in practical object recognition systems. The shapes were pre-classified using a k-NN technique. The normalized distance between a test feature vector $F_t(j)$ and a reference feature vector $F_r(j)$, $j=0,1,2$, was defined as

$$\text{DIST}(F_t, F_r) = \sum_j \frac{|F_t(j) - F_r(j)|}{|F_t(j) + F_r(j)|} \tag{5}$$

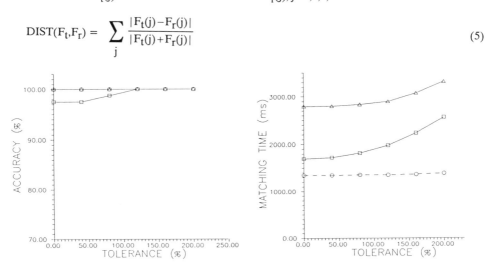

Fig.9. FINCAND=3. See Fig.5.   Fig.10 . FINCAND=3. See Fig.5.
(Δ and O coincide)

CAIP'91

In the case of the composite approach, the parameters FINCAND and TOLERANCE have the same meaning as for the multiresolution algorithm.

Fig.5 is an accuracy versus tolerance plot for FINCAND=2. This value proved to be optimal for both algorithms. It is easy to tune both algorithms to reach 100% classification accuracy. The matching time of the two approaches is similar. (See Fig.6.) It is reduced by a factor of 10 compared to conventional matching. The composite method is slightly faster and less sensitive to the setting of the tolerance parameter.

Finally, we investigated the influence of the FINCAND parameter. If FINCAND=1 (Figs.7 and 8), the difference between the two algorithms grows, but both become less accurate. Clearly, it is not advisable to force the algorithms to make the final decision without full-resolution matching. Notice that the accuracy of the feature-based pre-selector is 95%. When FINCAND=3 (Figs.9 and 10), the difference between the two techniques diminishes. The algorithms become more reliable at the cost of more computation.

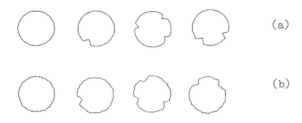

(a)

(b)

Fig.11. The original (a) and noisy (b) shapes used in second test.

Second test

A small set of 4 similar test shapes was considered. Noise was added to the contours of the test shapes. The original and the noisy shapes are shown in Fig.11. The original ones served as training patterns while the noisy ones were used as test samples. Each noisy shape was presented and classified in 5 different positions. In other words, teaching was done in much better conditions than recognition. This situation is realistic, especially when teaching is based on a CAD representation of the objects.

The proposed algorithm was able to reliably classify the test shapes while the composite technique failed. The multiresolution approach reached 100% classification accuracy if the starting level was 2 or less, in the whole considered range of the other two parameters. In the considered range of the parameters, the maximum accuracy of the composite method was 90%. To reach 100% accuracy, one had to increase FINCAND or TOLERANCE to such an extent that the pre-selector was of no use, since all the reference shapes were matched. This solution was more than 3 times slower than the multiresolution algorithm.

The superior performance of the proposed approach in the case of noisy shapes is partly explained by the Gaussian filtering that makes the method more robust. It is likely that the performance of the composite method can be improved by selecting other features which are less sensitive to noise. However, selection of the optimal set of features is, in general, a non-trivial task while the proposed approach uses a uniform and straightforward technique.

Conclusion

We have presented a method of using a contour pyramid as an aid to planar shape matching. It has been experimentally demonstrated that the proposed technique is computationally more efficient than conventional uniresolution matching. The difference may be essential for some real-time problems, e.g. in industrial recognition of large sets of objects.

The new technique has also been compared to another, composite method of speeding up the matching process. Although the performance of the composite method depends on the choice and the number of features, the experiments still provide useful information for a comparison of the two algorithms. The tests have shown that the accuracy and the execution time of the algorithms are typically similar. However, in certain situations the proposed technique may be preferable as straightforward and more robust.

Acknowledgement

This work was supported by a Director's Grant of Computer and Automation Institute.

References

Ballard, D.H. and C.M.Brown. (1982). Computer Vision. Prentice-Hall, Englewood Cliffs, NJ.

Burt, P.J. (1988). Smart Sensing within a Pyramid Vision Machine. Proc. of the IEEE, 76, 1006-1015.

Cox, P., H.Maitre, M.Minoux and C.Ribeiro (1989). Optimal matching of convex polygons. Pattern Recognition Letters, 9, 327-334.

Mérő, L. (1981). An algorithm for scale- and rotation-invariant recognition of two-dimensional objects. Computer Graphics and Image Processing, 15, 279-287.

Mokhtarian, F. and A.Mackworth (1986). Scale-Based Description and Recognition of Planar Curves and Two-Dimensional Shapes. IEEE Trans. Pattern Anal. Machine Intell. 8, 34-43.

Neveu, C.F., C.R.Dyer and R.T.Chin (1986). Two-dimensional Object Recognition Using Multiresolution Models. Computer Vision, Graphics, and Image Processing, 34, 52-65.

Pavlidis, T. (1978). A Review of Algorithms for Shape Analysis. Computer Graphics Image Processing, 7, 243-258.

Rosenfeld, A. and G.J.Vanderbrug (1977). Coarse-Fine Template Matching. IEEE Trans. Systems, Man, and Cybernetics, February, 104-107.

Witkin, A.P. (1983). Scale space filtering. Proc. 8th Internat. Joint Conf. on Artificial Intelligence, Karlsruhe, Germany, 1019-1022.

Yachida, M. and S.Tsuji (1977). A Versatile Machine Vision System for Complex Industrial Parts. IEEE Trans. Computers, 9, 882-894.

A NEW APPROACH TO CONSTRUCTING EXACT TESTS FOR DISCRIMINATION BETWEEN MODELS FROM SEPARATE FAMILIES OF HYPOTHESES

N. A. Nechval [1)]

INTRODUCTION

Let X be a real random variable having a distribution function F_θ, a member of a parametric family $\underline{F} = \{F_\theta : \theta \in \theta^\circ\}$ where θ° is a parameter space. It will be assumed that every member of the family has a density function f_θ (with respect to a dominating 6 - finite measure) so that the family may be described equivalently as $\underline{f} = \{f_\theta : \theta \in \theta^\circ\}$. Based on a random sample, $X_1, \ldots, X_n$, we would like to choose between the two hypotheses

H_1 : $X_1, \ldots, X_n$ was sampled from f_1

H_2 : $X_1, \ldots, X_n$ was sampled from f_2 $\hspace{2cm}$ (1)

where $f_1 \in \underline{f}_1 = \{f_{\theta_1} : \theta_1 \in \theta_1^\circ\}$, and $f_2 \in \underline{f}_2 = \{f_{\theta_2} : \theta_2 \in \theta_2^\circ\}$; $\underline{f}_1$ and $\underline{f}_2$ are assumed separate, i.e., an arbitrary member of one parametric family cannot be obtained as the limit of members of the other.

In a pair of articles Cox [3,4] considers this problem from the hypothesis testing viewpoint, where H_1 is taken as the null hypothesis and a value for the Type I error is fixed, and H_2 is used to indicate the type of alternative for which high power is required. For this approach he develops a large sample procedure based on the Neyman-Pearson likelihood ratio. These results are developed further by Jackson [5]. In the case of the hypothesis testing approach one generally has a preference for one of the two families (at the given significance level) and does not wish to accept the alternative unless the evidence in support of the alternative is fairly strong. The reason that one may prefer to deal with this problem from this point of view rather than the usual goodness-of-fit approach is that one may not wish to reject the null hypothesis model without an alternative model to take its place. In addition, one may not wish to perform a standard goodness-of-fit test, simply because such tests, as this study indicates, have lower power than procedures which take account of a specific alternative.

Atkinson [1] considers the problem (1) from the discrimination viewpoint. In this approach the two hypotheses are treated symme-

[1)] The author is with the Department of Control Systems, Civil
Aviation Engineers Institute, Lomonosov Street 1,
SU-226019 Riga,
U S S R

trically, i.e., $\alpha = \beta$, where α is the probability of rejecting the hypothesis H_1 when H_1 is true, and β is the probability of accepting H_1 when H_2 is true; in other words, we deal (in this case) with the equal probability test [8].

The above problem can be also considered from the viewpoint of minimizing the risk, or equivalently ($\alpha + \beta$), i.e., we deal, in this case, with the discrimination procedure which minimizes ($\alpha + \beta$).

In this paper a procedure is developed to construct exact tests for composite hypotheses. It is based on conditioning a likelihood function of the sample observations X_1, ... ,X_n on a sufficient statistic. The obtained result is then used to construct parameter-free tests. A number of procedures have been proposed for this problem. Possibly the best known is the procedure of Lehmann [6] for the problem in which the two models have unknown location and scale parameters. Lehmann has given the most powerful invariant test for discriminating between them. The procedure proposed in the present paper is not restricted to the case where $\underline{f}_1$ and $\underline{f}_2$ are location-scale families. It is relatively easy to apply and opens the way for finding solutions in the presence of small samples of the data.

TEST CONSTRUCTING PROCEDURE

In defining a procedure of constructing exact tests for discrimination between models, we must define both a test statistic and a decision rule indicating the action to be taken for each observed data sample $X^n = (X_1, \ldots, X_n)$.

The test statistic for the discrimination procedure from the hypothesis testing viewpoint (H_1 versus H_2) is the conditional likelihood ratio given by

$$W(X^n) = p_2(X_1, \ldots, X_{n-k}; T_n^{(2)})/p_1(X_1, \ldots, X_{n-k}; T_n^{(1)}), \qquad (2)$$

where

$$p_i(x_1, \ldots, x_{n-k}; t_n^{(i)}) = f_i(x_1, \ldots, x_{n-k}, t_n^{(i)}; \theta_i)/g_i(t_n^{(i)}; \theta_i),$$

$$i = 1, 2, \qquad (3)$$

is the probability density function of X_1, ... ,X_{n-k}, conditional on $T_n^{(i)} = t_n^{(i)}$, $T_n^{(i)}$ is a sufficient statistic for the family $\underline{f}_i = \{f_{\theta_i} : \theta_i \in \Theta_i^\circ\}$, $f_i(x_1, \ldots, x_{n-k}, t_n^{(i)}; \theta_i)$ is the joint density function of X_1, ... ,X_{n-k}, $T_n^{(i)}$, k ($1 \leq k < n$) is a minimum number of observations required for constructing a sufficient statistic

210

for $\underline{f}_i$, $g_i(t_n^{(i)};\theta_i)$ is a density function of a sampling distribution of $T_n^{(i)}$, $\theta_i \in \theta_i^\circ$.

Let $\emptyset(X^n)$ be a decision rule, where $\emptyset(X^n)$ is defined to be the probability of rejecting H_1 after observing $X^n=(X_1, \dots ,X_n)$. If the problem of discrimination between $\underline{f}_1$ and $\underline{f}_2$ is considered from the viewpoint of the most powerful test, then a decision rule is given by

$$\emptyset(X^n) = \begin{cases} 1 & \text{if } W(X^n) > C(T_n^{(1)},T_n^{(2)}) \\ à(T_n^{(1)},T_n^{(2)}) & \text{if } W(X^n) = C(T_n^{(1)},T_n^{(2)}) \\ 0 & \text{if } W(X^n) < C(T_n^{(1)},T_n^{(2)}) \end{cases} \quad (4)$$

where $C(T_n^{(1)},T_n^{(2)})$ and $à(T_n^{(1)},T_n^{(2)})$ are uniquely determined by

$$E_{H_1}(\emptyset(X^n);T_n^{(1)},T_n^{(2)}) = \alpha \quad (5)$$

and the following theorem holds true.

Theorem 1. The decision rule (4) represents a conditional test of size α of H_1 against H_2 which is most powerful for each $(T_n^{(1)},T_n^{(2)})=(t_n^{(1)},t_n^{(2)})$.

Proof. The proof is an immediate consequence of applying the Neyman-Pearson lemma to the conditional densities p_1 and p_2.

Corollary. If $T_n^{(i)}$ is a complete sufficient statistic for $\underline{f}_i$, a sampling distribution (under H_i) of the test statistic $W(X^n)$ does not depend on unknown parameter θ_i, $i=1,2$, then the decision rule (4) is reduced to

$$\emptyset(X^n) = \begin{cases} 1 & \text{if } W(X^n) > C \\ à & \text{if } W(X^n) = C \\ 0 & \text{if } W(X^n) < C \end{cases} \quad (6)$$

where C and $à$ are uniquely determined by

$$E_{H_1}(\emptyset(X^n)) = \alpha . \quad (7)$$

Proof. The proof is an immediate consequence of Basu's theorem [2] and Theorem 1.

The test that results from Corollary is referred to as the most powerful parameter-free test of size α of H_1 against H_2.

If the problem of discrimination between $\underline{f}_1$ and $\underline{f}_2$ is considered from the viewpoint of the equal probability test, then the parameters C and $à$ of the decision rule (6) are chosen so that $\alpha = \beta$.

If the above problem is considered from the viewpoint of the minimum risk test, then the following theorem holds true.

Theorem 2. The decision rule which minimizes the risk, or equivalently ($\alpha + \beta$), is determined as follows: given the sample X^n, choose H_i if

$$p_{H_i}(w) \geq p_{H_j}(w), \quad i,j=1,2, \ i \neq j, \tag{8}$$

where $p_{H_i}(w)$ is the probability density function of the test statistic $W = W(X^n)$ under H_i.

Proof. The proof is similar to that of Theorem 4.2.1 [7].

EXAMPLE

Let $X^n = (X_1, \ldots, X_n)$ be a random sample of independently and identically distributed random variables with density $f(x;\theta) \in \underline{f}_1$ or $f(x;\theta) \in \underline{f}_2$ where

$$\underline{f}_1 = \left\{ f_1(x;\theta_1) = 1/(b-a), \ x \in (a,b) \colon \theta_1 = (a,b), \ a,b \in R^1 \right\}, \tag{9}$$

and

$$\underline{f}_2 = \left\{ f_2(x;\theta_2) = (1/b)\exp(-(x-a)/b), \ x \in (a,\infty) \colon \theta_2 = (a,b), \right.$$
$$\left. a \in R^1, \ b \in R_+^1 \right\}. \tag{10}$$

The problem considered is that of selecting either $\underline{f}_1$ or $\underline{f}_2$ as the model for X^n. To obtain the test for this problem in a closed form we now evaluate p_1 and p_2. Let $X_{(1)} < X_{(2)} < \cdots < X_{(n)}$ be order statistics of X^n. It is easy to show that

$$p_1(x_{(2)}, \ \cdots, x_{(n-1)}; x_{(1)}, x_{(n)}) = \Gamma(n-1)/(x_{(n)} - x_{(1)})^{n-2}, \tag{11}$$

and

$$p_2(x_{(2)}, \ \cdots, x_{(n-1)}; x_{(1)}, \sum_{i=2}^n (x_{(i)} - x_{(1)}))$$
$$= \Gamma(n)\Gamma(n-1)/(\sum_{i=2}^n (x_{(i)} - x_{(1)}))^{n-2}. \tag{12}$$

In the test of uniformity ($H_1 : f \in \underline{f}_1$) against exponentiality ($H_2 : f \in \underline{f}_2$) the most powerful parameter-free test rejects H_1 if

$$W_u = \sum_{i=2}^n (X_{(i)} - X_{(1)})/(X_{(n)} - X_{(1)}) < C_u. \tag{13}$$

The density of W_u under the assumption of uniformity is

$$q_u(w_u) = (1/\Gamma(n-2)) \sum_{j=0}^{n-2} (-1)^j \binom{n-2}{j} (w_u - (j+1))_+^{n-3},$$
$$w_u \in (1, n-1), \tag{14}$$

where $d_+ = \max(0,d)$, that implies the distribution function of W_u,

$$Q_u(w_u) = \Pr(W_u < w_u)$$
$$= (1/\Gamma(n-1)) \sum_{j=0}^{n-2} (-1)^j \binom{n-2}{j} (w_u - (j+1))_+^{n-2}. \tag{15}$$

In the test of exponentiality ($H_2 : f \in \underline{f}_2$) against uniformity ($H_1 : f \in \underline{f}_1$) the most powerful parameter-free test rejects H_2 if

$$W_e = (X_{(n)} - X_{(1)}) / \sum_{i=2}^{n} (X_{(i)} - X_{(1)}) < c_e. \tag{16}$$

The density of W_e under the assumption of exponentiality is

$$q_e(w_e) = (n-1)(n-2) \sum_{j=0}^{n-2} (-1)^j \binom{n-2}{j} (1 - (j+1)w_e)_+^{n-3},$$

$$w_e \in (1/(n-1), 1). \tag{17}$$

Hence the distribution function of W_e is

$$Q_e(w_e) = \Pr(W_e < w_e)$$

$$= 1 - (n-1) \sum_{j=0}^{n-2} (-1)^j \binom{n-2}{j} \frac{1}{j+1} (1 - (j+1)w_e)_+^{n-2}. \tag{18}$$

To illustrate the tests described above, we consider the data taken from Shapiro and Wilk [9] where the following are the ordered 14 times between failures from a demonstration test of a sonar system: 15.25, 22.16, 32.62, 63.97, 65.65, 69.80, 85.80, 98.38, 113.07, 138.38, 154.06, 167.83, 180.90, 284.69. In the evaluation of these data, we have that

$$w_u = 4.76, \quad q_u(w_u) = 0.03, \quad Q_u(w_u) = 0.01, \tag{19}$$

and

$$w_e = 0.21, \quad q_e(w_e) = 7.17, \quad Q_e(w_e) = 0.34. \tag{20}$$

If the discrimination problem is considered from the viewpoint of the most powerful test (at the given significance level α), then the hypothesis of uniformity ($H_1 : f \in \underline{f}_1$) can be rejected at the significance level of more than 1% (if $H_1 \equiv H_0$), and the hypothesis of exponentiality ($H_2 : f \in \underline{f}_2$) can be rejected at the significance level of more than 34% (if $H_2 \equiv H_0$).

If the discrimination problem is considered either from the viewpoint of the equal probability test or from the viewpoint of the minimum risk test, then the data provide strong basis, from this analysis, to accept the hypothesis of exponentiality H_2.

In addition to the case discussed above, consider incomplete data situation which arises naturally in many fields, for example, life-testing. Suppose $X_r < X_{r+1} < \cdots < X_s$, $1 \le r < s \le n$, denote the order statistics of a doubly censored sample corresponding to a complete sample ($r=1$, $s=n$) of size n. It can be shown that

$$W_u = (\sum_{i=r}^{s} (X_i - X_r) + (n-s)(X_s - X_r)) / (X_s - X_r) \quad \text{and} \quad W_e = W_u^{-1} \tag{21}$$

are the test statistics with the probability density functions

$$q_u(w_u) = \frac{1}{\Gamma(s-r-1)} \sum_{j=0}^{s-r-1} (-1)^j \binom{s-r-1}{j} (w_u - (j+n-s+1))_+^{s-r-2},$$

$$w_u \in (n-s+1, n-r), \qquad (22)$$

and

$$q_e(w_e) = \frac{\Gamma(n-r+1)}{\Gamma(s-r-1)\Gamma(n-s+1)} \sum_{j=0}^{s-r-1} (-1)^j \binom{s-r-1}{j} (1-(j+n-s+1)w_e)_+^{s-r-2},$$

$$w_e \in (1/(n-r), 1/(n-s+1)), \qquad (23)$$

respectively.

LITERATURE

[1] Atkinson, A.C.: A method of discriminating between models. J.R.Statist. Soc., Series B, 32 (1970), 3, 323-345.
[2] Basu, D.: On statistics independent of a complete sufficient statistic. Sankhya 15 (1955), 377-380.
[3] Cox, D.R.: Tests of separate families of hypotheses. Proceedings of the Fourth Berkeley Symposium, Vol. 1, Berkeley: University of California Press, 1961, 105-123.
[4] Cox, D.R.: Further results on tests of separate families of hypotheses. J.R.Statist. Soc., Series B, 24 (1962),2, 406-424.
[5] Jackson, O.A.Y.: Some results on tests of separate families of hypotheses. Biometrika 55 (1968), 2, 355-363.
[6] Lehmann, E.L.: Testing Statistical Hypotheses. John Wiley and Sons, New York 1959.
[7] Nechval, N.A.: Detection of a change in a sequence of images based on the free statistics. SPIE Proceedings of the Technical Conference on Visual Communications and Image Processing, Vol. 1199, Philadelphia, Pennsylvania USA, 5-10 November 1989, Paper No. 1199-141, 12 pages.
[8] Nechval, N.A.: The equal probability test and optimal allocation of subjects to the groups when comparing a new drug and a placebo. Cybernetics and Systems: An International Journal 21 (1990), 503-512.
[9] Shapiro,S.S. and M.B. Wilk: An analysis of variance test for the exponential distribution (complete samples). Technometrics 14 (1972), 2, 355-370.

Fast Algorithm for Computing the Fractal Dimension of Binary Images

Reiner Creutzburg & Adolf Mathias

University of Karlsruhe
Faculty of Informatics
Institute of Algorithms and Cognitive Systems
P. O. Box 6980
D-7500 Karlsruhe 1
Phone: (+49)-721-608 4325
Fax: (+49)-721-696893

June 24, 1991

Methods for determining fractal dimensions of image objects have gained importance in recent developments of image processing [1-7]. Mainly for the classification of shape and textures of natural objects the fractal dimension has proven its usefulness [2-3,5-7].

The fractal dimension D of a set A in a metric space is defined by [1]

$$D = \lim_{\epsilon \to 0} \frac{\log(\mathcal{N}(A, \epsilon))}{\log \frac{1}{\epsilon}} \tag{1}$$

where $\mathcal{N}(A, \epsilon)$ denotes the smallest number of closed balls of radius $\epsilon > 0$ needed to cover the set A.

The aim of this paper is to introduce a new fast algorithm for computing the fractal dimension of binary images according to (1).

Consider a binary image that is represented as a matrix of binary pixels stored in a rectangular array $I(x, y)$. Let this image denote a subset of the set of all pixels in the plane.

In order to compute the fractal dimension of a digitized image, it is necessary to cover the set with the "balls" mentioned above. When processing binary images, it is convenient to use squares in place of the balls. This simplification allows a considerable speedup of the set's covering.

As an approximation to the covering of the set, we choose the "Minkowski sausages" [6] (see fig. 1). The fractal dimension can be computed by measuring the area covered by the Minkowski sausages with increasing radius ϵ.

The results of each step and the corresponding numbers of pixels are collected in a Richardson-Mandelbrot-plot giving the fractal dimension of the original image [2,3,6].

The main problem is the efficient computation of the Minkowski sausage with a certain radius.

A naive solution is obtained by simple shift operations and logical OR of the original and the shifted image. This has to be done for all shift offsets contained in the square with given radius ϵ leading to a number of $(2\epsilon + 1)^2 - 1$ shift- and OR-operations per ϵ-value.

An improvement can be obtained by an inductive approach for the determination of the Minkowski sausage of radius $\epsilon + 1$ when the Minkowski sausage of radius ϵ is given.

This can be done because all raster points of distance ϵ automatically lie in the environment with radius $\epsilon + 1$. Thus, the Minkowski sausage of radius $\epsilon + 1$ is obtained by simply adding the pixels with distance ϵ from the center to the Minkowski sausage with radius ϵ.

Instead of adding the pixels with distance $\epsilon + 1$ one by one, we can use the fact that every point in the Minkowski sausage with radius ϵ around a point is the result of an OR-operation of the center point with all points in its ϵ-environment. For increasing ϵ, we can OR the current image with shifted versions of itself instead of the original image. By this, we obtain increased Minkowski sausages with a constant number of operations for each step, applying logical OR on the current image and its shifts by all the steps between a point and the points in its neighborhood.

From the neighbourhood definition the shape of the ϵ-environment is derived. We used the well known maximum or chessboard metric. The use of this neighbourhood implies the OR-operation of each image with 8 shifted versions of itself analogous to the 8 points in each point's neighbourhood.

A further improvement can be made by a logical OR-operation of the image with its up- and down-shifts followed by the OR-operation of this new image with its right- and left-shifts. By this, the 8 shift-and-OR-operations per ϵ-increase can be reduced to 4 operations.

For the utilisation of the fractal dimension in shape recognition it is often necessary to consider the fractal dimension of the boundaries of binary objects instead of the objects themselves. For this purpose, a common edge detection operator has to be used before computing the fractal dimension.

A lot of practical examples (see figures 2-6) have been considered showing a good correspondence (see table 1) between the theoretical fractal dimension values D_{theor}, the fractal dimensions D_{mink} measured with the described algorithm and a standard algorithm [6] based on the grid dimension D_{grid}.

Fig. 1: Minkowski sausages of a binary object of fractal dimension 1.5

	D_{theor}	D_{grid}	D_{mink}
Test image 1	1.262	1.232	1.234
Test image 2	1.500	1.470	1.465
Test image 3	1.613	1.580	1.594
Test image 4	1.625	1.613	1.607
Test image 5	1.785	1.773	1.761

Table 1: Comparison of the fractal dimensions obtained by the two algorithms and the theoretical value

References

[1] Barnsley, M.: *Fractals Everywhere*. Academic Press: New York 1988

[2] Creutzburg, R; E. Ivanov: *Fast algorithm for computing fractal dimensions of image segments*. (in: V. Cantoni; R. Creutzburg; S. Levialdi; G. Wolf: *Recent Issues in Pattern Analysis and Recognition*. Springer: Lecture Notes in Computer Science **399** (1989), pp. 42-51

[3] Creutzburg, R; E. Ivanov: *Increasing the accuracy of fractal dimension computed from the Richardson-Mandelbrot-plot*. Proc. Intern. Conf. "Fractals '90", Lisboa 1990 (in print)

[4] Flook, A. G.: *The characterization of textured and structured particle profiles by the automated measurement of their fractal dimension*. Proc. Partikel-Technologie Nürnberg 24-26.IX.1979, pp. 591-600

[5] Keller, J. M.; R. M. Crownover; R. Y. Chen: *Characteristics of natural scenes related to the fractal dimension*. IEEE Trans. Patt. Analysis Mach. Intell. **PAMI-9** (1987), No. 5, pp. 621-627

[6] Mandelbrot, B. B.: *The Fractal Geometry of Nature*. W. H. Freeman: San Francisco 1982

[7] Pentland, A. P.: *Fractal based description of natural scenes*. IEEE Trans. Patt. Analysis Mach. Intell. **PAMI-6** (1984), No. 6, pp. 661-674

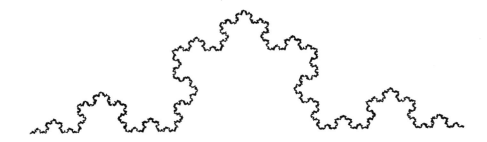

Fig. 2: Test image 1 with $D_{theor.} = 1.262$

Fig. 3: Test image 2 with $D_{theor.} = 1.5$

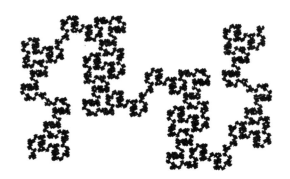

Fig. 4: Test image 3 with $D_{theor.} = 1.613$

Fig. 5: Test image 4 with $D_{theor.} = 1.625$

Fig. 6: Test image 5 with $D_{theor.} = 1.785$

A METRIC FOR COMPARING ATTRIBUTED RELATIONAL MODELS

Stephan Frydrychowicz *

Abstract

In this paper we want to present a general distance measure for matching attributed relational models. Such models are used in threedimesional computer vision. It can be shown that this distance measure is a pseudometric or a metric according to its assumptions. This fact is important for clustering if there is a great collection of models to compare with an object which was segmented in a picture for instance (s. [sha82]).

This general distance measure includes the best known metrics for matching attributed graphs or relational models. We will show that this distance measure includes the metric of [sha85] as a special case.

Relational models

First we will give a short definition of relational models, then we will present the general distance measure, for which we prove that it is a pseudometric or a metric. We will show how comprehensive this definition is by giving an example.

The following terms and basic definitions of relational models will be used.

Def. 1 (Relational model) *An attributed relational model* $(M; R_1, \ldots, R_k)$ *is a finite set* M *with a collection* $R_1, \ldots, R_k$ *of attributed i-ary relations* $R_i : M^i \to W_i$, *where* W_i *is the space of attributes.*

Remark: Instead of Relations $\hat{R} \subset M^i$ and attributes $\alpha : \hat{R} \to \hat{W}$ we use the characterization above. We can recast this by:

$$W_i = \hat{W} \cup \{(\text{nil})\}, \quad R_i : M^i \to W_i$$

$$R_i(m_1, \ldots, m_i) = \begin{cases} \alpha(m_1, \ldots, m_i) & : \quad (m_1, \ldots, m_i) \in \hat{R} \\ \\ (\text{nil}) & : \quad otherwise \end{cases}$$

In order to compare two models $(M; R_1, \ldots, R_k)$ and $(P; S_1, \ldots, S_k)$ we have to associate elements $m \in M$ with mates $p \in P$ first.

---

*Universität Erlangen-Nürnberg, Lehrstuhl für Informatik 5 (Mustererkennung) D-8520 Erlangen

Def. 2 (Association) *An association $f \subset M \times P$ is a relation with the following properties:*

$$(m,p) \in f \wedge (m',p) \in f \;\Rightarrow\; m = m'$$
$$(m,p) \in f \wedge (m,p') \in f \;\Rightarrow\; p = p'$$

We need the following abbreviations for a compact description:

Def. 3 (Common abbreviations) *For associations $f \subset M \times P$, $g \subset M \times Q$ and $h \subset Q \times P$ we define the sets $M_f \subset M$, $P_f \subset P$ and the associations $f^T \subset P \times M$, $h \circ g \subset M \times P$ by*

$$
\begin{aligned}
M_f &= \{m \in M \mid \exists p \in P : (m,p) \in f\} \\
P_f &= \{p \in P \mid \exists m \in M : (m,p) \in f\} \\
f^T &= \{(p,m) \mid (m,p) \in f\} \\
h \circ g &= \{(m,p) \mid \exists q \in Q : (m,q) \in g \wedge (q,p) \in h\}
\end{aligned}
$$

Given such an association, we have to weight the differences of all pairs R_i, S_i. This procedure will be described in the next section.

The General Distance Measure

We assume that for every element $m \in M$ and $p \in P$ we have costs $\mu(m), \mu(p) \in \mathbb{R}$, which will give an assessment of the case where m resp. p has no mate in the association. Further we assume that for every attribute space W_i a real function $\delta_i : W_i \times W_i \to \mathbb{R}$ is given. Later δ_i will be assumed to be a metric or a pseudometric. Now we define the costs $\eta_f(m')$ for each element $m' \in M_f$. We distinguish two versions and use the abbreviations $r_i = R_i(m', \ldots, m^{(i)})$ and $s_i = S_i(f(m'), \ldots, f(m^{(i)}))$.

version1	version2
$\delta_f'(m') = \delta_1(r_1, s_i)$	$\delta_f'(m') = \delta_1(r_1, s_i)$
$\delta_f^{(i)}(m') = \displaystyle\max_{m'', \ldots, m^{(i)} \in M_f} \{\delta_i(r_i, s_i)\}$	$\delta_f^{(i)}(m') = \displaystyle\sum_{m'', \ldots, m^{(i)} \in M_f} \delta_i(r_i, s_i)$
$\eta_f(m') = \displaystyle\max_{i=1, \ldots, k} \{\delta_f^{(i)}(m')\}$	$\eta_f(m') = \displaystyle\sum_{i=1, \ldots, k} \delta_f^{(i)}(m')$

Def. 4 (Weighting an association) *With these costs $\eta_f(m), \mu(m)$ and $\mu(p)$ we calculate the error of the association $f \subset M \times P$ by*

$$E_f(M,P) = \sum_{m \in M_f} \eta_f(m) \;+\; \sum_{m \in M \setminus M_f} \mu(m) \;+\; \sum_{p \in P \setminus P_f} \mu(p)$$

Def. 5 (General distance measure) *Now we define the distance of two relational models* $(M; R_1, \ldots, R_k)$ *and* $(P; S_1, \ldots, S_k)$ *with* $R_i : M^i \to W_i$ *and* $S_i : P^i \to W_i$:

$$E(M, P) = \min_{\substack{f \subseteq M \times P \\ association}} \{E_f(M, P)\}$$

Lemma (E is a metric/pseudometric)

Assertion:

1. If all (W_i, δ_i) are pseudometric spaces and $\mu = const \geq 0$, E is a **pseudometric**.

2. If all (W_i, δ_i) are metric spaces and $\mu = const > 0$, E is a **metric**, if we identify isomorphic relational models. [1]

proof:

For the first assertion (PM1) and (PM2) has to be proved and for the second assertion additionally (M1):

$$(PM1) \quad E(M, M) = 0$$
$$(PM2) \quad E(M, P) \leq E(M, Q) + E(P, Q)$$
$$(M1) \quad E(M, P) = 0 \Rightarrow M \equiv P$$

(PM1) For the identity $id : M \to M$ we have the inequality $E(M, M) \leq E_{id}(M, M) = 0$, because of $\delta_i(w_i, w_i) = 0$.

(M1) Assuming $E_f(M, P) = E(M, P) = 0$ and $\mu > 0$, we get $M \backslash M_f \cup P \backslash P_f = \{\}$. From this we conclude that $f : M \to P$ is one-to-one and onto. Owing to the metric property of δ_i we get

$$\eta_f(m') = 0 \quad \Rightarrow \quad \forall i : \delta_i(R_i(m', \ldots, m^{(i)}), S_i(f(m'), \ldots, f(m^{(i)}))) = 0$$
$$\Rightarrow \quad \forall i : R_i(m', \ldots, m^{(i)}) = S_i(f(m'), \ldots, f(m^{(i)}))$$

Therefore M and P are isomorphic.

(PM2) Because of $\mu = const \geq 0$ we get for each association f

$$E(M, P) \leq E_f(M, P) \quad = \quad (|M \backslash M_f| + |P \backslash P_f|) * \mu + \sum_{q \in M_f} \eta_f(q)$$

where $|..|$ is the number of elements in the set.

---

[1] Correctly we have only the assertion: E is a **pseudometric** and additionally that only isomorphic relational models have a zero distance.

Assuming that g,h are associations with $E_g(M,Q) = E(M,Q)$ and $E_h(P,Q) = E(P,Q)$, we get:

$$
\begin{aligned}
E(M,Q) + E(P,Q) &= E_g(M,Q) + E_h(P,Q) = \\
&= (|M\backslash M_g| + |Q\backslash Q_g| + |P\backslash P_h| + |Q\backslash Q_h|) * \mu + \\
&\quad + \sum_{m \in M_g} \eta_g(m) + \sum_{p \in P_h} \eta_h(p)
\end{aligned}
$$

Let $f = h^T \circ g = \{(m,p) \mid \exists q \in Q : (m,q) \in g \wedge (p,q) \in h\}$. Because of $M_f \subset M_g$ and $P_f \subset P_h$ as well as

$$
\begin{aligned}
|M_g \backslash M_f| &= |Q_g \backslash Q_h| \leq |Q \backslash Q_h| \\
|P_h \backslash P_f| &= |Q_h \backslash Q_g| \leq |Q \backslash Q_g|
\end{aligned}
$$

we get:

$$
\begin{aligned}
|M \backslash M_f| + |P \backslash P_f| &= |M \backslash M_g| + |M_g \backslash M_f| + |P \backslash P_h| + |P_h \backslash P_f| \\
&\leq |M \backslash M_g| + |Q \backslash Q_g| + |P \backslash P_h| + |Q \backslash Q_h|
\end{aligned}
$$

Consequently just

$$
\sum_{m \in M_f} \eta_f(m) \leq \sum_{m \in M_g} \eta_g(m) + \sum_{p \in P_h} \eta_h(p)
$$

remains to be shown.

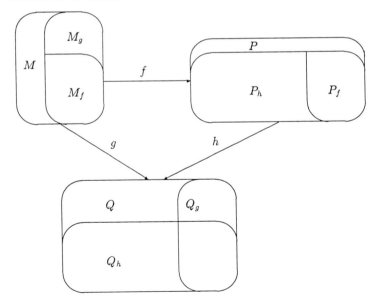

We prove this inequality for version no.1 of η, now. In this proof, we regard that the function

$$f|_{M_f} : M_f \to P_f, \quad f|_{M_f}(m) := p \quad \text{for each} \quad (m, p) \in f$$

and the analogously defined functions $g|_{M_g}$, $h|_{P_h}$ and $h^T|_{Q_h}$ are one-to-one and onto. With the abbreviations:

$$\begin{aligned}
\tilde{p}^{(i)} &= f|_{M_f}(m^{(i)}) = h^T|_{Q_h} \circ g|_{M_g}(m^{(i)}) \\
r_i &= R_i(m', \dots, m^{(i)}) \\
s_i &= S_i(f|_{M_f}(m'), \dots, f|_{M_f}(m^{(i)})) = S_i(\tilde{p}', \dots, \tilde{p}^{(i)}) \\
t_i &= T_i(g|_{M_g}(m'), \dots, g|_{M_g}(m^{(i)})) = T_i(h|_{P_h}(\tilde{p}'), \dots, h|_{P_h}(\tilde{p}^{(i)}))
\end{aligned}$$

we get:

$$\begin{aligned}
\delta_f^{(i)}(m') &= \max_{m'', \dots, m^{(i)} \in M_f} \{\delta_i(r_i, s_i)\} \\
&\leq \max_{m'', \dots, m^{(i)} \in M_f} \{\delta_i(r_i, t_i) + \delta_i(s_i, t_i)\} \\
&\leq \max_{m'', \dots, m^{(i)} \in M_f} \{\delta_i(r_i, t_i)\} + \max_{m'', \dots, m^{(i)} \in M_f} \{\delta_i(s_i, t_i)\} \\
&= \max_{m'', \dots, m^{(i)} \in M_f} \{\delta_i(r_i, t_i)\} + \max_{\tilde{p}'', \dots, \tilde{p}^{(i)} \in P_f} \{\delta_i(s_i, t_i)\} \\
&\leq \max_{m'', \dots, m^{(i)} \in M_g} \{\delta_i(r_i, t_i)\} + \max_{\tilde{p}'', \dots, \tilde{p}^{(i)} \in P_h} \{\delta_i(s_i, t_i)\} \\
&= \delta_g^{(i)}(m') + \delta_h^{(i)}(\tilde{p}')
\end{aligned}$$

Since the inequality is valid for all values of i, we get:

$$\eta_f(m') \leq \eta_g(m') + \eta_h(\tilde{p}') \qquad \forall m' \in M_f$$

and finally

$$\begin{aligned}
\sum_{m \in M_f} \eta_f(m) &\leq \sum_{m \in M_f} \eta_g(m) + \sum_{p \in P_f} \eta_h(p) \\
&\leq \sum_{m \in M_g} \eta_g(m) + \sum_{p \in P_h} \eta_h(p)
\end{aligned}$$

The inequality can be proved analogously for the version no.2 of η.

Example

Because of the limited space we will describe only one of the feasible applications ([bal82], [dav79], [sha85], [ull83]). We use the relational model in [sha85] and Shapiro's distance metric as an example for our general distance measure. We have to transform a relational model

$$(M; \hat{R}_1, \dots, \hat{R}_j) \quad , \quad \hat{R}_k \subset M^{i_k}$$

into our description. This procedure is described below:

- take $i_{max} = \max_{k=1,\dots,j}\{i_k\}$, therefore we have no i-ary relations with $i > i_{max}$. For each $i \in \{1, 2, \dots, i_{max}\}$ we define an i-aray attributed Relation R_i.

- If there are no i-ary relation in $(M; \hat{R}_1, \dots, \hat{R}_j)$, we define: $\quad R_i : M^i \to \{0\}$

- If $\hat{R}_{k_1}, \dots, \hat{R}_{k_{l_i}} \subset M^i$ are all i-ary relations, we define:

$$R_i : M^i \to \{0,1\}^{l_i}$$

$$R_i(m_1, \dots, m_i) = (w_1, \dots, w_\lambda, \dots, w_l)$$

$$w_\lambda = \begin{cases} 1 & : \quad (m_1, \dots, m_i) \in \hat{R}_{k_\lambda} \\ \\ 0 & : \quad otherwise \end{cases}$$

If we use the abbreviations

$$f(\hat{R}) = \{(p_1, \dots, p_i) \in P^i \mid \exists (m_1, \dots, m_i) \in \hat{R} \; \forall l : (m_l, p_l) \in f\}$$
$$f^T(\hat{S}) = \{(m_1, \dots, m_i) \in M^i \mid \exists (p_1, \dots, p_i) \in \hat{S} \; \forall l : (m_l, p_l) \in f\}$$

we can write for relational models $(M; \hat{R}_1, \dots, \hat{R}_j)$, $(P; \hat{S}_1, \dots, \hat{S}_j)$, with $|M| = |P| =$const, the metric which was defined in [sha85] by

$$\hat{E}_f(M, P) = \sum_{i=1}^{k} (|f(\hat{R}_i) \setminus \hat{S}_i| + |f^T(\hat{S}_i) \setminus \hat{R}_i|)$$
$$\hat{E}(M, P) = \min_{\substack{f : M \to P \\ bijective}} \{\hat{E}_f(M, P)\}$$

This metric is a special case of our general distance measure if we use the following definitions:

- we transform $(M; \hat{R}_1, \dots, \hat{R}_j)$, $(P; \hat{S}_1, \dots, \hat{S}_j)$ to our description $(M; R_1, \dots, R_{i_{max}})$, $(P; S_1, \dots, S_{i_{max}})$

- for each attribute space $W_i = \{0,1\}^{l_i}$ we define the metric:

$$\delta_i((w_1, \dots, w_{l_i}), (w'_1, \dots, w'_{l_i})) = \sum_{\lambda=1}^{l_i} |w_\lambda - w'_\lambda| \le l_i$$

- for the missing parts we choose

$$2\mu > \sum_{i=1}^{i_{max}} l_i |M|^{i-1}$$

By that we get for every association f and every $(m', p') \in f$:

$$\eta_f(m') = \sum_{i=1}^{i_{max}} \sum_{m'', \dots, m^{(i)} \in M_f} \delta_i \quad \le$$

$$\leq \sum_{i=1}^{i_{max}} \sum_{m'',\dots,m^{(i)} \in M_f} l_i \;\; = \;\; \sum_{i=1}^{i_{max}} l_i \, |M_f|^{i-1} \;\; \leq$$

$$\leq \sum_{i=1}^{i_{max}} l_i \, |M|^{i-1} \;\; < \;\; 2\mu = \mu(m') + \mu(p')$$

If we assume $|M| = |P| = $const just as in [sha85] we ensure with the demand above that an optimal association is one-to-one and onto. In that case we get, If we compute our general distance measure with version 2 of η:

$$E(M,P) \;=\; \hat{E}(M,P)$$

Conclusions

The example described briefly above confirms that the metric defined by [sha85] is included in our definition. Because of the limited space we could not describe more of the feasible applications in computer vision.

With only few restrictions we have been able to prove that our distance measure is a metric or pseudometric. This is very important for clustering. If there are many models given, we can match these with an object description by matching only the kernels of a few model clusters. Clusters with great distance measures can be refused.

References

[bal82]   D.H. Ballard and Ch.M.Brown: Computer Vision, Prentice-Hall, Englewood Cliffs, 1982, pp. 317-382

[dav79]   L.S. Davis; Shape Matching Using Relaxation Techniques, IEEE Trans. on Pattern Analysis and Machine Intelligence, vol. PAMI-1, no. 1, jan. 1979, pp. 60-72

[sha82]   L.G. Shapiro; Robert M. Haralick; Organization of Relational Models for Scene Analysis, IEEE Trans. on Pattern Analysis and Machine Intelligence, vol. PAMI-4, no. 6, nov. 1982, pp. 595-602

[sha85]   L.G. Shapiro; Robert M. Haralick; A metric for comparing relational descriptions, IEEE Trans. on Pattern Analysis and Machine Intelligence, vol. PAMI-7, no. 1, jan. 1985, pp. 90-94

[ull83]   J.R. Ullmann; Relational matching, in R.M. Haralick (ed), *Pictorial Data Analysis,* Springer-Verlag, New York/Berlin, 1983, pp. 147-170

A FEATURE-BASED APPROACH TO IMAGE MATCHING

Jan Flusser[1]

Abstract

A new feature-based approach to the matching of two images of the same scene with translational, rotational and scaling differences is presented. The cloused-boundary objects are extracted in the images. Their shapes are represented via invariant coding into shape matrixes. The shape matrix is then taken as an object feature and the objects are matched in the feature space.

I. INTRODUCTION

Analysis of two or more digital images of the same scene taken at different time, from different places and by different sensors often requires automatic matching of images. *Image matching* is a process of the determining of mutual correspondence between the objects in the images.

Object detection can be done by well-known segmentation techniques [2]. Two binary images with extracted objects are obtained as the results of the segmentation.

There are described many matching methods in [3] - [8]. These methods are based on combinatorial approach [5], graph matching [8], clustering [6], probabilistic relaxation [4], [7] and moment invariants [3]. Generally, they have high computing complexity or low reliability.

In this paper, a new feature-based approach to object matching in the case of translational, rotational and scaling differences between the original images is presented. There are two main problems to be solved: to find invariant, discriminatory and computationally effective object features and to construct a classification algorithm in the feature space.

In Section II, a space- and scale-invariant shape description by a binary *shape matrix* is given. The shape matrix is then taken as a feature of each object. In Section III, the matching algorithm in the feature metric space is described. In Section IV, numerical examples and practical results are shown.

II. INVARIANT SHAPE DESCRIPTION OF PLANAR OBJECTS

For given planar object G we define its shape matrix of size $n \times n$ as follows.

1. Find the centre of gravity $T = (x_t, y_t)$ of object G.

2. Find such point $M = (x_m, y_m)$ that $M \in G$ and $d(M, T) = \max_{A \in G} d(A, T)$, where d is Euclidean distance in R^2.

3. Construct the square with the centre in T and with the size of the side $2 \cdot d(M, T)$. Point M lies in the centre of one side.

4. Divide the square into $n \times n$ subsquares.

5. Denote S_{kj} the subsquares of the constructed grid; $k, j = 1, \ldots, n$.

[1]Institute of Information Theory and Automation, Czechoslovak Academy of Sciences, Pod vodárenskou věží 4, 18208 PRAGUE 8, CSFR

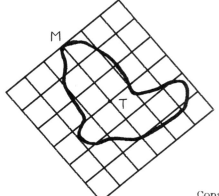

$$B \;=\; \begin{bmatrix} 0 & 0 & 0 & 1 & 0 & 0 \\ 0 & 0 & 1 & 1 & 0 & 0 \\ 0 & 0 & 1 & 1 & 0 & 0 \\ 0 & 1 & 1 & 1 & 0 & 0 \\ 0 & 0 & 1 & 1 & 1 & 1 \\ 0 & 0 & 0 & 0 & 0 & 0 \end{bmatrix}$$

Fig. 1

Construction of the shape matrix, n = 6

6. Define the $n \times n$ binary matrix B

$$B_{kj} = \begin{cases} 1 & \Longleftrightarrow \mu\left(S_{kj} \cap G\right) \ge \mu\left(S_{kj}\right)/2 \\ 0 & \text{otherwise,} \end{cases}$$

where $\mu(F)$ is the area of the planar region F.

An example of the shape matrix construction is shown in Fig. 1.

The shape matrix exists for every compact planar object G and for each n is defined unambiguously. It is easy to prove that the shape matrix is invariant to the displacement, rotation and scaling of the object. The shape of the object can be reconstructed from the shape matrix. The accuracy of the reconstruction is given by the size of the subsquares S_{kj}, i.e. we can reach more accurate shape description by increasing n. There exists an algorithm for the choice of optimal n.

Two different shapes are distinguishable by using of their shape matrixes, i.e. there exists such n that the shape matrixes of size $n \times n$ differ each other.

To determine the degree of similarity between two objects, their shape matrixes A and B are compared. The similarity relation **p** is defined by the following formula:

$$p(A, B) = 1 - \frac{1}{n \cdot n} \sum_{j=1}^{n} \sum_{i=1}^{n} |A_{ij} - B_{ij}|. \tag{1}$$

III. OBJECT MATCHING ALGORITHM

The presented algorithm for object correspondence determining consists of two main steps. First, the local information about the objects represented by their shape matrixes is used to find two pairs of the best corresponding objects. If these objects are known, the parametres of the geometric distortion between the images can be determined. The type of the distortion is supposed to be

$$\begin{aligned} u &= s\left(x \cdot \cos \alpha - y \cdot \sin \alpha\right) + p \\ v &= s\left(x \cdot \sin \alpha + y \cdot \cos \alpha\right) + q, \end{aligned} \tag{2}$$

where (x, y) and (u, v) are the coordinates in the first and second images, respectively.

In the second step, one set of objects is transformed into another using known distortion functions (2) and the correspondence between the other objects is then established.

The first step is the most important and complicated part of the algorithm, because in the first image could be extracted objects which were not extracted in the second one and vice versa.

Denote $F_1 \cdots F_N$, $G_1 \cdots G_N$ the objects extracted in the first and second images, respectively. Define the $N \times M$ matrix K by the relation

$$K_{ij} = p\left(F_i, G_j\right), \qquad i = 1, \ldots, N; \; j = 1, \ldots, M.$$

For each i find such $j_i \leq M$ that $K_{ij_i} = \max_j K_{ij}$.

In order to minimize the possibility of the false match, we define *the matching likelihood coefficients*. For each i we find such index $\ell_i \leq M$ that $K_{i\ell_i} = \max_{j \neq j_i} K_{ij}$.

Matching likelihood coefficient d_i is defined by the formula

$$d_i = K_{ij_i} \cdot \left(K_{ij_i} - K_{i\ell_i}\right), \qquad i = 1, \ldots, N$$

and expresses the degree of reliability, with which objects F_i and G_j correspond each other.

Now we can find indexes i_0, i_1 which describe the most reliable matching:

$$d_{i_0} = \max_i d_i, \qquad d_{i_1} = \max_{i \neq i_0} d_i.$$

In this way, we have determined two pairs of objects, which correspond each other with maximum likelihood:

$$F_{i_0} \approx G_{j_{i_0}} \qquad \text{and} \qquad F_{i_1} \approx G_{j_{i_1}}.$$

IV. RESULTS

To measure the performance of the proposed image matching algorithm, following experiments on the test and real images were carried out.

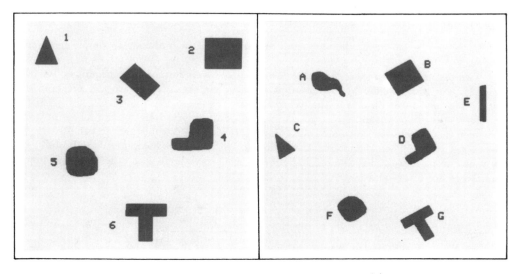

a)   b)

Fig. 2

The test images from *Experiment 1*

a) b)	1	2	3	4	5	6	d
A	88	61	68	83	45	76	440
B	62	85	81	69	80	65	340
C	**96**	65	68	84	49	78	1152
D	81	73	''1	93	59	77	1116
E	77	53	56	72	37	65	385
F	49	82	73	59	88	58	528
G	79	66	65	76	60	**98**	1862

Table 1

The matrix K and the matching likelihood coefficients
(all values of K are multiplied by 100).

	A	B	C	D	E	F	G
1	146,2	259,1	0	253,0	376,1	171,4	288,5
2	143,0	0,1	259,0	134,2	152,8	267,0	276,7
3	107,6	130,7	142,4	118,3	233,7	149,2	207,8
4	210,9	134,0	253,0	0,1	139,6	173,7	144,7
5	243,2	267,0	171,4	173,6	312,5	0,1	127,6
6	315,4	276,6	288,5	144,6	253,5	127,7	0

Table 2

Distances (in pixels) between the centers of gravity
of objects after the mapping.

EXPERIMENT 1

In the first experiment, the algorithm was applied to the matching of simple geometric shapes.

Two test binary images of the size 512×512 pixels were formed by a graphic editor (see Fig. 2). The images differ by a translation, rotation and scale. There are six objects in the first image and seven objects in the second image.

First, the shape matrixes of the size 16×16 of all objects were found. The similarity between the objects was calculated according to (1) for each possible pair and the matrix K was constructed. Then the matching likelihood coefficients were computed (see Table 1). It is visible from Table 1 that two pairs of objects which correspond each other with maximum reliability are $6 \approx G$ and $1 \approx C$.

a)	1	2	4	5	6
b)	C	B	D	F	G

Table 3

Correspondence between the objects in Experiment 1.

The parametres of the geometric distortion between the images (2) were computed: $p = -32.4$, $q = 237.1$, $s = 0.8$ and $\alpha = \pi/6$. Image 2b was mapped by means of them into image 2a and the correspondence between the other objects was established according to minimum distance (see Table 2 and Table 3).

It can be clearly seen by visual comparison of both images that the final correspondence determined by the proposed algorithm is correct everywhere.

EXPERIMENT 2

An interesting result was obtained in the case of two multitemporal images of the same part of the Earth's surface, taken from satellites SPOT and Landsat TM. The images had translational, rotational and scaling differences. Both images were segmented and closed-boundary regions were extracted. The extracted regions were limited to be not too large or too small. There were some regions that existed in only one of the images (see Fig. 3).

In order to determine the mutual correspondence between the regions, the above described

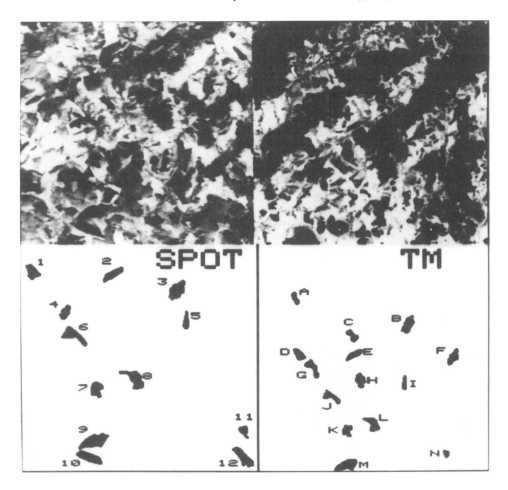

Fig.3
above: original images
below: extracted regions

SPOT	1	2	5	6	7	8	9	11
TM	D	E	I	J	K	L	M	N

Table 4

Correspondence between the regions

matching algorithm was applied. The result is shown in Table 4. Its accuracy is excellent: all determined correspondences are correct.

V. DISCUSSION

A new feature-based object matching algorithm is presented. It uses the binary shape matrix as an invariant feature of the object. The correspondence determining is a two stage process - the first stage is performed in the feature space, the second one is performed in the image plane.

The computing complexity of the whole algorithm is only $O(M \cdot N)$ that is the lowest complexity among matching algorithms published till now.

The algorithm can be extended to match two multispectral images [1]. The procedure for shape matrix size optimization can be derived [1]. It is also possible to generalize the first step of the algorithm by increasing of the number of used features.

The presented algorithm has numerous applications in computer vision, robotics, medical imaging and remote sensing.

REFERENCES

[1] Flusser, J.: *Object Matching in Computer Vision*, Research Rep. n. 1670, UTIA CSAV, Prague 1990 (in Czech)

[2] Haralick, R. M., Shapiro, L. G. : Image Segmentation Techniques, *Computer Vision, Graphics and Image Processing*, vol. 29 (1985), 100-132

[3] Hu, M. K.: Visual Pattern Recognition by Moment Invariants, *IRE Trans. Inf. Theory*, vol. IT-8 (1962), 179-187

[4] Ranade, S., Rosenfeld, A. : Point Pattern Matching by Relaxation, *Pattern Recognition*, vol. 12 (1980), 269 - 275

[5] Stockman, G. C., Goshtasby, A. : Point Pattern Matching Using Convex Hull Edges, *IEEE Tr. on System, Man, Cyb.*, vol. SMC-15 (1985), 631-637

[6] Stockman, G. C., Kopstein, S., Benett, S. : Matching Images to Models for Registration and Object Detection via Clustering, *IEEE Tr. on Pattern Anal. Machine Intell.*, vol. PAMI-4 (1982), 229-241

[7] Ton, J., Jain, A. K. : Registering Landsat Images by Point Matching, *IEEE Tr. on Geosci. Rem. Sensing*, vol. GE-27 (1989), 642-651

[8] Zahn, C. T. : An Algorithm for Noisy Template Matching, in : *Proc. IFIP Congress*, Stockholm 1974, 698-701

HYPOTHESES CONSTRUCTION/VERIFICATION in IMAGE UNDERSTANDING

D.A.Denisov, A.K.Dudkin (*)

ABSTRACT

The hypotheses construction/verification paradigm is analyzed. The Bayesian classifier as the hypotheses generator is suggested. The 2D object centered models for verification to be carried out are developed. The whole multistage decision making process is considered. The method application to the human chromosome identification problem is presented.

1. INTRODUCTION

The visual object identification problem is the "hot point" in computer vision and image understanding fields. Though there exists a well known matching paradigm as a ground for decision making, the concrete algorithmical mechanizms of this idea elaboration are still a wide space for exploration efforts.

The model invocation and hypotheses construction/verification processes were suggested recently as a powerful tools for decision making computational implementation when dealing with the complicated descriptive models [1] .

In the report the authors suggest the multistage technique for 2D object recognition on a base of hypotheses construction/ verification processes in the frame of matching the observed videodata with the objects models given [1,2] . The technique application to the automated human chromosome analysis and identification is presented.

2. THE HYPOTHESES CONSTRUCTION/VERIFICATION PARADIGM

The model invocation and hypotheses construction/verification processes are advocated by R.Fisher [1] as a powerful tools to attain the goal (interpretation) and are essentialy understood as objects and their subcomponents relationships finding, geometrical consistance establishing and position verifying when dealing with 3D computer vision tasks [1] . When transit from 3D scenes to 2D images the importance of the other aspects of the

(*) Leningrad Electrical Engineering Institute, prof.Popov
str.5, 197736, Leningrad, USSR

phenomenon have to be emphasized.

The first one is the sequential ("step-by-step") recognition character when we move from coarse objects sorting to fine
objects identification in the frame of the set of concepts caused by the final objective. This sequential character is compatible to human visual perception mechanisms [3]. In fact, very
often we are sorting objects according to their size first,group
them according to their shape similarity further and identify
them by more detailed analysis of the brightness pattern and
knowledge context.

The second aspect concerns the numerical features we use for
description aims. On one hand the noise affection and ambiguity
of the preprocessing results (image enhancement and segmentation,
object detection) make the numerical features the random variables and on the other - as a rule there exists insufficiency of the
discriminant power of the features used so that it's difficult
to discriminate reliably not only the goal objects, but their
nonintersecting groups as well.

This last notion justifies the consideration of the following situation.

Let

1. $\Omega = (\omega_1', \omega_2', ..., \omega_K')$ - the "classification alphabet", i.e.
the set of objects we want to identify (recognize);

2. $\Omega^* = (\omega_1'^*, \omega_2'^*, ..., \omega_M'^*)$ - the set of subsets from Ω such that:

$$\forall m , \omega_m'^* \subset \Omega , |\omega_m'^*| < K \qquad (1)$$
$$\exists n,m : \omega_n'^* \cap \omega_m'^* \neq \phi$$

3. The numerical feature set $\{x_1, x_2, ..., x_n\}$ and its subsets
allow reliably to discriminate objects within Ω^*

This situation banes the decision tree model utilization aiming at sequential recognition scheme building and leads to hypotheses construction/verification processes utilization. In fact,
the assignment of the unknown object to one of $\omega_m'^* = (\omega_{m1}', \omega_{m2}', ...)$
gives only the corresponding hypotheses needed to be verified.

The features categories can't be exhausted by numerical features estimating the size, shape, position and orientation of the
object. The knowledge context must be embedded into the identification process. That's why "vector model" is insufficient descriptive structure. On the other hand the frames and the semantic
nets essentially affect the matching algorithms and lead to significant complication of the whole process. Probably the multi-

stage sequential recognition scheme mentioned above is in some
sense the compromise between the traditional pattern recognition
algorithms (too poor to provide the effectiveness and reliability) and the universal artificial intelligence approaches (too
redundant in some practical cases).

The statistical character of the numerical features measured allows to use not only the statistical decision rules, but
also to estimate the plausibility of the decision. If we think
about the Bayesian decision rule for instance as a hypothesizer,
we'll find the elegant way to construct the hypotheses and simultaneously to estimate their plausibility values. In fact, the
row of the aposteriory probabilities ordered by the descreasing
their values gives both hypotheses themselves and hypotheses
plausibilities. These general ideas spoken out above were transformed into the particular identification technique.

3. THE TECHNIQUE DESCRIPTION

Let $X^T = (x_1, x_2, \ldots, x_n)$ be the vector of the numerical features characterizing objects size and shape[4] . Let $p(X)$ be
the density function of X . We assume that $p(X)$ is a mixture of
the gaussian distributions and therefore

$$p(X) = \sum_{i=1}^{K} \mathcal{P}_i \, f(X, M_i, \Sigma_i)$$

where K - the number of prespecified objects classes

$$\omega_1, \omega_2, \ldots, \omega_K$$

$\mathcal{P}_i$ - the mixture components apriory probabilities;

$M_i^T = (\mu_{i1}, \mu_{i2}, \ldots, \mu_{in})$ - mean vector of the i-th
mixture component;

$$\Sigma_i = \begin{pmatrix} \sigma_{i1}^2 & & \\ & \sigma_{i2}^2 & O \\ & & \ddots \\ O & & \sigma_{in}^2 \end{pmatrix}$$ - the diagonal covariance matrix of the
i-th mixture component.

To carry out the first stage of identification (recognition)
we suggest the Bayessian decision rule in the form:

$$d\mathfrak{z}_1 : \mathcal{X} \to \mathfrak{P}, \quad \mathbb{X} \in \tilde{\omega}_i \quad iff \quad \mathfrak{z}_i = \min_j \mathfrak{z}_j$$

$$\mathfrak{z}_j = \frac{1}{2} \sum_{k=1}^{n} \left[(x_k - \mu_{kj})^2 / \tilde{\sigma}_{jk}^2 + \ln \tilde{\sigma}_{jk}^2 \right] - \ln \tilde{\mathfrak{P}}_j \tag{2}$$

Thus the Bayessian classifier (2) provides the hypothesis about the object class - $\tilde{\omega}_i$ and the value of the hypothesis plausibility - $1/|\mathfrak{z}_i|$. The objects models in this case are concentrated in the mean vectors $\mathbb{M}_i$ and covariance matrixes Σ_i.

If there exist some assumptions on feature intervals such that

$$\forall k, i \quad \exists \Delta_k^{(i)} : x_k \in \Delta_k^{(i)} \quad iff \quad x_k / \mathbb{X} \in \tilde{\omega}_i ,$$

then we can build the decision rule in the form

$$d\mathfrak{z}_2 : \mathcal{X} \to \mathfrak{P}, \quad \mathbb{X} \in \tilde{\omega}_i \quad iff \quad \mathbb{X} \in H_i \subseteq R^h$$

$$H_i = \Delta_1^{(i)} \times \Delta_2^{(i)} \times \ldots \times \Delta_h^{(i)} \tag{3}$$

We can combine further the decision rules (2),(3) to achieve more reliability. In fact, the decision rule $d\mathfrak{z}_1$ gives us the row of the hypotheses aligned in accordance with the aposteriory probabilities decreasing. The decision rule $d\mathfrak{z}_2$ makes the redudant hypotheses filtering, rejecting those (for the unknown vector $\mathbb{X}$), which inconsistence with the rule. Such a combination is particularly useful in the situation (1) described above.

The hypotheses verification process is based on checking up the brightness pattern of the object. This brightness pattern as a rule needs to be described by some structural characteristics, reflecting the spatial peculiarities of the gray level values distribution.

When object brightness pattern model is given in the form of the brightness average profile along the akeleton axe -

$$B_i = (b_{i1}, b_{i2}, \ldots, b_{iL})$$

the verification process may be realized by matching the "observed average profile" (computed on the object observed) B^* with B_i. We verify not every hypothesis $\tilde{\omega}_i$ but the most plausible ones, derived from the previous stage of the identification. The matching can be carried out by using some metric $\varrho(B^*, B_i)$ (for instance Eucledian) and object centred template generator.

CAIP'91

The second verification mechanizm foreseen in the technique is based on the checking up the detailed object brightness structure by "existence" predicates utilization. Such predicates can be expressed by

$$P_i = (Y, T_1, T_2, \ldots, T_q) = \begin{cases} \underline{\text{true}}, \text{ iff some } \ \dot{\iota}\text{-th sub-} \\ \text{structure exists in location} \quad (4) \\ Y \quad ; \\ \underline{\text{false}}, \text{ otherwise;} \end{cases}$$

where Y - substructure's location characteristic;
$T_1, T_2, \ldots, T_q$ - prespecified parameters (thresholds), describing substructure's tolerant intervals.

The "$\underline{\text{true}}$" value of the logical decision function

$$LP_k = \overset{Q_k}{\underset{i=1}{\&}} P_i (Y, T_1, T_2, \ldots, T_q) \tag{5}$$

(Q_k - number of the predicates characterizing the object of class $\acute{W}_k$) gives the confirmation of the corresponding hypothesis and positive result of the verification process.

The both of the verification mechanizms are used in the technique.

4. THE TECHNIQUE APPLICATION TO THE CHROMOSOMES IDENTIFICATION

The decision making process on the base of the hypotheses construction/verification mechanizm in the problem of the normal chromosome analysis and identification was developed. The CHILD (CHromosome Identification Leningrad Design)system appeared as the result of the research undertaken [4].

The following numerical features were used to characterise the chromosome size(length), shape and integral brightness.

$$x^{(1)} = x_\ell / \frac{1}{2} \overset{NN}{\underset{\ell=1}{\sum}} x_\ell \qquad \text{(length)},$$

x_ℓ - length of the ℓ -th chromosome; NN - number of chromosomes in the metaphase cell.

$$x^{(2)} = x_\ell^{(U)} / x_\ell^{(B)} \qquad \text{(centromer index)},$$

$x_\ell^{(U)}$ - length of the upper chromosome's shoulder; $x_\ell^{(B)}$ - length of the bottom chromosome's shoulder.

$$x^{(3)} = N_{black} / N_{average}$$

N_{Black} - number of pixels within the chromosome region with the "black" brightness; $N_{average}$ - number of pixels within the chromosome region with the "average" brightness. This feature space allowed to apply the decision rule $d\mathcal{R}_1$ (2) to construct the hypothesis about chromosome class. Feature subspace $\mathcal{X}^* = \{\mathbb{X}^* : \mathbb{X}^* = (x_1, x_2)\}$ made possible to apply the decision rule $d\mathcal{R}_2$ (3) to filter some of the hypotheses. The intermediate alphabet Ω^* included subsets $\omega_m^* (m = 1, 2, \ldots, 20)$ which were reliably detected by covering them with the corresponding rectangulars in $\mathcal{X}^*$. During the verification stage being carried out the average chromosome brightness profile along the skeleton axe- B^* -has been computed to match it with the template profiles $B_k (k = 1, 2, \ldots, 24)$. Besides, the predicates P_i (4) and logical functions LP_k (5) were used to confirm or to reject the corresponding hypotheses. The predicates "caught" the existence or absence the concrete "bands" within the chromosome region while the logical functions described the whole "banding pattern" of the particular chromosome.

REFERENCES

1. Fisher R.: From Surfaces To Objects. Jon Wiley & Sons, Chichester, England 1989.
2. Ballard D., Brown C.: Computer Vision. Prentice-Hall, New-York 1982.
3. Neisser U.: Cognitive Psycology. Englewood Cliffs, New-York 1967.
4. Denisov D., Dudkin A., Saveljeva L.: The Computer Vision Information Technology in the Chromosome Analysis and Recognition. NOVINTECH, No2, 1991, 37-49, (in Russian).

KNOWLEDGE REPRESENTATION IN INTELLIGENT SYSTEM FOR IMAGE ANALYSIS

Boiko Balev

Institute of Mathematics
Bulgarian Academy of Sciences

George Sharkov [1]

Central Laboratory of Biophysics
Bulgarian Academy of Sciences

ABSTRACT

Knowledge-based approach for developing computer vision systems is one of the most successful new paradigms to make these large and complex systems flexible and efficient. We are developing an experimental knowledge-based system ISIA for analysis and interpretation of biophysical images. The reasoning of the system is based on abstract models of investigated biological objects and physico-chemical processes. The system is used for the purposes of processing, analysis and recognition of static or dynamic 2-D images and image sequences.

1. INTRODUCTION

The recent new quality state in image understanding is characterized mainly by applying AI methods and techniques which extend the functionality of computer vision (CV) systems. By using visual scene models of different complexity and hierarchy new CV systems allow integration of wide variety of algorithms. These intelligent CV systems usually exploit classical knowledge representation schemes - semantic networks [8, 9], models [3], logic programming languages and mainly production rules [4, 7] or hybrid knowledge representation techniques [6]. In dependence of their generality they use different types of knowledge for image processing algorithms and tools, spatial relations and constraints between scene primitives, structural models and respective mapping procedures to the primitives, strategies for guiding the focus of attention and for conflict resolution during the interpretation, etc. Some systems provide reasoning and interpretation of uncertain and fuzzy information as well as some features of adaptive reasoning and learning. Presently, object-oriented programming is one of the most successful approaches as a basis for developing intelligent CV systems. It allows high level of abstraction by structural representations and integrated rule-based logics as well as low level numeric computations.

In spite of the recent progress in computer technology and specialized DSP architectures, the reasonable approach for developing CV system is still a restriction to limited set of problems in a particular domain. Knowledge-based CV systems are used successfully in the field of biomedical imaging, where domain problems and objects are quite well structured and different restrictions and constraints could be specified. These systems have been applied for analysis of microscope, X-ray , NMR, scintigrafic and other images.

For the purposes of planning and analysis of biophysical experiments two knowledge-based systems have been developed at our laboratory [5]. They help in planning experiments on membrane electrofusion and formation of lipid membranes by using external electric fields. A specialized domain-oriented knowledge representation environment KREBS (Knowledge Representation Environment for Biological Systems) is used for building these systems [10]. In order to improve computer consultation we developed domain-oriented computer vision

---

[1] **Correspondence address:** Central Laboratory of Biophysiscs, Bulgarian Academy of Sciences, Acad. G. Bonchev Str., Bl. 21, Sofia 1113, BULGARIA

system ISIA (Intelligent System for Image Analysis). Presently, the system ISIA is used for the purposes of 2-D image or image sequences interpretation and data extraction from video tape records of experiments on protoplast dielectrophoresis (motion of cells in nonhomogeneous AC fields).

2. GENERAL STRUCTURE OF THE SYSTEM

The system ISIA is developed on the basis of knowledge representation environment KREBS (implemented in Common LISP for PC/AT), which provides object-oriented language, integrated production rule interpreter, logic programming language and fuzzy logic language. Generally, the system ISIA consists of numerical data base, symbolic data base (blackboard), low-level control interpreter, hierarchical domain model and inference engine. Numerical data base contains input images or image sequences, results of applying different DSP algorithms and segmented image. The blackboard maintains current information of the reasoning. The low-level control interpreter provides access to the numerical data base. It maintains the activation of low level image processing procedures.

3. THE DOMAIN MODEL AND KNOWLEDGE-BASED INTERPRETATION OF IMAGES

The models of real biophysical processes and objects are basically represented by different hierarchies of objects (classes, instances) at different levels of abstraction. The knowledge organization depends on the structural complexity of real objects. In general, this hierarchical structure follows the same knowledge organization principles as in the respective consultation expert systems. This means, that in addition to the inherited descriptions and relations for biological and physical objects, the system ISIA maintains similar network with their visual characteristics.

The knowledge and data information in ISIA is structured in different layers correspondent to the increasing of abstraction (Figure 1). For example, the input images and results of applying early vision image processing algorithms are at the lowest level of this hierarchy. The higher (middle) level contains task dependent basic (elementary) objects - lines, homogeneous regions, textures, etc. They are grouped into appropriate classes and subclassses (e.g. straight lines, complex lines, circle parts, etc.). These objects are compared to correspondent slots of the abstract objects from the high-level scene model. As a result, hypotheses for the presence or not of specified macro-object are generated and tested.

Low-level knowledge

Low level knowledge is represented basically by using procedural style. The supported common library (implemented in C-language) contains: basic algorithms for digital image processing (low-pass and median filtrations, edge detection, edge thinning, thresholding, histogram analysis, region segmentation, etc.); procedures for computation of basic properties of image objects and regions (e.g. average, highest and lowest intensity, area, minimum and maximum of the x and y coordinates, detection of characteristic line points - line ends, cross-points, line direction, object modification, Hough transformation, etc.); procedures for generating useful graphical primitives: pixel, line, cursor, circle, text; supplementary functions for graphic interface, hard-copy, file manager, hardware control, etc.

The appropriate algorithms for extracting visual structures are selected in dependence of the properties of expected objects and their specific visual characteristics. This control information is recorded at higher modeling levels. The recommendations are based not only

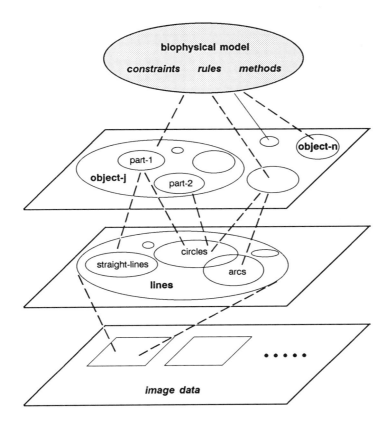

Figure 1. Knowledge and data structure in **ISIA**

on the domain expert expectations, but they express the experience from previous consultations. Formally, they are represented as empirical or heuristic control rules. In addition, the initial parameter values for the algorithms are supplied, but they are modified iteratively until some initial criteria are satisfied.

Middle level knowledge

The visual structures extracted from the image data have to be interpreted as parts of biophysical objects. In general, the matching process is top-down. It starts from the high-level abstract model of the biophysical process and propagates to the elementary regions of the visual image. At each level respective constraints should be satisfied and then the included rules for interpretation are locally checked and fired. At the middle level some forward chaining rules are evaluated in order to construct more complex and informative visual objects.

These middle-level objects are either lines produced by edge detection, or regions (results of region growing or thresholding of the grey image). Lines, for example, are represented as instances of the classes **simple-line** and **line:**

```
[simple-line
      area
      hypothesis_to_be
      grey-level = nil                    ; (average min max)
      gradient = nil                      ; (average min max)
      line-end-points= ()                 ; ((number0 x0 y0 direction0) ......)
      dir-list = nil                      ; (dir0 dir1 ........)
      dir-change = nil                    ; (pos neg posover negover change)
      ok-hough                            ; result (yes/no len (x y n exist int) (..3w) )
      hough-par                           ; (r xmin xmax ymin ymax)
      hough-results   ]                   ; (((x y n y3 n3 exist int)......))


[line
   :STATIC-VIEWS
      instance-of = '(simple-obj simple-line)
   :DYNAMIC-VIEWS
      is-a = '(meta-line)
   :ATTRIBUTES
      line-type
      line-parts = nil                    ; (arc0 arc1 .....)
      line-cross-points = ()  ]           ; ((number0 x0 y0 list-of-parts) ......)
```

In addition to standard attributes for all simple objects, these objects some specific
properties. Specialized methods and rules for information processing and interpretation are
inherited dynamically from the super-class **meta-line:**

```
[meta-line
   :METHODS
      in-llp = '(() (init-llp-obj self).......
      init-line = '(() (or (if (find-frame 'grey)...(split-line self) ...)))
      join-parts = '(() (sum-parts self) ... )
      find-end = '(() (if (> (=> self 'area) *delta*)
                          (find-end-of-line self)))
      init-arc = '(()(if (> (=> self 'area) *delta*) (progn ... ) )))
      hough-trans='(()(=> self 'hough-res '(:put ,(apply #'hough-cir...))))
      ...]
```

Commonly, the lines extracted by edge detection operators have complex unspecified
structure. In order to represent them at the low level they are decomposed to the set of
line-primitives (arcs and closed lines). Then, the following algorithm (inherited as a method
split-line from the class **meta-line**) is recursively applied to each instance of the object line:

```
ALGORITHM SPLIT-LINE (LINE):
    1.Detect the characteristic points of LINE - end points  and
           cross points (with 2 or more branches separated)
    2.IF number of end points = 2
        AND number of cross points = 0
      THEN LINE is arc
           return T.
    3.IF number of end points = 0
        IF number of cross points = 0
           THEN LINE is closed line
                return T.
           ELSE ;number of cross points >= 2 (i.e. object is COMPLEX-CLOSED-LINE)
                remove one cross point to break LINE
                and call SPLIT-LINE (COMPLEX-CLOSED-LINE).
    4.DEFAULT ;number of end points >0 AND number of cross points >=0
        FOR every end point analyze eight-connected points
            until cross-point is found.  Construct  ARC  with these points.
        IF  there is unmarked part of LINE -> REST-LINE
            call SPLIT-LINE (REST-LINE).
```

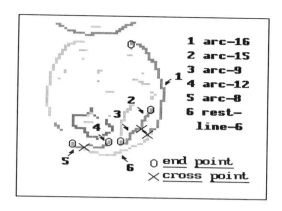

Figure 2. Example for a composite line splitting

For example, the splitting of a composite line from Figure 2 and applying other initializing procedures produces following data structures:

```
*  (report-lineobj 'line-6)
REST-LINE-6
((LINE-CROSS-POINTS) (LINE-PARTS) (LINE-TYPE . ARC) (AREA . 32)
 (PHYS-NUMBER . -32746)   (MAX-Y . 179) (MIN-Y . 167) (MAX-X . 148) (MIN-X . 126)
 (HOUGH-RESULTS
   ((143 142 1 143 2 7 6)(142 142 1 146 2 7 7)(141 143 1 144 2 7 7)
     (140 144 1 144 2 7 7) (139 144 1 145 2 7 7) (138 145 1 148 3 7 7)
     (137 153 2 147 3 7 7) (136 148 2 148 4 7 7) (135 149 4 150 7 7 7)
  .... (125 148 1 147 1 5 4) (124 148 1 147 1 5 4) 7)
 (HOUGH-PAR 28 123 143 136 161)
  (OK-HOUGH YES 7 (134 150 4 7 7) (134 150 7 7 7))   (CH-DIR . NEGATIVE)
  (DIR-CHANGE 0 4 0 2 0 0 0)
 (DIR-LIST (237 315 (146.172)(148.169)) (217 306 (142.175)(146.172))
  (207 306 (138.177)(142.175)) (207 297 (134.179)(138.177))
  (168 270 (129.178)(134.179)) (146 279 (126.176)(129.178)))
 (LINE-END-POINTS (1 126 176 153) (0 145 167 116))
 (GRADIENT) (GREY-LEVEL) (HYPOT . OUT-WHITE-CURVATURE))

ARC-16
((LINE-CROSS-POINTS) (LINE-PARTS) (PART-OF . LINE-6)
 (LINE-TYPE . ARC)  (AREA . 54) (PHYS-NUMBER . -32714)
 (MAX-Y . 168) (MIN-Y . 127) (MAX-X . 152) (MIN-X . 141)
 (HOUGH-RESULTS
   ((143 139 1 140 2 11 4) (142 140 1 140 2 11 4) (141 136 1 141 2 11 6)
     (140 137 1 142 2 11 6) (139 138 1 142 2 11 6) (138 140 1 143 2 11 7)
  ... (125 137 1 136 1 1 1) (124 0 0 0 0 0 0) (123 0 0 0 0 0 0)) 11)
 (HOUGH-PAR 28 123 143 136 161)
 (OK-HOUGH YES 11 (132 150 3 10 10) (133 152 7 10 10))
 (CH-DIR . NEGATIVE) (DIR-CHANGE 2 6 0 2 0 0 4)
 (DIR-LIST (315 54 (146.131)(143.128)) (297 45 (148.135)(146.131))
  (289 45 (149 . 138) (148 . 135)) (284 27 (150 . 142) (149 . 138))
  ... (259 0 (150 . 165) (151 . 160)) (237 126 (148 . 168) (150 . 165)))
 (LINE-END-POINTS (1 148 168 244) (0 141 128 161))
 (GRADIENT) (GREY-LEVEL) (HYPOT . OUT-WHITE-CURVATURE))

LINE-6
((LINE-CROSS-POINTS (0 145 167 (REST-LINE-6 ARC-15 ARC-9))
 (1 147 169 (ARC-16)) (2 126 176 (REST-LINE-6 ARC-12)))
 (LINE-PARTS REST-LINE-6 ARC-16 ARC-15 ARC-12 ARC-9 ARC-8)
 (LINE-TYPE . COMP-LINE) (AREA . 128) (PHYS-NUMBER . -32746)
```

```
(MAX-Y . 179) (MIN-Y . 127) (MAX-X . 152) (MIN-X . 122)
(HOUGH-RESULTS . :UNKNOWN)(HOUGH-PAR . :UNKNOWN)
(OK-HOUGH . :UNKNOWN) (CH-DIR . :UNKNOWN) (DIR-CHANGE) (DIR-LIST)
(LINE-END-POINTS (4 122 174 NIL) (3 138 173 NIL) (2 134 173 NIL)
 (1 148 158 NIL) (0 141 128 NIL))
(GRADIENT 97 62 150) (GREY-LEVEL 126 98 152) (HYPOT . :UNKNOWN))
 . . .
```

The produced elementary objects are referred to the subclasses of objects with given shape (arcs, splines, straight lines, etc.). Examples of such classes are **circle-arc** and **straight-line**:

```
[circle-arc
      is-a = '(meta-arc-cir)
      type                              ;gradient direction
      origin                            ;arc, loop or line-object
      dir-point-list                    ;((x0 y0)...
      restr-point-list                  ;((x0 y0)...)
      coord-list                        ;((R0 x0 y0)....)
      find-R                            ;(R rsqerr)
      find-x                            ;(x xsqerr)
      find-y                            ;(y ysqerr)
      centr-angle   ]                   ;(angle from to)

[straight-line
      is-a = '(meta-straight-cir)
      direction
      origin
      dir-point-list                    ;((x0 y0) ...
      near-parallel ]
```

High-level knowledge

At the highest level an appropriate matching to the parts of the abstract model is performed. By checking corresponding rules hypotheses for association of the image structures with parts of modeling objects are generated and tested. Then new verified instances of recognized objects are created in the blackboard. The generate and test cycle is performed until the adequate interpretation at highest modeling level is achieved. For unknown slot values the interpreter starts to check backward corresponding rules (listed in concluded-in facet). For example, when reasoning about the stages of the process dielectrophoresis, represented by the instance of the following KREBS object:

```
[dielectrophoresis-process
      sequence-investigation
           {data-facets = '((TYPE (system)) (EXPECT (atom)) (CONCLUDED-IN (r0)))}
      check-threshold
           {data-facets = '(...(CONCLUDED-IN (r14 r15 r16 R17)))}
      predict-next-positions
           {data-facets = '(...(CONCLUDED-IN (r27 r31 r28 r29 r30)))}  .......]
```

the motion of protoplasts is predicted by the rules like the following one:

> IF   distance between protoplasts is < short, and
>   protoplasts speed is > middle,
> THEN   (in next frame) protoplast speed is between 0 and high, and
>   calculate predicted location.

Before firing such rules the included linguistic variables (e.g. *short*, *middle* and *high*) are assigned to the respective values in accordance with the experimental conditions and image

244

features. For these purposes symbolic scales are used to transform the numerical values of some parameters to their symbolic description.

High level description of biophysical objects includes some meta-objects which consist of general physical constraints, specific rule sets and methods. Examples of such object **meta-protoplast-rules** and one of the indicated rules follow:

```
[meta-protoplast-rules
   hypothesis
     {data-facets = '(...(CONCLUDED-IN (r12 r13 r14 r15)))}
   check-hypot
     {data-facets = '(...(CONCLUDED-IN (r24 r25 r26)))}
   unification
     {data-facets = '(...(CONCLUDED-IN (r31 r32 r33)))}
   hough-check.....]
```

RULE R31:

IF   radius(PROTO) is equal to the radius(PROTO-HYPO), and
*   x-coord of PROTO-HYPO center is between predicted max and min, and*
*   y-coord of PROTO-HYPO center is between predicted max and min,*
THEN   unify PROTO-HYPO with PROTO.

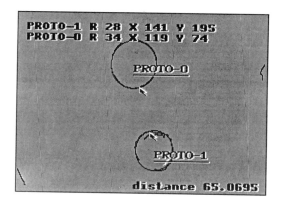

Figure 3. Result of interpretation of single frame

This knowledge base has been used for assistance in analysis of real experiments on protoplast dielectrophoresis. The input image sequence corresponds to the process stages and for each image frame the system generates symbolic description of the recognized objects and extracted data (see Figure 3 and Figure 4):

```
(FRAME-DESCRIPTION-8
(SPEED . 2.47392F-03)
(DISTANCE  (FINDPROTO-1 FINDPROTO-0 30.3268
          ((132 142)(130 114)(132 143)(129 113))))
(R 28 34) (Y 170 80) (X 135 126)
(PROTOPLASTS FINDPROTO-1 FINDPROTO-0)
(THRESHOLD . 60) (TIME . 200) (OUT-FILE . "C:\SEQ\OUTc-2")
(FILE . "c:\seq\s8"))
FINDPROTO-1
((SPEED 2.47392F-03 0 0.0075) (DISTANCE . 30.3268)
(PREDICT-Y 159 180) (PREDICT-X 125 145)
(OLD-CENTER 28 135 172) (CENTER 28 135 170)
(OTH-PRO-INST . FINDPROTO-0) (DELTA-TIME . 200) (UNI . T)
```

```
(NEAR-LINES LINE-12 LINE-11 ARC-8 LINE-9 LINE-8 ARC-5 ARC-2)
(EDGE-PARTS ARC-2 ARC-5 LINE-9)
(MAX-Y . 210) (MIN-Y . 133) (MAX-X . 164) (MIN-X . 106))
FINDPROTO-0
((SPEED 2.47392F-03 0 0.0075) (DISTANCE . 30.3268)
 (PREDICT-Y 70 91) (PREDICT-X 116 136)
 (OLD-CENTER 34 126 80) (CENTER 34 126 80)
 (OTH-PRO-INST . FINDPROTO-1) (DELTA-TIME . 200) (UNI . T)
 (NEAR-LINES REST-LINE-4 ARC-1 ARC-0 LINE-3 LINE-2 LINE-1)
 (EDGE-PARTS LINE-1 LINE-2 LINE-3)
 (MAX-Y . 125) (MIN-Y . 36) (MAX-X . 159) (MIN-X . 93))
```

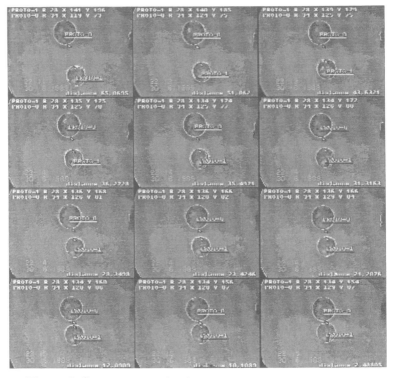

Figure 4. System output for interpretation of image sequence
(experiment on protoplasts dielectrophoresis).

4. CONCLUSIONS

In this paper we have presented knowledge base structure and knowledge representation
in ISIA system. The system reasoning is performed on the basis of the general domain
model by applying more specific (task-dependent) production rules, which are grouped into
appropriate rule sets. By changing and adjusting object descriptions, control and
interpretation rules, we can use the system for interpreting images from other sources (e.g.
fluorescence microscopy) and image sequences from other types of experiments.

Acknowledgements: We would like to thank Prof. D.S. Dimitrov and Prof. V.Tomov for
their support and helpful discussions.

REFERENCES

[1] Balev, B., Sharkov, G., Knowledge-Based Interpretation of Biophysical Images, Jorrand, Ph. and V. Sgurev (eds.), Artificial Intelligence IV - methodology, systems, applications, North-Holland, pp 405-414, 1990.

[2] Balev, B., Sharkov, G. Analysis of Biomedical Image Sequences with Knowledge-Based System ISIA, in: Proc. of 7-th Scandinavian Conference on Image Analysis, 1991, in print

[3] Brooks, R.A., Symbolic Reasoning Among 3-D Models and 2-D Images, Artificial Intelligence, vol.17, No1-3 1981, pp285-348.

[4] Darwish, A.M., Jain, A.K., A Rule Based Approach for Visual Pattern Inspection,IEEE-PAMI-10, No1,1988.

[5] Dimitrov, D., Tomov, V., Sharkov, G., Angelova, M., Liposome Production and Protoplast Electrofusion Expert Systems, in: Jorrand, Ph. and V. Sgurev (eds.), Artificial Intelligence II - methodology, systems, applications, North-Holland, pp 219-226, 1987.

[6] McKeown, D. et al., Automating Knowledge Acquisition for Aerial mage Interpretation, GVGIP, Vol 46, No1, pp 37-81, 1989.

[7] Menhardt, W. and Schmidt, K.H., Computer Vision on Magnetic Resonance Images, Pattern Recognition Letters 8, 1988.

[8] Niemann, H. (et al.), A Knowledge Based System for Analysis of Gated Blood Pool Studies, IEEE-PAMI-7, No5, 1985.

[9] Sagerer, G., Automatic Interpretation of Medical Image Sequences, Pattern Recognition Letters 8, 1988.

[10] Sharkov, G. and D. Dimitrov, Knowledge Representation and Reasoning in ES for Biophysics, in: Ras and Saitta (eds.), Methodologies for Intelligent Systems - 3, North-Holland, pp 150-159, 1988.

A BLACKBOARD SYSTEM FOR DISTRIBUTED ANALYSIS OF IMAGE SEQUENCES

K. Welz[1],   C.-E. Liedtke[1]

Abstract

The analysis of image sequences, which have been obtained by a TV camera from a natural scene, requires in general a large number of different tasks. Under real–time conditions many of these tasks have to be executed simultaneously. This paper proposes a multiprocessor architecture, which supports the system requirements for such kind of image sequence analysis problems. Interprocess communication and task distribution are realized with the blackboard principle. To study the system requirements of a multiple task analysis system we have chosen, as an example, the automated recognition of traffic signs from a moving car.

1. Introduction

Execution time for the analysis of natural image sequences depends on the complexity of the scene. The more relevant objects the scene includes, the longer is the time needed for execution. Therefore, the analysis of natural image sequences using sequential task execution is often not possible, when real–time operation is requested. Parallel processing is necessary to increase processing power and system reliability. Increasing time requirements of an application problem should be compensated by a modular system extension, without changing any application software. For this reason, the whole problem must be divided into small independent subtasks, which can be distributed to the available processors /1/. Parallel task execution requires the exchange and collection of data and execution results. Cooperation between the parallel working processors is needed in order to increase reliability, availability, and performance of the whole system /2/. Because of the uncertainty in interpreting natural image sequences, a pure top down or bottom up strategy is not possible. The required mechanisms have to enable cooperation within and between all levels of image analysis, i.e. the numeric and the symbolic processing level. Type and number of tasks waiting to be executed at the same time depend on the content of the actual scene. These tasks have to be allocated to the processors /2, 3, 4/. For application problems, where the types and numbers of tasks vary during execution, an automatic distribution of the tasks to the available processors will be more efficient than static allocation, because it more effectively balances computation and communication. By a dynamic distribution of processing power image processing tasks can be done with a smaller set of processors.

In particular applications, like the navigation of vehicles in natural environments, the real time performance can be the most important criterion. Efficiency and cost effectiveness is important, but is not in all cases of utmost concern. The primary intention of this project is to develop an architecture, which permits real–time operation for a large range of image sequence analysis problems, based on multiprocessing. It is not the primary purpose to maximize processor efficiency.

---

[1]   Institut für Theoretische Nachrichtentechnik und Informationsverarbeitung,
Universität Hannover, Appelstr. 9A, D–3000 Hannover 1, FRG

2. A Blackboard for Parallel Image Analysis
2.1 Blackboard Principle

In a top down approach to sequence analysis, which is envisioned here, tasks have to be generated during run time. These tasks must be allocated dynamically to the free processors. An advantage of an automatic distribution strategy is a high flexibility in case of system extensions.

For task distribution we will use the blackboard principle which provides information about executable tasks and processing results. Processors are able to write new tasks and results onto the blackboard. Idling processors can read a new executable task from the blackboard. Processing results will be distributed via the blackboard.

2.2 Blackboard Structure

A blackboard entry specifies a task. Each task has a unique *number*. Tasks may have different types of *destination*. A task with the destination attribute "broadcast" has to be executed by each processor. The destination attribute "broadcast" is suitable for the distribution of data, which are important for each processor. Having the destination attribute "any" a task may be executed by any processor. The destination attribute "definite" specifies that a task has to be executed on a definite processor or a definite set of processors.

Each task has a *priority*. A high priority guaranties that very important tasks or very complex tasks will be processed first. Answer tasks will get a high priority, too, so that processing results will be returned as quickly as possible. The blackboard is organized as a priority sorted waiting queue. When creating a new blackboard entry, the creation *time* will be noticed. Priority will increase with increasing waiting time. A dynamic priority avoids that tasks with low priority will never be executed, if there are tasks with a higher priority generated permanently.

To differentiate between executable tasks, waiting tasks, and tasks containing processing results a blackboard entry includes a *status* field. The *type* of a task specifies the algorithms to be executed. To achieve a good computation balance each processor should be able to execute as many different tasks as possible. A task entry has input or output parameters. The *parameter* field contains the length of the data block and the data itself.

2.3 Blackboard Realization

In Shared Memory Systems a blackboard can be realized as a globally accessible data base. All medium-and high-level processors have access to the blackboard. A disadvantage is the fact that a master processor is needed for blackboard administration. Access to the blackboard may become a bottleneck. For large systems this central distribution strategy is not efficient.

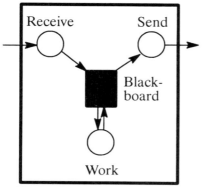

Fig. 1. Processes on a Dynamic
Blackboard Processor

Since we are mainly interested in large multiprocessor systems (not supercomputers), to avoid a system bottleneck only decentral schemes are considered. In loosely coupled systems with message passing we have the possibility to realize the blackboard principle for the data exchange as a dynamic blackboard. In a dynamic blackboard architecture blackboard entries will be distributed via the whole system. Each processor administers it's own local blackboard, which is organized as a priority sorted waiting queue. For this reason, at any time, each individual processor has access to a small part of the blackboard, only. Blackboard entries will be exchanged between the processors using special distribution strategies.

Fig. 1 shows that on each processor participating in the dynamic blackboard setup, three processes are running. All processes have access to a waiting queue, which contains a small part of the blackboard. The receive process receives tasks and writes them into the waiting queue. The work process may read a task from the waiting queue, executes this task, and writes processing results and/or new tasks into the waiting queue. The send process sends tasks, which have to be executed by other processors, and results to the next processor.

3 Results

In our present experimental setup the dynamic blackboard is realized on a transputer network, employing the transputer links for data exchange. First tests regarding parallel execution of image processing tasks are made. These tests measure speed up and overhead for a parallel task execution on the dynamic blackboard system. Fig. 2 shows the basic structure of our system, generally consisting of several rings of dynamic blackboard processors. To study the system requirements of the dynamic blackboard system we use the automated recognition of traffic signs from a moving vehicle. For these first tests we designed

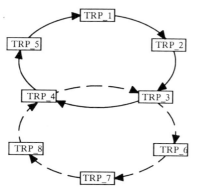

Fig. 2. Dynamic Blackboard System
consisting of two Processor Rings

a symmetrical organized dynamic blackboard. In this example we have only one blackboard (processor ring). The strategy of distributing tasks over the system is to send tasks to the next processors blackboard, when a processor is busy. Compared to other distribution strategies, where idling processors ask other processors for a task, our approach avoids additional overhead of idling processors.

The two conventional methods for parallel operation of image processing applications are data partitioning and functional partitioning. Data partitioning in image sequence analysis means that several processors execute the same task on different parts of the image. Functional par–

250

titioning means that different tasks are executed on different processors. The tasks which have to be executed in parallel in connection with the traffic sign recognition are for instance observing the left and right road edge, searching for new candidates for traffic signs along the road edge, and tracking /5/ as well as interpreting possible traffic signs. Fig. 3 illustrates the types of parallel execution in our system.

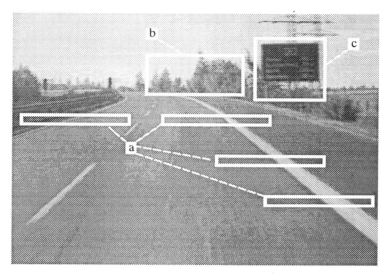

Fig. 3.   Road Scene with Windows for Road Edge Tracking (a),
Candidate Search (b), and Traffic Sign Tracking and Interpreting (c)

The strategy in finding road edges is the subdivision of the problem into an initial global analysis of the roadway and the tracking of the road edges. For the global analysis region orientated segmentation methods are used /6, 7/. When knowing the location of the road edges, it is sufficient to determine changes in the location in small control windows /8/, because of the little changes between two images. For this reason, tracking road edges can be executed in parallel for different locations within the TV image plane by different processors. The tracking of the road edges by several windows represents data partitioning. The results supplied by the parallel road edge tracking will be combined in a road model. The model knowledge controls the positioning of the windows for road edge tracking and candidate search.

A window for searching candidates for traffic signs can be set in that area where new traffic signs appear with a high likelihood. For the purpose of searching candidates for traffic signs we use different methods i.e. searching for triangles, circles, or areas of specific colors. This is an example for functional partitioning, because there are different tasks for the same window.

Having found a distant candidate for a traffic sign it cannot be identified, because of its small size. Hypotheses about the type of the detected traffic sign will be generated. These hypotheses will be verified in each new image. A hypothesis will be confirmed, rejected, or step by step refined. The smaller the distance to the traffic sign, the more information about the traffic sign is available, so that the hypothesis can be more specific. For the purpose of observing a traffic sign it must be tracked.

Fig. 4 shows the task graph for the automated recognition of traffic signs from a moving car. For each image the tasks 1 to 7 have to be executed. The tasks 8 to 11 have to be executed only, if a candidate for a traffic sign has been detected. These tasks are data dependent. The type and number of parallel working tasks is dynamically changing.

The execution time for the parallel execution of the tasks from the task graph from Fig. 4 in dependence on the number of working tranputers participating in the dynamic blackboard set up is measured. The test varies the number of working transputers from 1 to 5. In this example we have 8 tasks for "road_edge_tracking", 4 different tasks for "candidate_search", and two candidates for traffic signs, which have to be tracked and interpreted. Fig. 5 shows the execution time and Tab. 1 the speed up depending on the number of transputers.

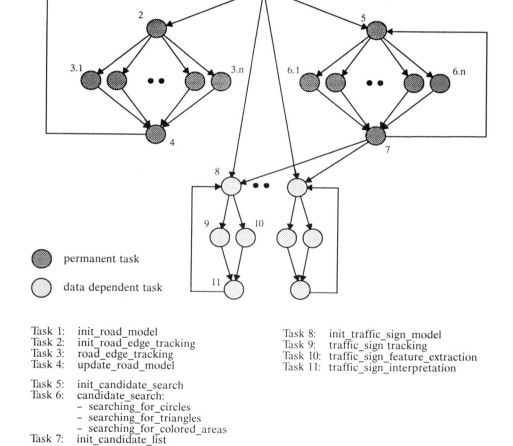

Task 1:   init_road_model
Task 2:   init_road_edge_tracking
Task 3:   road_edge_tracking
Task 4:   update_road_model

Task 5:   init_candidate_search
Task 6:   candidate_search:
          – searching_for_circles
          – searching_for_triangles
          – searching_for_colored_areas
Task 7:   init_candidate_list

Task 8:   init_traffic_sign_model
Task 9:   traffic_sign tracking
Task 10: traffic_sign_feature_extraction
Task 11: traffic_sign_interpretation

Fig. 4. Task Graph for Traffic Sign Recognition

252

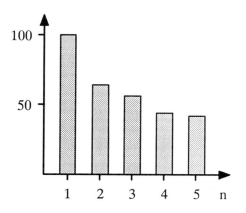

Number of Transputers n	Speed Up
1	1.00
2	1.54
3	1.79
4	2.26
5	2.38

Fig.. 5. Relative Execution Time Depending on the Number of Transputers n

Tab. 1. Speed Up Depending on the Number of Transputers n

4. Acknowledgements

The work has been supported by the Deutsche Forschungsgemeinschaft (DFG).

5. References

[1] Howe, Carl D., Bruce Moxon: "How to program parallel processors", IEEE Spectrum, September 1987.

[2] Ni Lionel M., Chong–Wei Xu, Thomas B. Gendereau: "A Distributed Drafting Algorithm for Load Balancing", IEEE Trans. on Software Engineering, Vol. SE–11, No. 10, October 1985.

[3] Lin Frank C. H., Robert M. Keller: "The Gradient Model Load Balancing Method", IEEE Trans. on Software Engineering, Vol. SE–13, No. 1, January 1987.

[4] Chou Timothy C. K., Jacob A. Abraham: "Load Balancing in Distributed Systems", IEEE Trans. on Software Engineering, Vol. SE–8, No. 4, July 1982.

[5] Liedtke C.-E., H. Busch, R. Koch: "Automatic Modelling of 3D Moving Objects from a TV Image Sequence", SPIE/SPSE Symposium on Electronic Imaging, Santa Clara, CA., USA, Feb. 1990.

[6] Turk Matthew A., David G. Morgenthaler, Keith D. Gremban, Martin Marra: "VITS–A Vision System for Autonomous Land Vehicle Navigation", IEEE Transactions on Pattern Analysis and Machine Intelligence, Vol. 10, No. 3, May 1988.

[7] Thorpe C., M. H. Hebert, T. Kanade, S. A. Shafer: "Vision and Navigation for the Carnegie–Mellon Navlab", IEEE Transactions on Pattern Analysis and Machine Intelligence, Vol. 10, No. 3, May 1988.

[8] Dickmanns E. D., Th. Christians: "Relative 3D–State Estimation for Autonomous Visual Guidance of Road Vehicles", Intelligent Autonomous Systems 2 (IAS-2) Amsterdam, 11–14 December 1989.

APPLICATIONS OF IMAGE ANALYSIS TECHNIQUES TO
THE CHARACTERIZATION AND QUALITY CONTROL OF NATURAL RESOURCES

MUGE, F.*; PINA, P.*; GUIMARÃES, C.*

ABSTRACT: In this paper case studies are presented covering applications of mathematical morphology based image analysis techniques to the quality control of cork products and to the characterization of different types of ornamental rocks. Image analysis techniques are used to determine defects shown by cork products. In order to detect and classify those defects, an automatic procedure was implemented, based on multithresholding and mathematical morphology algorithms.

In the second case study, ornamental rocks, the main purpose is to discriminate between different types of patterns occurring in ornamental rocks, in order to optimize the industrial operation of cutting and to constitute homogeneous stocks of material.

1. FIRST CASE STUDY

The utilisation and processing of commercial cork of *Quercus suber L.* depends very much on its structural quality influenced by the presence of various defects resulting from harvesting, from invading organisms and other causes.

In the manufacturing of stopper cork of champagne bottles, circular cork disks are used. On each of its two flat surfaces with a 3,5 centimeters diameter, can occur several natural defects, which conditionate the value of the final product. The main defects exhibited by these disks can be classified in two groups, (see picture 1):

- voids and *prego*
- coloured spots

Image analysis techniques were sucessfully used to identify and classify these groups of defects. Therefore, an automatic procedure was developped, consisting on the following steps:

1. Creation of a circular mask, within which all the image processing is executed.

2. Identification of all the defects, using the same automatic method.

3. Classification of voids and *prego* at once, and classification of spots in terms of its colour, using a more elaborated procedure.

---

* Research Group in Image Analysis, Dep. Mining Engineering, IST - Technical University of Lisbon

1.1. Creation of a circular mask

The cork disks have a standard dimension. Therefore, a circular mask with its dimension can be created with the purpose of processing images within it, (see picture 2). Some advantages are obtained with the creation of this geodesy, to know : time saving because the image processing is done in a more restricted area, as if it was in the initial field and identification of the voids which are contacting the border of the disk.

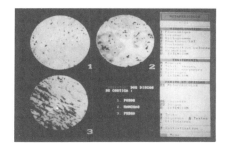

Picture 1. Main defects in a disk.

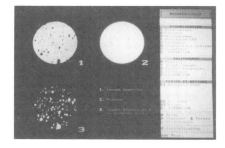

Picture 2. Mask creation.

1.2 Identification of the defects

In every digitalized image of a cork disk, three grey level populations can be determined. The darker population corresponds to the voids and *prego*, the middle one to the spots, while the brighter population represents the cork with no defects (healthy cork), as can be seen in picture 3.

Having a cork disk image with a grey level histogram with three peaks, automatic methods to determine these populations were issued. The one who conducted to better results is based on its later version due to Kapur et al. (1985) an automatic multithresholding technique using maximale entropy

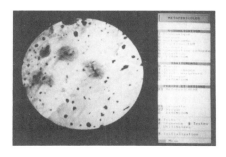

Picture 3. Image of a cork disk.

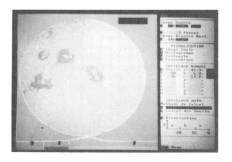

Picture 4. Image processing.

method. In order to better evaluate the information presented in an image, by obtaining the maximum contrast between each grey level population, a maximisation of the entropy of the image is performed. So, with this method, at the same time, three grey level populations corresponding to the three different structures (voids/prego, spots and healthy cork) are searched. The criteria for determine the existence or absence of each defect lies on the surface occupied by each grey level classe. The result of application of this method is shown in picture 4.

1.3. Classification of the defects

1.3.1. Voids and *prego*

Voids and *prego* are defects that belong to the darker population, having this way a similar grey level. The discrimination between these two types of defects can be achieved by the application of a shape criteria, once the *prego* is characterized by its elongated shape. So, this elongation factor can be obtained, for each particle, through the relation between Feret's maximum diameter and the corresponding orthogonal diameter (see picture 5). The measures allowing a disk classification in terms of porosity (which includes voids and *prego*) are its size distribution and the identification of those that touch the disk border. Size distribution is performed by using increasing size morphological openings (erosions followed by dilations of the set). The voids in the border of the disk can be identified performing an intersection between the set of all voids and the binary contour of the mask. The resulting set will constitute the marker for the reconstruction (geodesical dilation performed till idempotence) of only that kind of defect.

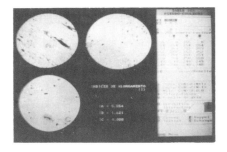

Picture 5. Identification of *prego*.   Picture 6. Color image processing.

1.3.2. Coloured spots

If the analysis of the surface occupied by the intermediate grey level class concludes about the occurrence of spots, a discrimination according to its colour is necessary. In what concerns the discrimination between the coloured spots (yellow and green are the main occurrences) it is necessary to process images acquired from a colour camera. The study of the three RGB components of the coloured image don't reveal enough contrast between spots of different colours. So, a conversion of the RGB components into another three components of a colour image, namely IHS (intensity, hue, saturation) is performed. The resulting image from H-component shows a sufficient contrast between the spots which allows the respective classification. In picture 6, one can see the results of this transformation.

2. SECOND CASE STUDY

In this case study the main goal is to discriminate between different types of patterns occurring in ornamental rocks, in order to optimize the industrial processing of cutting, and in the other hand, to constitute homogeneous stocks of material. This classification is often difficult to achieve due to the similarity of patterns presented, being, till today, executed by human visual inspection. Picture 7 shows a common pattern of veining occurring in a marble plate.

Picture 7 - Image of a marble plate

In order to improve the quality control of ornamental rock plates obtained during a cutting operation it is necessary to:

. Identify different patterns occurring in the larger plates before cutting
. Classify the cutted plates into homogeneous material stocks

A size criterion concerning the area occupied by the dark veinings was used to guide the cutting operation. In this case a regular grid was superimposed (Picture 8).

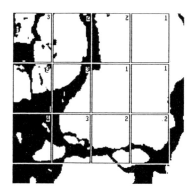

Picture 8 - Grid superimposition and classification

In each cell, the relative surface occupied by the dark veinings is measured and the cells are classified in classes according to the respective value. The origin of the regular grid can be translated and/or rotated in order to achieve the best recovery in terms of "good" marble plates (low level of dark veinings). Different patterns can occur within the same class. In order to distinguish between them, the following morphological criteria were used:

 i) **Covariance** - This function is used to detect preferential alignements (anisotropies) and the occurrence of periodicities.

 ii) **Linear size criterion** - This criterion is applied to detect differences in the thickness of the veins in each direction.

 iii) **Connectivity** criterion - This criterion is used to identify connected sets. The corresponding morphological transform is an homotopic thinning of the inicial set, called skeleton, which preserves the connexity number, i. e., the resulting image has the same number of particles and holes than the initial set.

As Serra (1982) points out, the methodology applied for the discrimination of objects consists on associating a specific criterion to each type of objects to be eliminated. The application of the criterion often "damages" all the particles present in the image, however some of them (those we wish to recognize) are characterized by tipical deformation.

3. CONCLUSIONS

In the first case study, identification and classification of defects occurring in cork, the methodology proposed based on an automatic procedure leaded to a good result which predicts a sucessful automation of the industrial process.

In the second case study, ornamental rocks, mathematical morphology showed to be an adequate tool for pattern recognition and discrimination.

REFERENCES

Kapur, J. N.; Sahoo, P. K.; Wong, A. K. C. - *A New Method for Gray Level Picture Thresholding Using the Entropy of the Histogram*, Computer Vision, Graphics and Image Processing, 29, 273-285, 1985.

Matheron, G. - *Éléments pour une Théorie des Milieux Poreux*, Ed. Masson, Paris, 1967.

Muge, F.; Pina P.; Guimaraes C. - *Applications of Mathematical Morphology Based Image Analysis Techniques to Mine Planning*, presented at 2 th CODATA, Leeds, Sept. 1990, to be published in "Sciences de la Terre".

Pina, P. - *Rapport de Stage - MATRA-Ms2i*, Internal Report, GIAI-IST, Lisbon, 1990.

Serra, J. - *Image Analysis and Mathematical Morphology*, Ed. Academic Press, Paris, 1982.

IMAGE PROCESSING IN CAIS - AN INTELLIGENT SYSTEM
FOR CHROMOSOME ANALYSIS AND CLASSIFICATION

Ekaterina Decheva [1]

INTRODUCTION.

Chromosome analysis is used for a wide variety of clinical, screening and biological measurement purposes. It is a useful tool in fundamental research of human chromosomes, in diagnostics and in environmental toxicology. Chromosome analysis is a technique of considerable importance to both clinicians and researchers. To cope with the increasing demands for speed and accuracy many attempts have been made in the past 25 years to investigate the possibilities of chromosome analysis automating. The classical approach is to analyze the image of a methaphase cell on a microscope slide.

The intelligent system CAIS is developed to perform chromosome analysis and classification and to find out the existence of possible chromosomal aberrations. The system is functioning in three steps: methaphase image preprocessing, object analysis and chromosome classification. The first two steps perform grey-level image processing. The preprocessing includes smoothing and segmentation of the methaphase image. The image is segmented using a global threshold computed from a histogram of all grey levels. As a result grey-level images of the isolated objects are obtained. The object analysis is performed to extract certain features needed for chromosome classification. The main features are chromosome length and centromere index. To calculate these features the chromosomes' contour is detected. Chromosome classification is based on the knowledge about the chromosome classes. It attaches the chromosomes to their appropriate classes.

The structure and the functioning of the system CAIS are discussed in details in [1]. This paper describes methaphase image preprocessing and chromosomes analysis.

PREPROCESSING.

The methaphase image is obtained from cells on a microscope slide.

[1] Institute of Mathematics, Bulgarian Acadamy of Sciences, Acad. G. Bonchev st., Block 8, 1113 Sofia, BULGARIA

For this purpose the microscope is equipped with a TV-camera connected to a computer. At first, the methaphase image is digitalized and stored into a 256x256 array. The elements of the array represent the gray values of the pixels in the image and are integers between 0 and 255.

Initially methaphase image smoothing is made using median filtering. Next a brightness histogram is built and three thresholds are calculated using the following formulae:

$$T_3 = 80\% * B_{max}$$
$$T_1 = B_{max} - T_3$$
$$T_2 = T_3 - T_1,$$

where B_{max} is the grey value where the brightness frequency has it's maximum (see figure 1).

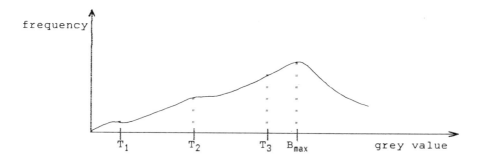

Figure 1. A brightness histogram

This method is based on the approach described in [2].

The three thresholds are used for image displaying in four colors. Object isolation is realized using T_1 as global threshold. This is done by a recursive procedure analyzing a 3x3 window with a center - the current pixel with gray value greater then T_1.

OBJECT ANALYSIS.

Object analysis is realized by procedures applied to each isolated object. Initially object contour detection is performed by LaPlassian filtering using 3x3 convolution on the current window with the kernel below [4]:

```
0   -1   0
-1   4  -1
0   -1   0
```

Then chromosome centromere is located using the method based on
the "closest approach" [2]. The two opposite contour points with
longest distance are determined first. They define the left and
the right contour part of the chromosome. Than the distances
between every left and right contour point are calculated. The two
opposite contour points with the shortest distance define the
centromere position. The location of the centromere is in the
middle of the segment connecting the two contour points. In order
not to misplace the centromere at the ends of the chromosome the
top and bottom contour points are ignored (see figure 2).

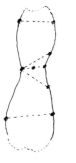

Figure 2.

Next the length of chromosome arms is measured. The length of each
arm is calculated as the longest distance between the centromere
position and each contour point of the arm (see figure 3).

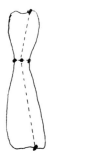

Figure 3.

The position of the centromere is displayed on the screen and the
operator can interactively make corrections if it is misplaced.

262   CAIP'91

The total chromosome length is calculated as a sum of the two arms lengths. Finally centromere index is computed as a ratio between the length of the short arm and the length of the chromosome. This approach can be successfully applied also to bent chromosomes (see figure 4).

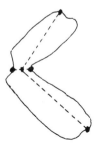

Figure 4.

CONCLUSIONS.

The purpose of this paper is to describe an approach to the methaphase image processing. It differs from the approaches used in the existing systems for automatic chromosome analysis. The main difference is in centromere detection and chromosome measurement. Currently most systems [3] are based on the location of the principal axes of the chromosomes and on some geometrical corrections like rotation and straightening in the case of bent chromosomes. This method is extremely complicated. In the presented system CAIS the chromosome analysis is based on the object contour. The procedures for preprocessing and analysis are using also some computer graphics methods [5]. The advantage of this approach is it's simplicity. Another point of interest is that object isolation, centromere position detection and chromosome length measuring follow the way of manual karyotyping.

The system supports some other functions like image file input/output, image negating, image binarization, graphic image editing, etc. that are not discussed in this paper.

The CAIS system is realized in TURBO C on IBM-PC/AT computers.

REFERENCES.

[1] Decheva E., V.Valev. Knowledge based automated chromosome analysis system - a conception. Third International Conference on Computer Analysis of Images and Patterns CAIP'89,1989,Leipzig,GDR.

[2] Kate T.K ten. Design and implementation of an interactive karyotyping program in C on a VICOM image processor. I2 Report, Systems and Signals Group, Section Pattern Recognition, Department of Applied Physics, Delft University of Technology, 1985.

[3] Lunsteen C., J. Piper (eds.). Automation of Cytogenetics. Springer, Berlin, 1989.

[4] PIP EZ. MS DOS Software Library for the PIP-512/1024 Video Digitizer, MATROX Electronic Limited, 1986.

[5] Rogers D.F., J.A. Adams. Mathematical elements for computer graphics. Moscow, 1980 (in Russian).

SEGMENTATION AND AGGREGATION OF TEXT FROM IMAGES OF MIXED TEXT AND GRAPHICS

SH Joseph, Mechanical & Process Engineering Dept, Sheffield University, Mappin St, Sheffield S1

INTRODUCTION

The prime consideration in segmenting text out of images that contain graphics has been the distinctive large size or high level of the connected components that are not text symbols. To detect which of the residue are text we must look to relations between components. This can be done by constructing text strings and comparing characters within. Excessive identical repetition or string length [3], or lack of word breaks [9] have been taken to indicate graphical objects. These methods are hindered by errors in binarization which result in false connection between components. If such errors join actual characters to each other they may be parted under strong assumptions about the characteristics of the string that contains them [2] or by OCR on the fragments due to trial parting places [4]. If, however, they join actual text to actual graphics, they have been separated only in special cases when the graphics are tightly defined [1, 5, 7]. The aggregation of text into strings can be done by testing components for proximity [9], optionally preceded by tests for collinearity [3].

Some more general approach is required if we are to process the wide class of documents that assume the human ability to segment and aggregate characters with graphics which touch or even intersect. Such an approach must be part of a total which attempts to interpret the whole document. It must operate in a manner that relates clearly to the rules defining the structure of the document so that the class of processable documents can be identified and extended as desired. As well as handling blocks of text (paragraph/line/word/character) it should deal with labels and signs. This then is a case of the general problem of matching a description to error-prone data. It is possible in some cases to overcome errors by best match techniques [6, 8], but these are only feasible for localised, discretised structures. The present problem is one in which the discrete letters are joined to the large, continuous graphical structures in the drawing.

An alternative technique, sometimes found in general vision systems [8] is to use an initial segmentation to refine and extend the analysis. Errors in initial segmentation at character level can be corrected by using the structure defining rules to refine the segmentation. For example, a character in a word connected to a neighbouring line could be recovered by seeking the missing character in a string, or by seeking the label for a pre-existing line. This implies the existence in the image of objects which can be identified with a high degree of certainty, so that they can be used as the basis for prediction of uncertain cases. If the technique is to work, the confidence of prediction must not be excessive given the strength of the context, otherwise many false positives will arise. Also, this confidence must be upgraded as certainty rises, so that false negatives are minimised.

The problem remains of properly defining and handling these certainties and confidences, and assessing the performance of the resulting system. There is no established method for building and using context in this way; in this situation the requirement must be for a system in which we can experiment with methods and see the results at every stage clearly displayed. Only when we have established a qualitative grasp of some appropriate methods can we pass on to the quantitative optimisation of their performance, and to seek the optimal structure for the system which applies them.

Custom programming of such context based extraction is prohibitive unless we are very selective about the contexts we encompass. Fortunately, technical drawings are highly conventional, and the standards contain a good quantity of hierarchical rules to describe allowed styles of drawing. In these a number of repetitive or cyclic entities (broken lines, hatching, words) are found, which provide well define contexts for their aggregation element by element.

The present work reports some new context based methods employing the ANON engineering drawing conversion system, discusses their performance, and assesses their implications for system design.

THE IMPLEMENTATION OF CONTEXT BASED SEGMENTATION

ANON contains a hierarchically organised set of schemata (or frames) describing prototypical drawing constructs. In its present form the system includes schemata corresponding to solid, dashed and chained lines, solid and dashed circles and arcs, cross hatching, physical outlines, text (both letters and words), witness and leader lines and simple forms of dimensioning.

Each schema contains a geometrical and structural description of the construct it represents, a set of state variables noting the current condition of that representation and a number of procedures and functions written in the C language. ANON combines the extraction of primitive descriptions with their interpretation. All image analysis is performed in the context of the current schema a particular hypothesis regarding the local content of the drawing.ANON's control system is rule-based. Rules are written in the form of an LR(1) grammar and applied by a parser generated using the unix utility yacc. While this use of a parser as an inference engine is restrictive in that rules must be expressed in a format that can be interpreted by yacc, the advantages of the approach easily outweigh the problems it causes.

Thus the current schema provides the context for the extraction process. We will consider the extraction of problematic text as a series of contexts, describing the examination of the image and the criteria that are applied in each.

CONTEXT 1: FAILED GRAPHICS

Fig 1. (below) shows a piece of text at two thresholds demonstrating the inescapable connection of graphics and text found in real examples of engineering drawings.

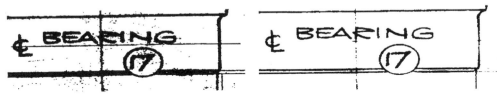

ANON seeks stroke type ink marks as the basis for all its constructs; these will be at least twice as long as the maximum expected line width. These strokes are developed into graphical primitives such as line, curves and broken curves, and the primitives assembled into high level entities. If the initial strokes lie in text then the processing applied is quite inappropriate, and no legal graphical entity is found. The control rules reflect this, in that an object 'nongraph' is instantiated when an error occurs while developing a graphic primitive. This object then applies processing suitable to the extraction of text: that of contour tracking to extract a connected component.

This is illustrated in Fig 2. (above). The letter 'R' is connected to linework, and is rejected as too large, as would be any part of the 'E' or 'A' which are joined together. The letter 'N' is accepted as generating a contour with a suitably small bounding box.

False positives arise through graphics failing to develop when they should. Many of these will arise from marks that are connected to large regions of black, and so will be caught by the subsequent contour tracking. Those that do not will be accepted as isolated text, but should not be built into strings. They will often be found as part of graphics subsequently, and flagged as overlapping conflicting by the entity storage system. Reduction of these errors is sought by improvement to the graphics extraction method: the alternative, to build putative strings out of them, then reject them as graphics after all, is an inappropriate arrogation of processing that clearly fits the graphics context better.

False negatives occur when text objects fit graphics descriptions. Not many of these persist, as the subsequent extraction is structured so that, for example, coincidental collinearities are rejected at higher level. An example that remains is the capital 'O' / small circle confusion. We consider that the graphics schemata need to be able to extract small circles and store them without reference to the kind of context that would be necessary to reject 'O's. These circles will stay and be flagged as overlapping conflicting when the rest of the word is detected. False negatives will also occur when failed graphics embraces several connected components including text, but does not initiate contour tracking in one which is actually text. This would be overcome if the text were part of a string and if the string were initiated from a different letter. Otherwise, it is likely to be a case of an isolated letter related to graphics (see below).

The contour tracking carried out by the 'nongraph' is used to determine the principal bounding box of the connected component of which is is part. If that box falls within predetermined size limits then the next context is instantiated, that of text.

CONTEXT 2: TEXT

In this context we have a connected component of a suitable size which did not develop into a graphical structure. Such objects are valid in drawings as symbols isolated from other text, and are accepted as such as a part of our drawing schema. In future developments we propose to implement the relation of these symbols to other graphical entities in our image description. Much more commonly, though, they are found in strings forming numbers or words. Accordingly, the text object searches for neighbouring letters so that this string context can be instantiated. An outward radial search is performed in the image for ink marks (Fig. 3, right) and those found are contour tracked to identify their connectivity. As we now seek a second letter, the charac-

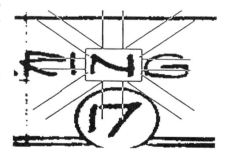

teristics of the current letter can be used to refine our search. A limiting box is applied to the contour tracking, based on its start location and the size of the current letter. This is shown in Fig. 4, (right) where the contour around a neighbouring graphics

object contacts the limiting box, and is rejected. If, on the other hand, the track lies within the box the string context is instantiated with the two letters as input. Fig. 5 (left) illustrates this for the 'G'.

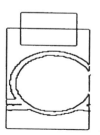

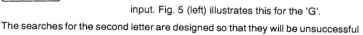

The searches for the second letter are designed so that they will be unsuccessful if the current letter was a false positive from the previous nongraph context, and thus not be built into strings.

To obtain a false positive second letter a suitably sized connected component must fall into the search area. Such a component could be graphics or text, and could be related or unrelated to the first letter. Related components that are not part of strings can only be dealt with by extending the system description to include the context of which they and the first letter are part. Unrelated components in this context would certainly constitute bad typography or draughtsmanship, and be confusing even to the human observer. A more subtle false positive arises when the rules for seeking the second letter are inadequate. For example, the rule that "the next letter in the string is the nearest one" does not hold in toleranced dimensions. This case is best dealt with by extending the image description to include 'tolerancing text' explicitly.

False negative second letters will arise from letters connected to linework, or several letters connected to each other. It is possible to adjust the limiting box to accept two connected letters as a next letter, without unacceptable levels of false positives. False negatives also arise from a failure to find the second letter within the search area. This will be corrected if the string can be found starting at another letter, but short, badly connected strings are likely to be found as separate letters rather than as strings.

CONTEXT 3. STRINGS

A string is instantiated from two letters or from a letter found to label a leader line. The string direction is taken as that joining the centroids of their bounding boxes, and the string height is taken as the extent of their bounding boxes measured normal to that direction.

The string context extends itself by seeking further letters to complete a word. These are sought as ink marks in a target region calculated from the string dimensions and interletter gap (see Fig. 6, right). The marks are then contour tracked, within a limiting box;

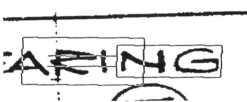

a connected com-

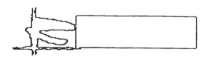

ponent lying entirely inside the box is accepted as an additional letter in the string ('I' in Fig. 7, left). Thus this context is similar to that of a letter, but more precise due to the increased localisation of searching and testing. False positives are at a very low rate, and this permits more elaborate procedures to overcome false negatives due to text connected to graphics.

By a straightforward extension to the contour tracking algorithm it is possible to obtain a 'contour in a box' which follows the contour while it lies inside the limiting box, but follows the box boundary otherwise. This contour contains more useful information than a normal contour, as it reports only on components within the allowed area of interest. Fig 8 (left) shows such a contour in the case where a letter is connected to linework. For cases of letters that are connected to the box boundary by a simple line passing through or by them, it is possible to cut out the effects of that line, once it is identified, as follows. First, the parts of the contour that are attributable to the line itself are defined simply as those parts of the contour lying closer to the line than one line width away. We then wish to determine whether the contour can be explained as a letter whose sole connection to the box is due to the distracting line. This is done by discarding parts of the contour attributed to the line; the residue can then be tested for suitability as the next letter in the usual way.

268

This method is readily extended to a case where a letter is connected in a more complex manner to the limiting box. Here, we discard from the above residue parts of the contour which are connected to the box, and test this second residue as before. Identification of the distracting line is performed by examination of the limiting box for black marks, and attempting to grow lines from them. Candidate distracting lines are then used alternately as input to the above excision procedure; if any of these produce an acceptable residual contour it is taken to be the next letter and is used to extend the string.

Fig. 9 (above, left) shows the parts of the contour discarded under this procedure, and Fig. 10 (above,right) the residue accepted as part of the string.

The 'EA' that is a single contour (see fig. 11, left) is next accepted as a letter in this context, although it would be rejected as such in the 'failed graphics' context.

Finally, in Fig. 12 (right) a text object outside the string is encountered and rejected as contacting the limiting box.

False negatives will clearly still occur if the connection to the limiting box is more complex, or if line extraction fails. In the former we have approached the limit of human intelligibility; in the latter we employ context based line tracking which also approaches human capability.

False positives may occur if graphics features are coincidentally present which have the appropriate residual contour after line excision. This again is confusing to the human observer.

CONTEXT 4. WORDS AND DIMENSIONS

Words are instantiated on the exhaustion of a string at both its ends. They are accepted as isolated entities in the drawing. The only action taken by this context is the search below or to the right of a string for a parallel close line to be a leader line labelled by the word . If such a line develops into a dimension object then the word is taken as the text of that dimension.

False positives arise from false negative next letters in strings; no attempt is made to overcome that by additional searches in this context. Established leader lines search for text at the expected location of their labels and instantiate a string with the first such letter found, using the direction of the leader as the string direction. Extraction of single letter labels is thus obtained only from the dimension graphics, and the second letter of a two letter label can thus be extracted despite distracting lines.

DISCUSSION

The above description indicates the power of context based extraction to overcome some of the classic problems in text segmentation, as well as the worth of the ANON system in providing a framework for its operation.

It is clear that the present methodology is in an early stage, where its crude outlines are being laid down. Current work focusses on experiments with contexts and criteria with two aims: to draw up guidelines for good practice in system construction, and to quantify the false detection rates described above.

REFERENCES

[1]Abe K, Azumatani Y, Mukouda M and Suzuki S, Proc 8th ICPR p.1071, Paris, 1986.

[2]Baird HS, Kahan S and Pavlidis T, Proc 8th ICPR p.344, Paris, 1986.

[3]Fletcher LA and Kasturi R, IEEE Trans PAMI, 10, 910, 1988.

[4]Holbaek-Hanssen E, Braten K and Taxt T, Proc 8th ICPR p.144, Paris, 1986.

[5]Kasturi R, Bow S-Z, Gattiker J, Shah J, El-Masri W, Mokate U and Honnenahali S, Proc 9th ICPR p.255, Rome, 1988.

[6]Maderlechner G and Kreich J, Proc 2nd Int. Conf. on Image Processing, p 139, IEE London, 1986

[7]Maeda Y, Yoda F, Matsuura K and Nambu H, Proc 8th ICPR p.769, Paris, 1986.

[8]Matsuyama T and Hwang V, Proc 9th IJCAI, p 908, 1985.

[9]Meynieux E, Seisa S and Tombre K, Proc 8th ICPR p.442, Paris, 1986.

STRATEGIES IN IMAGE ANALYSIS

Fuchs, S.; Gruber, G.; Cong, T. V. [1]

1. Problem statement

If we understand image analysis as describing an image not in the sense of signal theory but in terms of semantic then we have to think about some model information, consisting from relations between semantic entities and signal space. Such an image interpretation process has to answer one of the two following questions:

(Q1)   The classical pattern recognition formulation: What is it?

(Q2)   The computer vision formulation: Where is it?

Optimal methods and approximations of it are well known to find answers to the first question. But the problem arises:

(P1)   How may be found an optimal solution to the question (Q2)?

The solutions to question (Q1) are typical buttom-up-procedures and on the other hand we can try to answer analogously the question (Q2) but by a top-down procedure using also the statistical decision theory. Fig. 1 shows the two problems stated in an analogous way and in such manner, that Bayesian decisions follow.

bottom up   top down

Given:

- signal $\underline{x}$ - model (prototyp) M

- set of classes (models)   - set of signals (Image I)
  $\{M_k \mid k=1...K\}$ $\{\underline{x} \mid \underline{x} \subseteq I\}$

-                   set of decisions $\equiv$ set of Interpretations

  $\{e_j \mid (e_j=(\underline{x},M_j), \ j=1..K) \ v \ e_0\}$ $\{e_{\underline{x}} \mid e_{\underline{x}} = (M,\underline{x}) \ \underline{x} \subseteq I\}$

-                              cost function

  $C(e,k)$ k true model $C(e_{\underline{x}},\underline{x})$ $\underline{x}$ true signal

-                              probabilities

  $\{P(M_k \mid \underline{x}) \mid \underline{x}, \forall M_k\}$ $\{P(\underline{x} \mid M) \mid M, \forall \underline{x} \subseteq I\}$

-                      Bayesian solution:

  $e_{\hat{n}} = \underset{\forall e}{\text{argmin}} \ \underset{\forall k}{\Sigma} \ P(M_k|k) \ C(e,k)$ $e_{\underline{x}} = \underset{\forall \underline{x}}{\text{argmin}} \ \underset{\forall \underline{x} \in I}{\Sigma} \ P(\underline{x}|M) \ C(e_{\underline{x}},x)$

Fig.1: Comparison of problem statements and bayesian solution for the bottom up and top down procedure respectively

This is a principal solution of the problem (P1). But this theoretic result is mostly useless because of the combinational explosion. Therefore in some realised image interpretation systems mixed bottom-up/top-down procedures are used /1/. A second problem arises:

[1]   TU Dresden, Fakultät Informatik, Institut DBKI, Mommsenstr. 13, O-8027 Dresden

(P2)   How to construct systematically such mixed procedures and how to optimise them?

At first we want to describe a solution of a concrete task and give than some generalizations.

2. An example of applying a mixed strategy

We selected the following task:

Identify the number of the car presented in a black-white TV frame.

The image is produced under some standardized conditions:

(C1)   Fixed positioning of the camera with respect to the hind part of the car (with negligible derivations)

(C2)   Small variations of illumination

(C3)   Short pick -up time (only for a half interlaced picture)

(C4)   The whole frame consists of rough two hundred times more pixels than the number plate occupies.

From the condition (C4) follows that it is not efficient to interpret the whole frame, which may be structured in a difficult manner. There is an obvious conclusion: to select a "region of interest" (ROI) focussing the analysing process to the interesting part of the image. But because the ROI must be known before be analysed, the first part, is a top-down procedure. It has to be started from one or more ROI models. When this or these ROIs are found the top down process is stopped. Then in a bottom-up process we have to estimate the fields each bearing a single character. Finally we have to classify the segment signal into the character classes (Fig. 2)

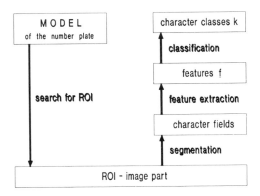

Fig.2: The steps solving the problem

The top-down process

This process searching for the number plate has to handle at least 4 degrees of freedom expressed by the questions for:

(1)   Number of ROIs?

(2)   Position(s) of ROI(s)?

(3)   Extent of ROI(s)?

(4)   Shape of ROI(s)?

The questions (3) and (4) may be decided destingtively based on apriori knowledge. The question (1) for the number of ROIs can be decided apriori too. The pick-up is controlled by the

272   CAIP'91

car being observed so, that only <u>one</u> number plate is placed on the image and therefore only one ROI is necessary. But the search for the number plate may fail indicating a region which may be similar to a number plate but is no one. For this case it is useful to analyse more than one candidates for ROI to select the best interpretation result. On the other hand the costs causing by the search and by the interpretation increase with the number of ROIs. Therefore the number of ROIs has to be optimised.

Let be:

- $C1$ The calculation costs for search and interpretation of one ROI
- C_{int} the medium interpretation risk of an ROI being a number plate
- C_{max} the costs of an useless interpretation (ROI is not a number plate)
- $P1$ the probability of success using only one ROI

It is possible to show that for the case $P1 > 1 - C1/(C_{max}-C_{int})$ the risk will be minimal using only one ROI.

The question (2) for the position of the ROI is realy an optimisation task which is to be solved at the observed image. The realised solution consists of a top-down search process using models, described by

- the shape and the extent of number plates (used as search windows running through the image)
- the topologic feature : The ROI region is completely embedded in another region.

$$e(R) \in T \quad \text{if region R is completly embedded}$$
$$e(R) \in F \quad \text{else}$$

- the medium contrast x_c of the region R with respect to the surrounding one.
- the amount of energy x_f in specific horizontally measured frequency intervals, which are typical for character strings.

As decision rule of top-down search we used:

R = "number plate"-ROI <u>if</u>$[(w_0 + w_1 x_c + w_2 x_f) > 0] \wedge [e = T]$

R = "not a number plate", (continue the search) <u>else</u>

The bottom-up process

The realised bottom-up process consists of 3 parts and it uses only a binary image signal:

(1)   Segmentation in character fields
(2)   Feature extraction
(3)   Classification

In these steps we have used only known methods:

The segmentation determines the borders of character fields at the local minima of a line profil inside the ROI. Then the contour line of the black component in each field is extracted as a polygon of digital straight segments (DSS).

The classifier used to recognize the characters was based on the bayesian decision rule in an approximated manner. It takes in account apriori information as the probability of character classes and conditional probabilities of the following feature vectors:

$$\underline{x} = \begin{pmatrix} x_1 \\ x_2 \\ x_3 \\ x_4 \\ x_5 \\ x_6 \end{pmatrix} \begin{array}{l} \text{number of holes} \\ \text{number of vertical lines} \\ \text{number of horizontal lines} \\ \text{number of rectangles} \\ \text{number of free ends} \\ \text{number of components} \end{array} \qquad \underline{y} = \begin{pmatrix} y_1 \\ y_2 \\ y_3 \\ \\ y_4 \\ y_5 \end{pmatrix} \begin{array}{l} \text{area} \\ \text{length of contour} \\ \text{centre of gravity} \\ \text{of the hole} \\ \text{number of DSS} \\ \text{measure of symmetry} \end{array}$$

Under the assumptions that the features are independent of each other, that the probabilities $p(y_i|k)$ are normal distributed and that the $P(x_i|k)$ may be stored directly we get the following decision rule:

$$\hat{k} = \underset{k}{\text{argmax}} \ \ln P(k) + \sum_{i=1}^{6} \ln P(x_i|k) - \sum_{j=1}^{5} \ln \hat{\sigma}_{yj} - \tfrac{1}{2}\sum_{j=1}^{5} ((y_j - \mu_{yj})^2 / \hat{\sigma}_{yj})$$

The reference values $P(k)$, $P(x_i|k)$, $\hat{\sigma}_{yj}, \mu_{yj}$ were estimated in a learning process.
The performance tested on a real test sample is encouraging.

3. Generalisation

In the example we used a mixed top-down/bottom-up-strategy based on the heuristic principle (H1) selective focussing determining the top-down part (Fig. 2, Fig. 3.1).

From other realised systems we can abstract other principles.

(H2) Rough preliminary analysis and successive refining: This principle combined with (H1) may be used also to search for a ROI in a top-down process if the ROI model is formulated at a lower resolution level of the signal (Fig. 3.2). As a suitable data structure a quadtree or other hierarchical representations are used /2/.

(H3) Cycles including hypothesis generation and verification: In this case a hypothesis about the model is derived from a constraint part of the image where as the verification checks an additional part specified by the hypothetical model (Fig. 4). The search for the interpretation organised as reiteration may be optimised by controlling the hypothesis generation by the results of the preceding verification. But the optimisation is rather complicated on account of the expected steps.

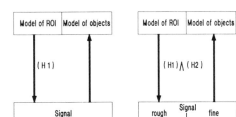

Fig.3.1: The use of (H1)
"selective focussing"

Fig.3.2: The use of
(H1) and (H2)
"rough preliminary
analysis and
refining"

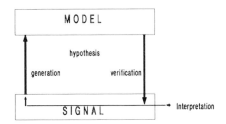

Fig. 4: (H3) Cyclic hypothesis generation and verification

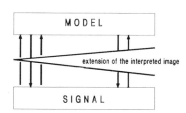

Fig. 5: (H4) Predecisions on keys

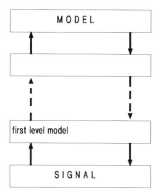

Fig. 6: Successive abstraction

(H4)   Predicisions based on keys: Such an heuristic is used beginning a cyclic interpretation process at easily detectable models or at clear interpretable signals (keys) and deciding ultimatively after each maching and going on the neighbourhood up to now uninterpreteted (Fig. 5). This process includes suboptimalities.

(H5)   Successive abstraction: There are some application tasks which may be naturally ordered in some hierarchical levels. The adapted process architecture is built up by layers (Fig. 6).

4. Conclusion

Some heuristics and the derived architectures of the analysis process are shown. For one of these, the "selective focussing", an example including with the optimisation of steps is demonstrated.

5. References

/1/   Bunke,H. *Modellgesteuerte Bildanalyse*. B. G. Teubner, Stuttgart: 1985
/2/   Rosenthal,D.A. *An inquiring driven vision system based on visual and conceptual hierarchies*. UMI Research Press, Ann Harbor, Michigan 1981

Three-Dimensional Array Grammars and Object Recognition

P. S. P. Wang

MIT AI Laboratory, Cambridge, MA 02139

and

College of Computer Science

Northeastern University, Boston, MA 02115

ABSTRACT

A new concept of 3-d universal array grammar is introduced for representing 3-d patterns. It uses parallelism for pattern generation. Many interesting 3-d objects can be represented by this universal 3-d array grammar, which can be used for 3-d object recognition, description and understanding.

Keywords: 3-d array grammars, universal array grammars, pattern generation, object representation, parallel generation

I. INTRODUCTION

The research and development of two-dimensional(2-d) pattern recognition, scene analysis, computer vision and image processing have progressed very rapidly in recent years. Among various models employed for pattern representation and analysis, the array grammar has attracted constant attention because it has several advantages over others. It is a powerful pattern generative model generalized from Chomsky's phrase structure grammar[8]; is sufficiently flexible to be extended to higher dimensionalities[10]; has been shown more accurate than some other methods for 2-d clustering analysis[14]; can be highly parallel and as powerful as tessellation or cellular automata[4]; and can provide a sequential/parallel model that serves as a compromise between a purely sequential model, which takes too much time for large arrays, and a purely parallel one, which normally requires too much hardware for large digital patterns[12]. Besides, it provides a good setting to get inside and indepth views of multi-dimensional parallel computation, automata and language theory[1,13].

In this report, we introduce a new approach for representing three-dimensional (3-d) objects by 3-d array grammar. The concept of 2-d universal array grammar[15] is also extended here to 3-d array grammar. This is to overcome the NP-complete difficulty of grammatical inference problems. Also, in the conventional syntactical pattern recognition[3], if the number of classes under consideration is very large, the pattern matching and classification involve so many grammars (or a very large grammar resulted from unions of many smallers ones), that it becomes too time consuming to be practical. 3-d universal array grammars provide an alternative to solve such problems.

II. NOTATIONS, DEFINITIONS AND EXAMPLES

We adapt the basic definitions and notations of array grammars from earlier work in the literature.[16]

Definition 2.1

A 3-d array grammar is G = (Vn, Vt, P, S, #),

where Vn: Set of nonterminals,

       Vt: Terminals,

       S $\in$ Vn   Start symbol,

       # $\in$ Vn U Vt   Blank symbol,

P: $\alpha \rightarrow \beta$, $\alpha(x,y,z) \rightarrow \beta(x,y,z)$

During derivation, the locations of each nonterminal that should be applied (replaced) are specified(by their (x,y,z) coordinates).

CAIP'91

Definition 2.2

Parallel derivation: when a rule is applied, it is applied to all nonterminals of the α simultaneously (under specifications).

$$L(G) = \{R \mid S ==^*> \ R \in V_t^{++} \text{ and } connected(according \text{ to the } 6 - neighborhood)\}$$

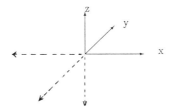

3-d 6-neighborhood

Example 2.1:

Gu = (Vn, Vt, P, S, #), where   Vn = {S}, Vt = {*} and

```
P: (1) S #  --> S S            (5) Sa #  --> Sa S
                                  [where a means the left symbol is above right sybmol]
           #          S
       (2) S     --> S          (6) Sb #  --> Sb S
                                  [where b means the left symbol is below right symbol]

       (3) # S  --> S S          (7) S      --> *

           S          S
       (4) #     -->  S
```

At the beginning, S is at (0,0,0). Notice that, the neighborhood of

(0,0,0) is {(0,0,0),(1,0,0),(0,1,0),(0,0,1),(-1,0,0),(0,-1,0),(0,0,-1)}

In general, the neighborhood of (i,j,k) is

{(i,j,k),(i+1,j,k),(i,j+1,k),(i,j,k+1),(i-1,j,k),(i,j-1,k),(i,j,k-1)}

Consider * as a unit cube * =

Example 2.2:
```
         1           1           1           1
   S # ==> S S # ==> S S S # ==> S S S S # ==> # # # # #
                                               S S S S S
   2             2             2             2
 ==> S S S S S ==> S S S S S ==> S S S S S ==> S S S S S
       S S S S S     S S S S S     S S S S S     S S S S S
                     S S S S S     S S S S S     S S S S S
                                   S S S S S     S S S S S
                                                 S S S S S

   5     5     5     5     7                    5*5*5 cube
 ==>   ==>   ==>   ==>   ==>                    (Solid)
```

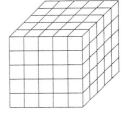

```
                                         4 4 4
Derivation sequence: 1 1 1 1 2 2 2 2 5 5 5 5 7 or 1  2  5  7
                     n-1 n-1 n-1
In general a derivation sequence 1   2    5    7 is for an nxnxn cube, n>=1.
```

Example 2.3:

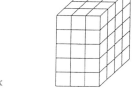

```
         2    3    4
      1     2    5    7
   S ==>   ==>  ==>  ==>   3*4*5  brick (Solid)
```

```
                        m-1 n-1 p-1
In general: m*n*p solid brick sequence is  1    2    5    7, where m,n,p>=1.
```

Note: if no positions (locations) specified during derivation process,
by default, all locations wherever applicable are applied.

Example 2.4:

```
        n-1   p-1
      1     2
   S ==>   ==>   {(0<=x<=n-1, y=0, z>0), (0<=x<=n-1, y=p-1,z>0),
                  (x=0, 0<=y<=p-1, z>0), (x=n-1, 0<=y<=p-1, z>0)}
                  m-1
                5      7
                ==>    ==> n*p*m hollow (up) brick

        n-1 p-1    m-1
   or    1   2   C 5    7, where C is the set of cells defined above in { }.
```

A figure of n*p*m hollow(up) brick is shown in the following firue. Please compare the figures in Examples 2.1 -2.6 with those object figures in [2,5,6, 7,9,11].

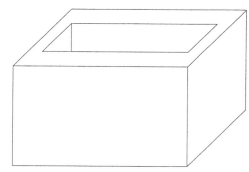

Example 2.5: 5*5*3 pyramid

top views:

278

```
      4    4
      1    2                 5                            5        7
S ==>    ==>   S S S S S  ==>                      ==>          ==> 5x5x3 pyramid
              S S S S S   {(1<=x<=3,1<=y<=3,z=0)}=C  (2,2,1)=C
              S S S S S           1                     2
              S S S S S
              S S S S S                                 _
                                   _____              _|_|_
              ----------         _|_|_|_|__         _|_|_|_|_
side views:|_|_|_|_|_|         |_|_|_|_|_|         |_|_|_|_|_|
```

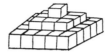

```
      4 4
   or 1 2  C  5  C  5 7
        1     2
```

Gu can be considered as a "universal" AG (3-D), which can generate
a rather large class of 3-D objects, each represented by a parsing
(derivation) sequence.

Example 2.6: Wire-like objects [2,9]

(i)

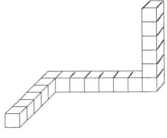

$$2^5\{(x \geq 0, 5, 0)1^6\}\{(7, 5, z \geq 0)5^5\}7$$

(ii)

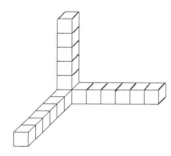

$$2^6\{(x \geq 0, 5, 0)1^6\}\{(0, 5, 0)5^5\}7$$

(iii)

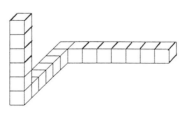

$$2^6\{(x \geq 0,\ 6, 0)1^7\}\{(0, 0, z \geq 0)5^5\}7$$

III. DISCUSSIONS AND CONCLUSIONS

The above mentioned 3-D array grammars not only can generate a lot of interesting 3-D objects, but also can be used for 3-D object learning, understanding and description. For example, according to the sequence of rules (universal array grammar), Figure 2.6(i) can be described as: a wire-like object with 6 units of segments stretching toward x-axis, followed by a 7 units of line segments stretching toward y-axis, followed by a 6 units of line segments stretching toward z-axis. It is the author's hope that this ground work can also pave a road for further studies of 3-d formal model for object pattern recognition and to stimulate research in 3-d object clustering analysis involving noisy and distorted patterns.

IV. BIBLIOGRAPHY

1. C.Cook and P.S.P.Wang, "A chomsky hierarchy of isotonic array grammars and languages", *Computer Graphics and Image Processing*, v8, 144-152 (1978)

2. S.Edelman, H. Bulthoff, D.Weinshall, *Stimulus familiarity determines recognition strategy for novel 3-D*, MIT AI Lab. Memo. 1138, July 1989.

3. K.S.Fu, *Syntactic pattern recognition and applications*, Englewood Cliffs, N.J., Prentice-Hall, 1982

4. W.I.Grosky and P.S.P.Wang, "The relation bewteen uniformly structured tessellation automata and parallel array grammars", *Proc. IEEE ISUSAL 75*, Tokyo, Japan, 97-102 (1975)

5. T. Marill, *Computer perception of three-dimensional objects*. MIT AI Lab Memo. 1136, August 1989.

6. T. Marill, *Recognizing three-dimensional objects without the use of models*. MIT AI Lab. Memo. 1157, September 1989.

7. D. Marr and H.K. Nishihara, Representation and Recognition of the spatial organization of three dimensional shapes. MIT AI Lab. Memo 377, August 1976.

8. A. Rosenfeld, *Picture languages: formal models for picture recognition*, Academic Press, New York, 1979

9. R. N. Shepard and J.Metzler, "Mental rotation of 3-D objects" *Science* 171, pp.701-703(1971).

10. R.Siromoney, "Array language and Lindenmayer systems- a survey", *The Book of L*, G. Rozenberg and A. Salomma (ed), Springer Verlag, 1986

11. S.Ullman, *An approach to object recognition: aligning pictorial descriptions*. MIT AI Lab. Memo. 931, Dec. 1986.

12. P.S.P.Wang, "Finite-turn repetitive checking automata and sequential/parallel matrix languages", *IEEE Trans. Computers*, v.30, n5, 366-370 (1981)

13. P.S.P.Wang, "Hierarchical structures and complexities of isometric patterns", *IEEE Trans. PAMI*, v5, n1, 92-99 (1983)

14. P.S.P.Wang, "An application of array grammars to clustering analysis for syntactic patterns", *Pattern Recognition*, v17, n4, 441-451 (1984)

15. P.S.P.Wang, "On-line Chinese character recognition" *6th IGC Int. Conference on Electronic Image '88* 209-214 (1988)

16. P.S.P. Wang(Ed.), *Array grammars, patterns and recognizers World Scientific Publishing Co. (WSP)*, 1989.

17. P.Winston with S.Shellard, (ed) *Artificial Intelligence at MIT - Expanding Frontiers*, MIT Press (1990)